The Foundation Stone

Henry Yates Satterlee and the Creation of
Washington National Cathedral

Richard Greening Hewlett

Published by
Montrose Press
Rockville, MD

© Copyright June 2007
Richard Greening Hewlett

The Foundation Stone:
Henry Yates Satterlee and the Creation of
Washington National Cathedral

Library of Congress Control Number 2007927657

ISBN 978-0-9728874-4-1 (hard cover)
ISBN 978-0-9728874-5-8 (paperback)

Author: Richard Greening Hewlett
Editor: Diane Ney
Book Designer: Elody R. Crimi

TABLE OF CONTENTS

LIST OF ILLUSTRATIONS

FOREWORD

Richard Hewlett has written an engaging and vivid biography of the first Bishop of the Diocese of Washington, Henry Yates Satterlee, and his vision for building the Cathedral of Saint Peter and Saint Paul, the Washington National Cathedral. Bishop Satterlee was highly influenced in his episcopacy by the teaching of Jesus that challenged and proclaimed the temple of his time to be a "house of prayer for all people." Bishop Satterlee's adaptation of this Old Testament phrase, a phrase also echoed by Jesus, is central to a proper understanding of the Cathedral's beginnings and its place in the religious, political, and ethical community of our nation and the world today.

Deeply concerned about the moral and ethical issues that could be obscured by the chaos and distractions of partisan politics in the nation's capital, Bishop Satterlee feared there would be no advocate for the permanent residents of the great federal city. He set out to endow the Cathedral pulpit and its programs with prophetic power, saying: "if there is one city where religious impressions need to be strengthened and religious principles upheld, it is in the capital of our country."

He saw the need for the cathedral to become a gathering place for those interested in addressing the issues of an emerging global community as well as a place of sound teaching and learning, especially as it affected the city's youth. The three schools on the Cathedral Close, Beauvoir, Saint Albans School for Boys and the National Cathedral School for Girls were all born out of Bishop Satterlee's educational imperative for the young.

Satterlee believed that this new cathedral, like the great cathedrals of the Middle Ages, should belong to the common folk who helped build them. In the Middle Ages, cathedrals were known as "palaces of the poor" and stood as vast architectural counter-weights to the castles of kings and princes. Satterlee's cathedral, when built, would continue that ancient cathedral understanding and be open to the common person. It would not be influenced by the financial interests of a few people who might modify the independent principles of cathedral life, outreach, and ministry. Because the Washington National Cathedral, as incorporated by an act of the Congress, does not have a governing congregation like other

Episcopal churches and cathedrals, it retains its autonomy and independence as envisioned by Bishop Satterlee.

His understanding of preaching in this new cathedral was best captured in one of his writings: "Cathedral preachers will be free, like Christ in the Temple to rebuke class sins, the political sins, the national sins of the people, free to stand forth to denounce corruption, unpatriotism or immorality whether in a dominant political party or in the highest rulers of the land. Think of the tremendous moral power of a great cathedral preacher who dares from the pulpit of a free church in a free state, to hold up the mirror of Christ's pure Gospel, with the highest ethical standard before the eyes of those who neglected the responsibilities their country has laid on them, or who forgot that public office is a public trust. All great prophets of the Bible rebuked the national sins as a moral disease, which honeycombs the life of the people. Dante is gone but do we not need to make room in our American Church for the prophetic voice."

Bishop Satterlee, some might say, was ahead of his time. Others might say that he dangerously ventured into the no man's land of mixing religion with politics. But his passion for building a great cathedral for national purposes continues to drive the vision of Washington National Cathedral as it enters the twenty-first century. His vision of a prophetic people's cathedral for the District of Columbia, the nation, and the world will continue to inform and shape its life, vision, and ministry for the next one hundred years.

The Right Reverend John Bryson Chane, M.Div., D.D.
Eighth Bishop of Washington

PREFACE

Just a century ago, on September 29, 1907, Henry Yates Satterlee, the first Bishop of the Episcopal Diocese of Washington, laid the Foundation Stone for the great cathedral he and others planned to build in the nation's capital. Present on that memorable occasion were President Theodore Roosevelt and members of his cabinet, a justice of the Supreme Court, members of Congress, the Anglican Bishop of London, the presiding Bishop of the Episcopal Church, thirty-five bishops from all parts of the nation, the clergy of the diocese, and an estimated gathering of 35,000 people who flocked to Mount St. Alban to witness the ceremony.

That day marked the high point in Bishop Satterlee's life. It was the fruition of his eleven years as bishop and was the last time he would preside over a service on the Cathedral Close. In less than four months he would die of pneumonia when he persisted in following a grueling schedule for weeks on end. He would never see another stone laid on the cathedral site, much less the magnificent edifice that would take shape over the next eighty-three years.

Why, then, does the legacy of this diocesan bishop who died almost a hundred years ago continue to resonate in the purpose and character of the national Episcopal Church? In dispelling the patrician image of Episcopalianism in the years of social and economic upheaval following the Civil War, Bishop Satterlee and other leaders – politicians, industrialists, old money and new – redefined the vestiges of class left from the nation's beginning a century before. Through the story of Satterlee's journey from patrician New York family to the spiritual father of what many consider America's national cathedral, this book explores the shaping of today's Episcopal Church as a national "house" of prayer for all people.

That a leader of such lasting influence is relatively unknown outside the inner circles of the Episcopal Church is not surprising. Institutional memories fade quickly, and Satterlee never put himself forward on the national stage. With the passing of each generation of leadership within the church, Satterlee became a revered but largely unknown prophet, even as his prophecies were realized. It wasn't until the late 1970s, when Washington National Cathedral collected its unprocessed records dating back to the early 1890s to establish its archives, that Satterlee's "private record" was discovered. In this document Satterlee set down his inmost thoughts, frustrations, and occasional joyful moments of accomplishment from the spring of 1896 until the summer of 1907. This document gives us an extraordinary insight into what really happened behind the formal record in the minutes of the board of trustees and official correspondence during those years. It also captures the flavor of events Satterlee describes, with all the dilemmas, disagreements, and compromises that plagued the founders. Rather than limit this book to a conventional edition of the *Private Record*, I have chosen to integrate it into the text as a separate chapter within the narrative.

Chapter 1 covers the formative years of Satterlee's life: his upper-class childhood in New York, his early exposure to art and architecture in Europe, his decision to enter the ministry, his stance on the controversial issues that were sweeping the Episcopal Church while he was in seminary, and his apprenticeship as rector of a country parish in the Hudson Valley.

Chapter 2 follows Satterlee's career as rector of a large parish in New York City, where he applied many of the ideas he had developed in his country parish. With the financial support and leadership of several elite families, he expanded the mission of the parish to reach the homeless, poor, and uneducated on the lower East Side. Drawing on the work of social reformers in London, he succeeded in building a city mission that attracted attention both in the city and the national church and preceded his election in 1895 as the first Bishop of the new Diocese of Washington.

Chapter 3 turns away from Satterlee to attempts by the Bishop of Maryland and Washington clergy and laity to raise funds and build a cathedral in the nation's capital, beginning in 1890. The controversy, misunderstanding, and suspicion that engulfed that effort demonstrated that talented, experienced, and well-intentioned people cannot succeed in such an enterprise without strong leadership. By the time Satterlee came to Washington in 1896, the cathedral project was in shambles. The account of these difficult years identifies the problems he faced in accepting this checkered inheritance.

Chapter 4 describes Satterlee's years in Washington in the form of a commentary on the *Private Record,* which is reproduced in full in Chapter 5. Chapter 4 covers parts of the story that Satterlee neglected or did not choose to include in the *Private Record*. The chapter makes clear that without his leadership the great Gothic cathedral on Mount St. Alban would not exist today.

Chapter 5 opens with an account of the origins of the *Private Record*, followed by an edited version of the complete typescript found in the Cathedral's records in 1980.

Chapter 6 covers the last five months of Satterlee's life, from the laying of the Foundation Stone in September 1907 until his death in February 1908. The chapter ends with an analysis of Satterlee's legacy, his influence on the architectural design of the Cathedral, and his three prescriptions of the Cathedral's mission that continue to serve as a guide for the future.

The world in which Henry Satterlee worked and lived a century ago scarcely exists today. By our standards his was a naive and innocent age in which Americans still believed in endless progress toward human betterment and the possibility of world peace. Satterlee's grand vision of the cathedral in Washington as a magnet drawing Christian churches of many denominations into a union for national and world mission would be difficult for most Americans to take seriously today. Yet the Cathedral that stands on Mount St. Alban bears the mark of his commitment to excellence in art and architecture and his profound conviction that the Cathedral can bring people of all faiths closer to God for generations to come.

A familiar site on the Hudson River in Satterlee's youth. Painting, "Becalmed off Halfway Rock," by Fitz Hugh Lane, 1860. Image © Board of Trustees, National Gallery of Art, Washington.

1. THE TRAINING GROUND

During his first fifty years Henry Yates Satterlee could never have imagined that the crowning achievement of his life would be the creation of a national cathedral of the Episcopal Church in Washington, D.C. Born in New York City in 1843, he had never during those five decades lived more than a few miles from the Hudson River. He had built his reputation as rector of two parishes in the Diocese of New York, one seventy miles up the Hudson and the other on the lower East Side in the city. He had rejected several attractive offers of more prestigious positions that would have taken him away from New York. He had never taken leadership in building a church. He had expressed reservations about raising funds for a cathedral in New York City because it might compete with parish growth. He had never pushed himself forward for leadership positions in the Diocese of New York or the Episcopal Church nationally. How, then, could such a man be called to organize a new diocese in the nation's capital and to build one of the largest cathedrals in the world? What was it that qualified Henry Satterlee for this challenging task? The fact is that his entire career before 1895 can be seen in retrospect as a training ground for that task.

THE YOUNG PATRICIAN

In the two decades after the War of 1812 New York City and the Hudson Valley were still part of a stable society in which elite minorities established and maintained the standards of culture and morality. In 1832 Frances Trollope in her *Domestic Manners of the Americans* praised the city's upper class as "a small patrician band"—"the Medici of the Republic"—whose genteel way of life met the highest European standards.[1]

During the 1840s there were at least six Satterlee families living in the upper-class neighborhood in lower Manhattan in sight of the Battery. Like many of the elite in the city, the Satterlees had come from England in the late seventeenth century and over four generations had migrated south into New York State, either to the city, as "Yankees," or to the Hudson Valley, as "Knickerbockers."[2] Edward Rathbone Satterlee, born in Saratoga Springs in 1780, was one of the Knickerbockers. He attended the Albany Academy and studied under Joseph

Henry, who later became the Secretary of the Smithsonian Institution and one of the most prominent scientists in America. Presumably Edward's education, which was exceptional for those times, gave him an advantage in business. He became a wealthy merchant and a prominent citizen in Albany, where he spent the rest of his life. Interested in art and music, he collected paintings and at one time was president of the Albany Gallery of Fine Arts. These accomplishments clearly established him as one of the elite.

His son Edward, born in Albany in 1815, early showed an interest in literature and art. Tall and handsome, young Edward had many friends and enjoyed the social life of Albany. Letters he wrote years later to his family reveal him to be well educated with a fluent and easy writing style.[3]

It was not surprising that this popular young patrician should win the affection of Jane Anna Yates, a member of a distinguished New York family. Jane could claim a grandfather who was a colonel on General Schuyler's staff during the American Revolution. The next generation of the Yates family produced four sons of prominence, including Joseph Christopher Yates, governor of New York, 1823-1825, and Henry Yates, the future bishop's grandfather, who became a New York state senator, mayor of Schenectady, and a founder of Union College. Jane, an attractive woman but physically handicapped in a childhood accident, took advantage of this misfortune by devoting herself to reading and study. She was an avid student of the history of ancient religions, French literature, and music. Coming from an old Dutch family on her mother's side, Jane spoke Dutch and French fluently.[4] Both Edward and Jane were clearly the offspring of patrician families. They were married in Schenectady in April 1838 and settled in Albany, where their first child, Mary, was born in 1840.

Edward shared his father's devotion to art, but he was more interested in painting and writing than in business. Like many patricians in generations following the founder, Edward was comfortable with drawing on the family inheritance to live a life of cultivated leisure. Literature and especially art were the center of his life, and he became an accomplished amateur painter. Edward's copy of a Rembrandt at one time attracted the attention of Sir C. Purdon Clarke, at that time director of a London museum and later of the Metropolitan Museum in New York.[5]

Soon after his daughter's birth, Edward moved his family to New York City, where he took up residence at 112 Greenwich Street near the Battery. There, on January 11, 1843, Henry Yates Satterlee was born. Why Edward moved to the city is a mystery, but it seems likely that he had hopes of establishing himself as an artist with the financial help of his father or even from wealthier Satterlee cousins who lived there. Apparently his plans failed, and he moved Jane and his two children back to Albany in 1845.

In Albany, Edward became a partner in his father's business and moved his family into the Dutch mansion where Jane's father, Henry Yates, lived.[6] The house, located on several

The Yates mansion near Albany

acres on the outskirts of the city, had been at various times the home of three governors of New York. Over the next decade four more Satterlee children arrived in a household bustling with excitement and energy. Mary Satterlee later recalled that her younger brother was "a healthy, happy boy, fond of reading, especially of making all sorts of collections of insects, minerals, etc." The Yates mansion was a center for hospitality. Mary never forgot the grand fancy-dress ball in 1847. Her parents appeared as King Charles I and Queen Henrietta, and she and young Henry were dressed as pages. Over the next nine years the Satterlee children thrived in the pastoral surroundings of their grandfather's home. Henry began schooling with a private tutor and then moved up to the Albany Academy. With his family and perhaps his tutor, Henry learned to speak what he later called "New York" Dutch.

What Henry later recalled as an idyllic life was soon to end, however. After Grandfather Yates died in 1854, Edward decided to move back to New York City with his family. Perhaps by that time he judged his financial resources adequate to permit him to lead a comfortable life in the city, where he could be part of the growing and vibrant community of sculptors and painters. The city had changed greatly during the decade he had been in Albany. Thousands of immigrants from Ireland and Northern Europe had flooded into the lower East Side. The old elite families that had clustered around the Battery in the 1840s had now moved northward, first to Union Square at Fourteenth Street, and by the mid-1850s to Twenty-third Street, where they lived in five-story brownstones. The "new-money" elites, who were amassing huge fortunes in railroads and manufacturing, were building mansions as far north as Thirty-fourth Street. Edward found a house for his family one block east of Broadway on Twenty-third Street. His cousin Edward R. Satterlee, a wealthy stockbroker, lived a few doors away in a large house overlooking Madison Square Park.[7] The location was decidedly upper class.

For a young patrician, the normal path for education led to the prestigious Columbia Grammar School, where the venerable Charles Anthon immersed Henry in the classics. Two years later, in 1858, Henry passed the entrance examinations for Columbia College, still the choice for elite New York families before the Civil War. His matriculation at Columbia, however, was postponed by what turned out to be one of the most significant adventures of his life.

A TASTE FOR ART AND ARCHITECTURE

For an art lover and artist like Edward Satterlee, the museums, cathedrals, and palaces of Europe held an irresistible attraction. Now that Henry had finished grammar school, Edward made plans for an extended trip to Europe. With his wife Jane, Edward took along his daughter Mary and Henry, now just fifteen. His hope was that the trip would lead Henry to follow him into the art world. The family sailed for England in September 1858 and for nine months toured Europe from London and Paris to Vienna and Rome in the grand style of the English aristocracy. Henry's early exposure to the classics in both literature and the arts enabled him to appreciate the museums, palaces, and libraries that the family visited in the capitals of Europe. His one extant letter from this trip reveals a young man with a discerning eye for art and architecture, an ability that would serve him in good stead in the cathedral project. About the Berlin Museum he wrote:

> Among the most celebrated [paintings] are: "A boar hunt" by Rubens and Snyder and several pictures by Raphael representing the Madonna. In an adjoining room is a large unfinished picture by Raphael representing "The Adoration of the Magi" which is only to be seen on application. It is beautifully drawn and if it had been finished would undoubtedly have been one of his masterpieces. . . . We visited several studios in Berlin one of them belonging to Cornelius, the celebrated painter and sculptor, it was very fine, although it was mostly composed of drawings. Some of these were beautifully executed. . . .[8]

The magnificent views of the Bay of Naples and the Amalfi Coast inspired the young traveler to write several pages of colorful description as the small steamer made its way to the

Isle of Capri. Once back in London, Henry spent days in the library at the British Museum, browsing through books on English history.

The grand tour opened a new world to the young Satterlee, who put his experiences to good use in his college essays and term papers. He could now write tales about the mysterious disappearance of young French noblemen entrapped by the seductive but deadly charms of a beautiful woman or about finding a roll of papyrus in the tooth of the Great Sphinx in Egypt. The stories and essays were vehicles for exploring the power and beauty of the English language. As he wrote in an eleven-page essay:

> At this time, the sixteenth and seventeenth centuries, the English language attained its greatest purity and beauty, more forcible and more capable of expressing sublimity than any other language written, it was at the same time fitted to express the greatest pathos and sentiment. . . . Since that time Stars of the first Magnitude have appeared in the firmament of English literature and have exerted a powerful but beneficial influence upon the lesser lights Milton Dryden Pope Cooper and a host of others, whose names are world renowned, and "familiar to our ears as household words" have lived since that time and have polished enriched and refined the English language until it became what it now is.[9]

The overseas experience also had a lasting impact on Satterlee far beyond his school years. It made him for life an ardent Anglophile who would look to England for standards in art, architecture, literature, philosophy, and theology. It gave him a taste of French, German, and Italian culture. The excursions to Egypt and the Holy Land gave him insights into the Mediterranean world that later would enable him to procure some of the most distinctive artifacts for the Cathedral.

When the family returned to New York in 1859, Henry set off for Columbia College. He later recalled trudging up Fifth Avenue to Forty-ninth Street in an October downpour, trying to balance an umbrella with a stack of books in his arms. His first day at college was hardly a success. Within hours he received two reprimands from the faculty, first for sitting with the seniors instead of with the freshmen and then for recklessly volunteering an erroneous translation in Latin class. His year abroad had perhaps given him an intellectual advantage over his classmates but put him behind others in class work. Although he continued to live at home, he took an active part in college activities. He soon became president of the debating society and in 1861 delivered the Delta Phi Junior oration. The curriculum of the college was probably reflected in the library, which contained no more than 15,000 books, concentrated in theology, law, science, ancient and modern history, and literature. The class work that Satterlee kept in his files for the rest of his life was limited to essays, fictional stories, and poetry.[10]

THE MILITARY OPTION

Agreeable as college life was, military service proved a growing attraction to Satterlee as the nation plunged into the Civil War. If his motivation had been simply the Union cause, he might have enlisted in a New York regiment. He may well have been attracted by the color and pageantry of the military academy at West Point, which was close to his father's summer estate on the Hudson. When he seriously considered entering the army, his father, with the best patrician intentions, reluctantly consented on the condition that he obtain an appointment to West Point through his own efforts. With no clear sense of vocation, Henry could imagine making a career in military service. Armed with letters to congressmen from several New York districts, Henry set off for Washington in pursuit of an appointment. The only result was another interruption in his college work; all spaces at West Point had already been filled.[11] He was forced to give up his hopes to join the army, but the military services would have a prominent place in his life as a bishop and cathedral builder. He would select high-ranking army and navy officers to serve on the Cathedral's board of trustees, call upon military staff officers to assist him on technical matters, and enlist the Marine Band to play at Cathedral celebrations.

THE CALL TO THE MINISTRY

It seems likely that Henry Satterlee's efforts to join the army simply represented a patriotic desire to serve his country in time of war rather than a serious intention to make the military his career. For a nineteen-year-old college student, several options must have appeared open. As a young patrician he could easily have moved into the business world in the footsteps of his Grandfather Satterlee and several of his cousins in the city. Edward Satterlee was still hoping that his son would find a place in the art world. Another option, given Henry's interest in literature, was to become a writer or even a poet for literary magazines, feasible choices for a young man from a wealthy family. However, as he approached graduation from Columbia in 1863, he felt drawn to the ministry.

Henry had never been an active member of any church, but religion did have a place in his childhood. Although both the Satterlee and Yates families had come from England, some of their forbears had married into Dutch families in the Knickerbocker region of Upstate New York. Thus, both of Henry's parents had some cultural if not religious ties to the Dutch Reformed Church, where Henry presumably was baptized. His mother was attracted to the Episcopal Church, and while they lived in Albany, she rented a pew in St. Paul's, where she attended afternoon services, often with her son Henry in tow. The few extant letters to her children reveal her to be a prayer-centered person with a simple but intensely real faith.

Her four surviving children all became communicants in the Episcopal Church, but she was never confirmed.[12] Bishop Charles H. Brent in his biography describes young Satterlee as a man with a religious bent, although during his college years he was not associated with any one church or denomination. Brent suggests that Satterlee came to the ministry through his immersion in the study of ethics and his practice of fasting as a form of self-discipline. One of Satterlee's student essays makes clear his devotion to Victorian morality. In a student paper entitled "The Power of the Will," he wrote:

> The power of the will is exemplified in so many ways, and its operations so manifest as bearing not only upon the moral condition and his influence over mind and matter, but also has a bearing on the moral condition of nations, their rise and progress, that it affords a wide field for the speculator and a subject of deep thought for the moralist.

> Man is endowed by the Creator with certain powers of mind that if rightly exercised or wrongly, will produce good or evil alone depending wholly upon the intellectual zeal or moral power he possesses.

> This power can be strengthened by self-improvement for the Creator has given those qualities to each man and he intends that he shall strengthen and increase and to every one he has given in a greater or less degree the power of ruling himself & others.[13]

According to Brent, "It was the ministry as such, and not some one aspect of it as interpreted by a given church, which claimed him [Satterlee] at the outset."[14] With no previous commitment to any denomination, Satterlee sought the advice of a number of prominent men who were available to him through family connections. Milo Mahan, a professor at Columbia and uncle of the famous American admiral, recommended that Satterlee consult Arthur Cleveland Coxe, rector of Calvary Church on Gramercy Square, just four blocks from the Satterlee residence on Twenty-third Street.

Calvary had grown and prospered since the 1840s as a convenient place of worship for the old-monied elite, like the Satterlees, who lived nearby. A large church built in Gothic style, Calvary relied for financial support on pew rents, which the wealthy were willing to pay in order to reserve for Sunday services a pew, properly marked with the family name. To accommodate middle- and lower-class families, Calvary had been one of the first parishes in New York to build a separate chapel, located on East Twenty-third Street, just east of Fourth Avenue. For the chapel, the clergy and staff of the parish church provided worship services and programs that mirrored those of the larger church.

It was Coxe who steered young Satterlee into the Episcopal ministry. The son of a Presbyterian minister, Coxe was a historian and theologian who had become one of the prominent Episcopal clergy in the Diocese of New York. He took a liking to the serious young man who was seeking to find himself, and he soon became Satterlee's mentor. The two became close friends and stayed in touch after Coxe left New York in 1865 to become Bishop of Western New York in Buffalo.

The Episcopal Church in 1862

The Episcopal Church, as Satterlee may have learned in his discussions with Coxe, was in terms of membership small among Christian denominations in America. Originated as part of the established Church of England in colonial times, the parishes clustered along the Atlantic Coast had barely survived in the thirteen states after the American Revolution. Many of the clergy were loyalists and left America with the British troops. With no experience with bishops or cathedrals, most Americans had little interest in, or appreciation for, an episcopal church. Nor did the ritualistic liturgy provided in the Anglican *Book of Common Prayer* have much appeal in the newly created states.

The remnants of the Anglican churches began organizing in state conventions that in some cases (as in Maryland) were established by state legislatures. During the first five years after the war it was not at all clear that a single Episcopal Church at large could be created. Episcopalians in the middle and southern states tended to accept lay participation in the church hierarchy and to stress similarities with other Protestants. The Connecticut-based New England church denied the laity a role in the government of the diocese and stressed the role of bishops in the apostolic succession, which other Protestants could not accept. These issues and others delayed the formation of the Episcopal Church as a denomination until 1792, when it at last had a governing body (General Convention), a prayer book, a national constitution, and a procedure for creating new bishops.[15] Even then it would be four decades before the dioceses in all of the thirteen original states sent representatives to the General Convention and elected their own bishops.

In 1862 the Episcopal Church had relatively little presence beyond the Northeast. Torn asunder by the Civil War, nine southern dioceses were not represented at the General Convention that year. In the border states from Maryland to Kansas, churches had been destroyed and their congregations scattered. On the frontier west of the Appalachians, the Episcopal Church was weak or virtually non-existent. By the 1850s dioceses had been created in all the states between the mountains and the Mississippi, but beyond the states bordering the west bank of the river, there were no dioceses except in Oregon and California. Beyond the Mississippi Valley were only two missionary districts, one of which covered 750,000 square miles and eventually would include ten states. In this vast domain Bishop Joseph C. Talbot had only seventeen resident clergy in 1865.[16]

The church at large in 1862 was more a loose confederation of independent dioceses than a unified body with central administration. In 1789 the General Convention had followed the lead of the federal government in adopting a constitution that provided for a bicameral legislative body consisting of an upper house of bishops and a lower house of clerical and lay delegates. The two bodies met in the General Convention every three years to enact canon law and adopt resolutions affecting the life and governance of the national church. During the long intervals between meetings of the convention, its officers worked as individuals without staff support. The titular head of the church was the presiding bishop, elected by the house of bishops but by custom the most senior bishop in order of consecration. This arrangement meant that the presiding bishop was often elderly and found it difficult to perform his clerical functions in addition to his duties as the Bishop of his diocese. The presiding bishop had no executive authority beyond coordinating the election and consecration of bishops.

Most of the members of the Episcopal Church in 1862 resided in the dioceses along the Atlantic seaboard from Virginia to Maine. In these states the Church had parishes in every large town, where in many cases church membership reflected social status—in ascending order from Baptist, to Methodist, to Presbyterian, with Episcopal at the top of the social ladder. The Diocese of New York alone had more than twice the number of clergy in all the dioceses west of the Mississippi; Connecticut and Maryland each had almost as many, and Pennsylvania more than all the western dioceses.[17] The Church, however, was strongest in the large cities—Baltimore, Philadelphia, New York, and Boston. In New York City the Episcopalians had more churches than any other denomination in the middle decades of the century. The social elite, both the old-monied families like the Satterlees and the railroad and banking tycoons of the Gilded Age like the Vanderbilts and Morgans, rented pews for unprecedented amounts in the Episcopal parishes. The rectors of the newly rebuilt Trinity Church at the head of Wall Street and of the sumptuous Grace Church at Broadway and Tenth Street enjoyed national recognition as Christian leaders. *The Churchman*, published in the city, served as the major Episcopal periodical in the northern states. And the seminary that Satterlee would attend was still *the* seminary of the Episcopal Church in the United States, although other dioceses had established similar schools by the 1860s. New York City was, in many respects, the heart of the Episcopal Church.[18]

The Seminarian

After graduating from Columbia College in June 1863, Satterlee headed west on Twenty-third Street to the General Theological Seminary, then housed in two buildings on Chelsea Square. As it had for years, the seminary was struggling to survive with little income and a small faculty of five or six professors. So dire was the financial situation when Satterlee arrived that the seminary was launching a special fund drive to raise $20,000, an effort that was only partly successful. Such problems were probably lost on young Satterlee, who suddenly found himself in the midst of exciting, even revolutionary, developments that were sweeping the Episcopal Church at the time. For thirty years the seminary had been the port of entry for new concepts of theology and liturgy that were pouring into the Episcopal Church from the mother Church of England.

Beginning in 1833 John Henry Newman, John Keble, and other clerics at Oxford University published a series of tracts attacking what they saw as the sterile, secular, humanistic, and lethargic character of the Anglican Church. The Tractarians proposed to reform the Church by returning it to its catholic roots. They saw the apostolic succession of bishops and independence from secular government as essential to renewal of the Church and stressed the centrality of the sacraments in worship. Edward B. Pusey, also at Oxford, saw reform in returning to the "purity" of the early centuries of the Christian era before the Church was "corrupted" by Roman Catholic excesses. Pusey advocated relying on a sense of community rather than on the church hierarchy to counter the erosive forces of modern, industrial, and secular society.[19]

During the same decades before the Civil War, a second wave of reform swept into America, this time from Cambridge University. While the Oxford Movement focused on theology, John Mason Neale and others in the Cambridge Camden Society proposed liturgical and architectural reform. Under the Cambridge influence, many Episcopal parishes in America began to convert their churches from unadorned, "auditory," pulpit-centered arrangements with a simple four-legged communion table under the pulpit to Gothic-style designs, deep chancels, elevated stone altars, and stained-glass windows. Trinity Church, Wall Street, Grace Church on lower Broadway, and later St. Thomas farther up Fifth Avenue all were built in the Gothic style.

Prior to 1840 Episcopalians had been divided into two parties that differed on theological emphases but agreed on forms of worship. The high-church party stressed the necessity of the episcopacy for a legitimate church, while the evangelical party stressed the importance of personal conversion. This complexion of the two church parties began to change with the arrival of Oxford and Cambridge ideas. Younger members of the high-church party began to associate more catholic forms of worship with their theological concepts, with the most advanced high-church party members (the Anglo-Catholics) advocating adoption of liturgical elements closely modeled on the Roman Catholic Mass of that time. Evangelicals for their part either tried to hold on to the older, simpler forms of worship (low churchmanship) or advocated selective adoption of catholic elements (broad churchmanship). Distinctions between the parties were not always clear and they changed from decade to decade, but in the years before the Civil War General Seminary had become the bastion of the high-church party, mainly to stand against the inroads of the evangelicals.

The new concepts coming from Oxford and Cambridge received vastly differing interpretations in the Episcopal Church. Much of the diversity stemmed from the fact that the Church consisted of a loose confederation of independent dioceses rather than a united denomination. The most controversial issues concerned ritual and liturgy. The use of clerical vestments changed as cassocks and surplices with stoles replaced the simple black preaching robe and bishops began wearing distinctive vestments. Many parishes suffered fierce disputes over such innovations as sung services, candles on the altar, vested choirs, and weekly celebrations of Holy Communion.[20]

The high-church party, at least as Satterlee found it at the seminary, had adopted the historical and theological precepts of the Oxford Movement: adherence to the catholic tradition of the "primitive" Christian Church of the fourth century, the centrality of the apostolic succession, and the orders of ordained ministry. From Pusey the party adopted the sacramental community as the model for the modern parish, which would stand not only as a bulwark against secularism but also as a mission of Christian hope for the downtrodden in modern industrial society. From the Cambridge Movement the high-church party adopted the use of modest clerical vestments and liturgy strictly in accordance with the *Book of Common Prayer*, but with none of the elaborate vestments and ceremonial of the Anglo-Catholics. Also from the Cambridge tradition, the high churchmen favored the altar-centered church and the Gothic style of architecture.[21]

By the time Satterlee entered the seminary the high churchmen felt confident if not complacent that they were winning the battle with the evangelicals. But during Satterlee's second year at seminary a new disturbance came from the Anglo-Catholic side, when George Franklin Seymour, the new dean, inserted more ritualism in chapel services over the strong objection of high-church members of the faculty.[22]

The complexities of these seemingly endless disputes over churchmanship and the incredible hostility they generated within the Episcopal Church are perhaps of serious interest only to church historians. But the fact that these battles were still being waged in Satterlee's time is vital to understanding his career in the ministry. When he entered the seminary in 1863, his experience and knowledge of the Episcopal Church depended largely on what he had learned in a year of discussions with Coxe. Like an adult sheltered from childhood diseases, his inoculation with the vaccine of high churchmanship had a profound and permanent effect on his ministry. At every step in his career, including his years in Washington, the enduring principles of the high-church school were clearly evident. At the same time, he seems to have sensed the futility and discord engendered by the liturgical battles of the nineteenth century. While he operated from high-church principles, he refused to stand with the party or even to admit that he was a member of any school. As Frederick D. Huntington, his friend and mentor, wrote to him thirty years later when he was elected Bishop of Washington, "That you belong to no party, school, or clique and are independent of them all, so that your election cannot be claimed as advantage by anyone, or made to serve anyone, is a reason why you did accept the burden."[23] He could apply what he learned in seminary without identifying himself with the high-church party.

During his seminary years Satterlee maintained his close friendship with Coxe. Because many high-church Episcopalians at the time did not accept the validity of baptisms by other denominations, Satterlee was baptized a second time, this time by Coxe on Easter eve in 1864. The next day, Easter Sunday, Horatio Potter, the Bishop of New York, confirmed Satterlee in Trinity Church, Wall Street.[24] The following year Coxe left Calvary to become Bishop of Western New York, but the new bishop kept up a running correspondence with "his boy" for the rest of his life. Coxe later appears in Satterlee's *Private Record* as a supporter of the Washington project.

THE APPRENTICE PASTOR

Satterlee tried to gain practical experience in church work while he attended seminary. For a time in 1865 he took charge of the "colored" Church of the Messiah in New York City and taught Sunday school at Calvary. That summer, probably at the suggestion of Bishop Potter, he agreed to serve as lay reader at Zion Church, in Wappingers Falls, New York, seventy miles up the Hudson from Manhattan. The rector, George B. Andrews, had started the parish in 1833 in the small village at the head of Wappingers Creek. Now eighty years old and feeble, Andrews welcomed the tall, energetic twenty-four-year-old seminarian. Because there was no pension plan in the Episcopal Church, Andrews had no choice but to remain as rector for the rest of his life. Before the end of the summer both Andrews and most of his congregation found Satterlee the answer to their prayers and asked him to come to Zion as assistant minister. The request was premature because Satterlee was just entering his third year at General Seminary, but Bishop Potter saw wisdom in the idea and ordained Satterlee to the diaconate on November 21, 1865. He preached his first sermon at Zion three weeks later.[25]

Walking a country road in the autumn of 1865 Satterlee chanced to meet Irving Grinnell, a young man about his age. The two men found they had much in common. They had all the credentials of the old-monied elite in New York City. Both had graduated from Columbia College, and Grinnell had been a member of a Unitarian church just a block from Calvary Church in New York City. Irving's father, Moses Grinnell, had made a fortune as a shipbuilder and as an agent for packet lines. He was among the first prominent Republicans in New York and had welcomed the newly elected president, Abraham Lincoln, to his daughter's home on Fifth Avenue in February 1865. An avid sportsman, Irving was active in the New York Yacht Club, a bastion of the elite. He had worked in his father's firm for a few years before marrying Joanna Howland, the daughter of a wealthy New York importer, and purchasing the Howland estate, Netherwood, a 2,500-acre estate high on a bluff overlooking the Hudson, just north of New Hamburg and Wappingers Falls.[26]

Life in Wappingers Falls was a far cry from Satterlee's surroundings in Lower Manhattan, but he did not find it unfamiliar. He had spent many vacations and holidays at his father's estate across the Hudson at West Point, and during his school days he had hiked and camped with pals in the Catskills.[27]

In the first half of the nineteenth century the towns along the upper Hudson had been transformed from local agricultural communities into marketing centers that provided food, fabric, and manufactured goods to New York City and the world beyond.[28] Flash floods at the falls on Wappingers Creek had long since washed out the flour mills built there, to be replaced in 1834 by a calico printing plant established by James Ingham, a native of Manchester, England. With the introduction of machinery for printing from copper rollers,

Wappingers Falls, where the textile mills were located

the plant grew rapidly to be the largest industry in Dutchess County. By the time of Satterlee's arrival, employment in the calico plant was approaching a thousand workers, and a new plant to manufacture denim overalls, sack coats, and jackets had created 250 additional jobs. Most of the families that had followed Ingham to America had counted themselves as members of the Church of England and could be expected to look upon Zion as their church home.[29]

On June 28, 1866, Satterlee received his degree from General Seminary and two days later married Jane Lawrence Churchill, daughter of Timothy Gridley Churchill, a wealthy New York merchant who served on several city commissions during the Civil War. Jane's mother, Patience Riker Lawrence, had an old-monied elite pedigree even more impressive than the Churchills. The Rikers and the Lawrences had been large landowners in eastern Long Island in the seventeenth century, and the Lawrences show up in city records as having a large country mansion on the upper East Side in the 1760s and a four-story Federal house on Lower Broadway in the 1780s.[30]

Henry had first met Jane, or Jennie as Henry and the family called her, at West Point in the summer of 1863 after his graduation from Columbia. As their friendship blossomed, Jennie was easily accepted into the Satterlee family, and during the summer of 1865 the young couple ran a summer Sunday school at West Point with Henry's mother. Like most upper-class Victorian matrons, Jennie lived in the shadow of her husband. We know virtually nothing about her background, education, or interests except what can be gleaned from the dozens of letters that she wrote to her husband, children, and family. She was in fact a partner in her husband's ministry, taking a leadership position in parish work and serving as his personal secretary during his years in Washington.[31]

Housing proved a difficulty when Henry arrived in Wappingers Falls with his bride. Dr. Andrews was still living in the rectory, and there were no houses that Satterlee could afford to rent on his salary, which had just been raised from $500 to $750 per year. It seems that the young couple, like many members of the elite, enjoyed social and cultural status without wealth. The problem was solved when Grinnell offered the young couple a cottage on his Netherwood estate. Captivated by Henry's commitment and enthusiasm, Irving and Joanna quickly took active roles in Zion Church.[32]

The Satterlees and Grinnells, all in their twenties at the time, soon became a foursome of talented young people who seized the opportunity to rebuild old Zion parish and Wappingers Falls in their own image. The inspiration of the young foursome lay in their sense of responsibility for social and moral improvement of the working classes, an obligation they accepted as members of the upper-class elite. Sociologist Suzanne Keller sees social elites as "a minority of individuals designated to serve collectively in a socially valued way." They are, Keller asserts, "ultimately responsible for the realization of major social goals and for the

Irving Grinnell in later life

Satterlee as Assistant
Minister, Zion Church

continuity of the social order."[33] The Satterlees and Grinnells clearly fit this definition.

Satterlee had already lifted the spirits of the congregation with his fresh leadership, and he was now looking for ways to reach out to the unchurched in the surrounding community. True to his high-church convictions, he saw the parish as encompassing the entire community, and he looked to the working-class families in their modest homes as well as to the upper-class gentry living on their summer estates near the Hudson as targets for mission. By visiting the homes of his parishioners, he soon knew them all and could begin to see how they and others could be drawn into the spiritual community of the parish. He set out to improve the sanitary conditions of the workers' homes and opened a reading room in the parish hall. In time he and others in the parish established a workingmen's club and organized a debating society. He saw the need for a home for the girls who had come to the town to work in the factories and a school for boys who had dropped their education to take jobs. A few months after he moved to Wappingers Falls with Jennie he opened a night school for boys, and Satterlee and Grinnell served as teachers two nights a week. When he discovered that the town had no library, Satterlee inspired Grinnell to start one. In time Grinnell established a permanent library, which still operates today under the Grinnell Library Association.

Satterlee saw all these endeavors, including a failed attempt to create a temperance society in the town, not as secular activities but as an integral part of Christian ministry. His aim, as he explained some years later, was "to make the Parish Church . . . a warm spiritual home." He was also able to enlist the support of the owners and managers of the mills in

Zion Church, Wappingers Falls

Wappingers Falls, some of whom had estates on the banks of the Hudson. "The one ruling idea," Satterlee wrote, "was to break up class prejudices by genial personal contact in these different social gatherings which were held under the shadow of Church influences, and by the principle of cooperation in all forms of church work from the election of the Vestry down to the choice of officers in a workingmen's club."[34]

When Satterlee first came to Zion as a lay reader in 1865, the average attendance at Sunday service was about forty. Three years later the congregation had grown so much under Satterlee's leadership that the old church, built in 1833, was no longer adequate. With Andrews' support, Satterlee won the congregation's approval for enlarging and renovating the church and then organized a building committee and fund-raising campaign. Work began

16

immediately after the Christmas services in 1868. When Bishop Potter came to preach at the first service in the new church in July 1869, the plain interior had been transformed into a Gothic style. Three arches had been constructed in the west end to form the chancel. The pews had been rearranged to create a center aisle, the old flat ceiling had been removed, and a new vaulted roof had been installed. For the opening service a choir of twenty-five organized by Jennie occupied the new chancel pews.[35] It would be hard to imagine that Satterlee did not have a role in the decision to adopt the new design in line with high-church principles.

Satterlee's energy, self-confidence, and firm but compassionate leadership made Zion an exceptional country parish even before he became rector. Although he was actually in charge of the parish most of the time, he was careful to defer to the rector. He did not hesitate to make decisions, but always after conferring with Andrews. As the years passed, Satterlee took over more and more of the preaching and the conduct of worship. In those years he carefully wrote out his sermons, but his preaching was spontaneous, often passionate, as he tried to generate enthusiasm and commitment in the congregation. Preaching was just one tool of his ministry, which centered on personal relationships, social intercourse, pastoral work, and teaching. He ran the Sunday school himself, taught classes, selected and trained teachers, and wrote a manual for teachers with a list of reference books and four pages of questions and answers to be used in classes for each Sunday of the church year.[36]

As Satterlee saw new opportunities for ministry, he found members of the parish to organize them. He could always count on the Grinnells to fill the breach. In 1873 Joanna was running the aid and employment department and Irving was teaching the Sunday morning Bible class which in time reached two hundred men. In 1874 Satterlee finally realized his dream of creating a home for factory girls "on one of the leading avenues of the village and . . . thoroughly furnished with every article of convenience."[37] With these solid achievements, young Satterlee completed his apprenticeship.

When Dr. Andrews finally died at the age of ninety in 1875, Satterlee quickly took the reins as rector. He began publishing a yearbook that described the functions and membership of the twenty-eight organizations that at one time or another were active in the parish.[38] Now running out of space in the village for these activities, he encouraged the parish to set up a Sunday school and sewing school for women in nearby New Hamburg and then made plans to hold Sunday services there. The New Hamburg mission became the center for the parish missionary department that Satterlee created "to promote interest in the Foreign and Domestic Missionary work of the Church, and particularly to assist the Women's Auxiliary in sending boxes of clothing, etc., when needed."[39] Leadership in missionary work, both at the local and national level, soon became a hallmark of Satterlee's career in the Church.

By the spring of 1880 Satterlee had realized most of his hopes for creating a vibrant, active parish at Wappingers Falls. Membership had grown to more than three hundred

Street scene, Wappingers Falls, 1880

families, and more than a thousand persons were now associated with the activities of Zion parish. These accomplishments, however, had come at a price. He was exhausted physically and mentally. Now that he had a full-time assistant and a capable staff, he took the first extended vacation he had had in nine years.[40] He and Jennie sailed for Europe in time to attend the passion play at Oberammergau before proceeding to Italy, Egypt, and the Holy Land. As he wrote in long letters to his sister Mary, who had gone with the family on the grand tour in 1858, the trip brought home to him as never before the reality of the New Testament accounts of Christ's ministry. "Going up to Jerusalem I read the Psalms of Ascent (CXX to CXXXIV), which were chanted by the Jewish pilgrims when they went up to the Holy City. And I always tried to read on the spot the Scripture narrative of every place I visited."[41] His experiences in the Holy Land were later to have a profound influence on his plans for the fabric of the Washington Cathedral.

During the fourteen months that the Satterlees were traveling in Europe and the Middle East, the people at Zion Church were preparing a surprise for their return by raising funds for construction of a new parish hall on property that Satterlee had purchased next to the church. Delighted by their initiative, Satterlee began immediately to work on the design

18

of the building. The parish hall was completed in 1882, but the last of the debt was not paid off until Satterlee covered it privately years later with his own funds.[42]

The extended travel abroad marked the end of a significant chapter in Satterlee's life. After finding himself as a college student, he had settled on the ministry in the Episcopal Church. He had seized an opportunity to prove himself in the parish at Wappingers Falls and emerged from that experience as a capable leader and beloved pastor. What he had learned at Zion Church would serve him well as he moved on to New York City and Washington, D.C. He was now ready for even greater challenges that lay ahead.

Lower East Side, New York, 1920s

2. A House of Prayer for All People

The Return to Calvary

By the 1880s Satterlee's accomplishments at Zion Church were bringing his name to the attention of churchmen in New York City and beyond. In the city he already had name recognition as a member of the "old" social elite, the merchant class that came into money before the Civil War. Little of the "old" money had come down to Henry Satterlee, but his social position was significant, not only to him but to the church. After Coxe left Calvary, Bishop Horatio Potter had taken the young clergyman under his wing and at times offered grandfatherly advice about problems encountered at Zion Church. Satterlee developed a personal friendship with Henry Codman Potter, who was rector of Grace Church, at that time the parish of preference for the socially elite in the city. The younger Potter, the bishop's nephew, was but one of the city rectors whom Satterlee brought to Wappingers Falls to participate in parish programs.

Most significant of all, Satterlee had never completely broken his ties with Calvary Church and Coxe's successor, Edward A. Washburn, who invited him in 1878 to join the Clerical Club, a group of city clergymen who met periodically to hear papers written by members. Years later Satterlee recalled reading a paper on "Sacrifice" at his first meeting with the group. Because those present represented a broad range of churchmanship, Satterlee's paper was roundly criticized for its high-church arguments. He was, however, clearly able to hold his own in the club. In addition to Henry Potter and Washburn, the members included John Cotton Smith; Arthur Brooks, rector of the Church of the Incarnation; Charles C. Tiffany, rector of Zion Church; E. Winchester Donald, rector of the Church of the Ascension; and Heman Dyer, a former college president and clerical activist in New York.[1] Being the first "country" clergyman to be invited to join the club was in itself a mark of distinction. Satterlee qualified for the club on his own merits, but his upper-class status was probably a factor in his selection.

Under the circumstances, Satterlee was certain to be a leading candidate for the rectorship at Calvary when Washburn died in the fall of 1881. The prospect of taking over one of the most prominent parishes in the city certainly had its professional attractions, but Satterlee had strong misgivings about leaving his country parish. He cherished the genuineness and simplicity of rural and village life, the keen sense of place, and strong ties to the past. Decades later he would recall his first meeting with the Dutchess County convocation of clergy held in a barn at Low Point before the church was built there. He had never forgotten the stories told by elderly clergy about their grandfathers during the Revolutionary War. Surely there would be the pain of leaving the loving and caring Christian community he and Jennie had helped to build in Zion parish. They had become so much enmeshed in the lives of the people in Wappingers Falls that breaking those ties would involve guilt as well as pain. They would also find it hard to leave the comfortable home that the Grinnells and the parish had built for them at Netherwood, where their two children had been born, Churchill in 1867 and Constance in 1874.[2] By the time the call to Calvary did come in February 1882, Satterlee had other offers: the rectorship of Zion Church, New York City; positions at Trinity Church, New Haven, Connecticut, and at the cathedral in St. Louis, Missouri; and the presidency of Griswold College in Iowa.[3] Calvary, however, was too close to Satterlee's heart to be rejected outright. It was still in a sense his home parish, even after seventeen years at Wappingers Falls.

Calvary Church, New York. The rectory is the building on the right.

Now in its third location, on Gramercy Park at Fourth Avenue and Twenty-first Street, Calvary was a large and impressive Gothic church designed by James Renwick, Jr. Its most recent rectors had been Bishop Coxe of Western New York and Dr. Washburn, a great preacher and internationally known cleric, who with Arthur Penrhyn Stanley, the dean of Westminster, was a leader of the broad-church movement in the Anglican Communion. In an effort to heal the rifts in the American church, Washburn had been a founder of the Church Congress, which held periodic meetings of bishops, prominent clergy, and laymen of all points of view and of other denominations who were attempting through free and open discussion to move the Church in new directions.[4] Satterlee was clearly not a leader in the Church Congress during these years, but his close connections with Washburn and Calvary placed him in the middle of Congress activities and introduced him to such prominent leaders of the movement as William Reed Huntington and Phillips Brooks.

In his first meeting with the Calvary vestry, Satterlee warned that he was neither a great preacher nor a Low Churchman, but this admission did not discourage the parish leaders. They asked him to reconsider. Privately, Satterlee was troubled by the shaky condition of Calvary parish. Although the church had been able to hold some of the wealthy, socially elite families that had supported the parish in the past, there was a growing movement of the upper classes to residential areas closer to Central Park. The area south of Twenty-third Street and east of Broadway was now absorbing blue-collar and immigrant families. Some parish leaders thought Calvary should sell out and move north with its congregation. In the past the parish had suffered financial crises that threatened its very existence. Only the loyal support of families who continued to pay pew rents kept the parish alive. For Satterlee the practice of supporting a church by renting the pews was wholly unacceptable and contradicted his high-church commitment to an all-inclusive Christian community. Equally ominous, the upper-class, conservative lay leadership was getting old and parish programs had stagnated as Washburn concentrated his efforts on preaching and his interests outside the parish. Other parishes might have offered less of a challenge, but for Satterlee Calvary was too close to his heart and too much in need of help. Late in March he made his decision and he preached his first sermon as rector of Calvary on Easter Sunday, 1882.[5]

Rebuilding Calvary

Satterlee soon found the condition of the parish even worse than he had expected. Seventy of the pews remained unrented and the church was heavily in debt. He found that some of the vestry were seriously considering selling out for $250,000 and moving uptown as other parishes had done. The new rector argued patiently but firmly that Calvary historically had been a part of the community as the first church of any Christian denomination north

Satterlee as Rector, Calvary Church

of Fourteenth Street and east of Broadway. Fifty years of missionary efforts had connected the parish with "people of power," as Satterlee put it. Even more important, if Calvary left, it was unlikely that a new congregation would come in to take "her deserted place."[6]

Once Satterlee had convinced the vestry to keep the church on Gramercy Park, he began to look for ways to rebuild the parish. Finding little of the closely knit, spirit-centered community that had emerged at Wappingers Falls, he was overwhelmed by the task ahead. Sunday worship followed the established pattern of Morning and Evening Prayer, with only one Communion service a month. For a high churchman, one Communion a month seemed inadequate. The choir was isolated in the west balcony, where the paid choristers went out to smoke during the sermon. This practice offended Satterlee's sense that worship was a close-knit community of believers, not a commercial production. The arrangement of the chancel, which he thought looked "like a big parlour," offended his high-church tastes. But most discouraging of all was the parish's dependence on the pew rent system, which made it impossible to reach out to the broad spectrum of people living in the community. As long as the vestry refused to abolish the pew rents, rebuilding the parish as a worshiping community would be extremely difficult.

Satterlee found these obstacles all but unsurmountable. For all of his first year at Calvary, he later admitted in private notes, he did nothing because he did not know what to do. He tried to reassure himself on paper: "All these troubles come from thinking of self instead of others. . . . This requires careful watchfulness and prayer daily. . . . You know not the work for which God is preparing you. . . . The fear is not to be exaggerated on the one hand or to be minimized as ridiculously small on the other. It is a constitutional bias that is not to be yielded to for one moment. It is an unreality and to give way to it is to lose the spirit of love and power and of a sound mind." He later wrote on this document that this "was the hardest battle of my life."[7]

When at last he was ready to act, Satterlee started with changes in liturgy and

worship, which were the prerogatives of
the rector in the Episcopal Church. His first
decision was to bring the organ from the
west balcony to the chancel, where a vested
choir of parishioners would now sing. This
change brought the congregation together
as a worshiping community. He moved the
altar from the center of the chancel to the
east wall with a reredos and communion
rail to create a sanctuary in high-church
style. Now there would be a Eucharist at the
early service every Sunday and at the main
morning service once a month. Morning
Prayer would be read at the principal service
on other Sundays, and the clergy, including
Satterlee whenever he was available, would
conduct Morning and Evening Prayer every
day of the week. There would also be a
Eucharist on saints' days recognized in the

Interior, Calvary Church

Book of Common Prayer and on major feast days.[8]   Thus he established the liturgical style
that he would carry to Washington and that would become the standard for cathedral worship
there for seven decades.

A Place in the Diocese

While Satterlee struggled to find a future for Calvary, he turned his interests outside
the parish. New opportunities for service had arisen in the diocese just as he was moving
back to the city. Within a matter of weeks of his return, Bishop Horatio Potter, now eighty
years old, announced that he could no longer carry the full burden of leadership and
requested the election of an assistant bishop. That fall the diocesan convention elected Henry
Codman Potter, then rector of Grace Church on lower Broadway. Potter and Satterlee, born
the same year, had similar backgrounds. Both had spent their childhoods in upstate New
York, both had family ties to Union College, and both had avoided identity with any church
party. Potter, who had grown up in a high-church family, had gone to the Virginia Theological
Seminary rather than General, and as bishop could maintain a neutral position on matters of
churchmanship. Satterlee's independent stance on churchmanship was clearly established.
And both men were eager to open the Episcopal Church to new avenues of mission.

Henry Codman Potter

In other ways the two men differed. Potter, the son of a former Bishop of Pennsylvania and nephew of Horatio Potter, seemed to have a perfect pedigree for an Episcopal bishop. Furthermore, he had a confident and flexible style that made him a good leader and earned him entry into New York society.[9] In contrast, Satterlee had come to the Episcopal Church only as an adult. He was reserved, even somewhat shy, wary of moving too far from the familiar surroundings of parish life. But the two men knew each other well, and Satterlee could expect that he would be called upon to work closely with the new bishop in revitalizing the diocese.

Just as promising for Satterlee as Potter's election was the news that William Reed Huntington, rector of All Saints Church in Worcester, Massachusetts, and already one of the most influential leaders in the Episcopal Church, would come to New York to take Potter's place at Grace Church. Satterlee already knew Huntington and his cousin Frederick D. Huntington, the Bishop of Central New York, both of whom were members of the Clerical Club and active in the Church Congress. Both Henry Potter and the two Huntingtons would remain Satterlee's close and trusted colleagues for the rest of his life.

Another clergyman arriving in the city at that time was William S. Rainsford, who was taking on the task of rebuilding the ministry of St. George's Church, just six blocks south and east of Calvary on Stuyvesant Square. Since the departure of its famous rector, Stephen H. Tyng, in 1878, the parish had fallen on such hard times that the vestry in 1882 was willing to risk its future on the tall, handsome, fair-haired, thirty-two-year-old who had toured the country as a missioner for the Episcopal Church. Popular, charismatic, and impulsive, Rainsford was the perfect choice to revive Tyng's evangelical style of preaching and liturgy. Born and educated in England, he had worked in the East London missions organized by the Anglican Church and thus was well prepared to create a social ministry at St. George's for the poor and oppressed on the lower East Side. As Satterlee's closest Episcopal neighbor, Rainsford would be a direct competitor in terms of churchmanship and social ministry. At the same time, the common interests of the two men in extending the mission outreach of the Church made them frequent allies.[10]

Missions, Domestic and Foreign

Also in 1882, probably through Bishop Horatio Potter, Satterlee was appointed a member of the board of the Domestic and Foreign Mission Society of the Episcopal Church. Quickly taking a leadership role on the board, he was able to convince the society a few years later to construct its new office building on property next to Calvary on the same block of Fourth Avenue. This arrangement gave Satterlee easy access to missionaries coming to New York from all parts of the world. One of his innovations at Zion had been to organize an active mission program that would reach out to missionary districts in the West and to countries overseas.[11] Now at Calvary Satterlee was well positioned to promote missionary efforts both within his parish and in the national Church.

The idea that parishes should undertake missionary work was an idea not widely accepted in the Episcopal Church at that time, but Satterlee was out to remove that bias. In an article in *Harper's Weekly,* he pointed out that "such mission work is not confined to any one age or body of Christians, but is as old as Christianity itself." Soon after his arrival at Calvary he began working with other city clergy to promote preaching missions in the city. In his mind, missionary work was not just carrying the Gospel to foreign lands and cultures, but had to appeal to the thousands of unchurched people in the city. There was enough support for the idea by 1885 that Bishop Henry Potter appointed a committee to plan for a city-wide mission during the Advent season. In addition to Satterlee, the committee included, among others, Rainsford and Benjamin F. De Costa, rector of the Church of St. John the Evangelist, who was destined to be a leader in the Social Gospel movement in New York. The purpose of the mission, as described in the *New York Times*, was to attack "the evil of class churches and the lack of spiritual ministry to the rich." Extending the reach of the Church beyond the privileged classes and addressing the social evils that afflicted the lower classes were high on the agendas of both Satterlee and Rainsford. The plans came to fruition that Advent, when more than twenty churches participated by holding three to six services daily for ten to sixteen days. Satterlee was fortunate in having Daniel S. Tuttle, the Bishop of Missouri, and Robert W. B. Elliott, missionary Bishop of Western Texas, as the missioners at Calvary. Tuttle had earlier invited Satterlee to join his cathedral staff in St. Louis, and the two became good friends during the Advent mission at Calvary. The relationship would prove valuable to Satterlee years later when Tuttle became the presiding Bishop of the Episcopal Church.[12]

The Advent mission was so successful that the *New York Times* chose to comment on it as "something so unusual as to claim notice outside strictly religious circles."

The Episcopal churches here are greater in number than those of any other Protestant body and also than those of the Roman Catholics, and many of them are, too, among the wealthiest and most important ecclesiastical corporations in the city. Deriving its origins from the Church of England the American Episcopal Church has always been noted for its quiet, orderly, and conservative way of doing its work. . . . Hence this church has never favored a system of revivals, as other denominations have done, and has eschewed all connection with schemes of sensational or exciting preaching, [or] extemporaneous prayers. . . . During the last few years, however, some of the Episcopal clergy—mostly young and zealous men—have been desirous of doing something better for the spiritual welfare of the great city of New York. . . . Anxious to emulate the course of the English church, several of the clergy in New York, with the cordial approval of Bishop Henry C. Potter, arranged a plan of services to be held in the Advent season of 1885. . . . There can be no question, we think, . . . as to the fair measure of success which it attained.[13]

SOCIAL MINISTRY AT CALVARY

With little hope of abolishing the pew rent system, Satterlee reached out in other ways to the working class and indigent families in the community. He took steps at once to strengthen the work of Calvary Chapel, established in 1856 as one of the few free chapels in the city. Other parishes soon discovered the free chapel as a partial solution to the pew rent system, which restricted attendance in the parish church to the privileged, except for a few free seats in the balcony. Satterlee was frustrated that he could not create a single, closely knit worshiping community in the parish as long as the chapel existed, but at least it enabled him to minister to those who could not afford a pew. He placed the senior clergyman on his staff in charge of the chapel with an assistant. With the same liturgical style as the church and a somewhat reduced schedule of services, the chapel was an independent operation mirroring all the activities of the larger church.

To reach the unchurched, Satterlee set up Galilee Chapel in a battered storefront building on Twenty-third Street near First Avenue in 1883. The following year Rainsford opened a mission in the back room of a saloon nearby on Avenue A. The lower East Side, just a few blocks east of Calvary Church, had become one of the worst slums in the city, crowded with poor families, recent immigrants, and the destitute. Merchants and small shopkeepers had now all but abandoned East Twenty-third Street, a main thoroughfare just two blocks north of the church, when elevated railroad stations were erected over the street at both Second and Third Avenues. The noise of the trains and the soot and cinders spewed out by the steam locomotives drove away middle-class businesses and left some abandoned buildings. It was precisely here that Satterlee was determined to center his missionary outreach in the city.[14]

THE GALILEE EAST SIDE BUILDINGS OF CALVARY PARISH.

Satterlee quickly found that the Galilee Mission posed challenges he had not faced in Wappingers Falls, where the population was relatively homogeneous. Now he was appealing to people with diverse cultural backgrounds. High-church liturgy used at Calvary meant nothing to the unchurched who were lured into Galilee Mission. Satterlee later reported: "The neighborhood was so bad, that 22 panes of glass were broken in the windows while service was going on, and I had the jagged end of a bottle thrown at me while I was speaking one night. The mission service was a sort of Methodist experience meeting adapted to the Church."[15] It was clear that city missions required clergy with special talents and training.

To find such men, Satterlee wrote to an Anglican bishop who had told him about settlement work in London. "I know from personal experience and observation how far you are spiritually in advance of us in England. There is no work in the City of New York like the best work that is being so largely done in London." Satterlee was certain many English clergy had the required qualifications, but he realized they might find it difficult to work in America. To cover that possibility, he sent off a letter that same day to Dwight L. Moody, the internationally known lay evangelist, who had run city missions in Chicago. Satterlee may well have heard Moody preach at a great revival in New York City in 1875. "Though you do not, of course, sympathize with many of the convictions which I hold as a churchman," Satterlee wrote, "still we have so much in common, and you are so familiar with the kind of work I propose starting."[16] In this way Satterlee was reaching out to others who had experience in developing city missions.

In 1885, when he could find or borrow the money, Satterlee began acquiring abandoned buildings along the south side of Twenty-third Street, near First Avenue. By 1887 the parish had opened a workingmen's lodging house, called the Olive Tree Inn, on the upper floors of several buildings. On the ground floor were a reading room and a restaurant that was providing meals at minimum cost to 150 men each day. Satterlee always maintained, as

29

did many social reformers of his day, that doling out free food would only destroy the self-respect of the poor. He insisted instead that fees, however small, be charged for "everything but the Gospel."[17]

At the same time social ministries were growing within the parish. The Industrial School taught girls how to sew and make garments; the Kitchen Garden taught table setting, dish-washing, and waiting on the door; the Relief Department provided home visitors, help to people in distress or seeking employment, and personal counseling; the Chinese Sunday School provided language training, Bible classes, and religious education on Sunday afternoons for Chinese immigrants recruited from the hundreds of small family laundries that dotted the city. The people of Calvary were members of a score of organizations outside the parish.[18]

DRAWING ON THE ELITE

With a staff of five clergy, four choirs in the church and two in the chapel, two Sunday schools including more than one hundred teachers and seven hundred students, and dozens of organizations designed to meet special needs, Satterlee devised his own techniques for managing this growing enterprise. In one sense he had no organizational plan at all. As new needs or opportunities arose, he set out to address them regardless of cost or the impact on other activities. He then looked for someone within the parish who he believed could carry out the task. Often the person selected felt unequal to the responsibility, but most found it impossible to refuse the rector's challenge. He was an inspiring leader fully committed to the importance of the work he was undertaking, and those tapped for greater responsibility were flattered by his confidence in them. Once the new organization had a name, a statement of purpose, a roster of members, and a budget, Satterlee gave the group free rein. The group reported its activities each year in the parish Year Book, a printed volume of more than two hundred pages. Widely distributed within the parish, the Year Book was more than an activity report—it was also a vehicle for program evaluation and financial control.[19]

Over and above their value as a reference guide and a record of accomplishment, the *Year Books* were clearly designed to be a source of inspiration and optimism. What they did not always reveal were the depths of the rector's disappointments and frustrations. Inevitably, some of his recruits were not up to the tasks assigned to them. Because the low fees charged in the Galilee missions never met expenses, Satterlee was frequently appealing to individuals for funds or digging into his own pocket to meet shortfalls. Some of the Galilee projects, especially the workingmen's club, were failing to attract enough patrons to justify their existence.

Many of the people whose names appeared in the Year Book later supported Satterlee on the cathedral project. Among the young men he recruited during his first years at Calvary were George Zabriskie, Alexander M. Hadden, and Frederick W. Rhinelander. Hadden, about thirty years old, described himself as "a man not over occupied in business, going about in society, and somewhat of a club man." He took an interest in Satterlee and volunteered to serve as a private secretary without salary. Over the next few years, Hadden "rather unwillingly" accepted the leadership of two of the largest mission operations in the parish. He would continue to serve Satterlee behind the scenes for more than twenty years.[20] Rhinelander served on the vestry, became one of the Satterlees' close personal friends, and married Satterlee's daughter, Constance. His younger brother, Philip Mercer Rhinelander, grew up in the parish, later entered the ministry, served as one of Satterlee's principal associates in Washington, and later became the Bishop of Pennsylvania. Zabriskie's name would be found on the rosters of many committees and organizations, both in the parish and the diocese.

As one of the young laymen wrote to the Calvary vestry, "I do not know of any other church in the City of New York which has a larger, more substantial body of young men workers, between the ages of twenty and forty, and these are ready to stand in the breach and shoulder very real burdens." At Calvary, young members of the elite who were bored with their empty lives found themselves capable of undertaking projects that would have a lasting and visible effect on the world around them.

Also a part of the younger generation of the upper-class elite were the rector's now grown children. Like his father, Churchill had received his early education at home with private tutors, traveled to Europe with his parents as a teenager, and then gone to Columbia College. His father did not push him to enter the ministry, but growing up in Calvary parish, where he met bishops, missionaries from all parts of the world, and talented upper-class New Yorkers, young Churchill abandoned thoughts of business or law and went off to the General Theological Seminary in 1890. He never had a parish in New York City, but he remained close to his father by almost daily correspondence with his father and family.[21] Had he not died of a heart attack at age thirty-four in 1904, he might well have become a bishop himself. Constance with her mother stepped into many positions at Calvary and was always at her father's side as a helpmate and secretary both in New York and Washington. Following her father's death, Constance was for three decades an active leader in the Washington Cathedral Association in New York City.

The Year Book rosters also contained familiar names from the older generation. First and foremost was Jane Lawrence Satterlee, the rector's wife, who among other things directed choirs and the Chancel Guild, taught classes, maintained the social agenda in the rectory next to the church on Twenty-first Street, and served as the rector's primary source of guidance and inspiration throughout his ministry. Close to Satterlee personally were a number of lay leaders who represented some of the wealthiest and most socially elite families in the city. Dr. William C. Rives III was the son of a Virginia landowner and member of the Richmond

Junto, who had served in Congress and had been ambassador to France in the 1840s. Young Rives was a graduate of Harvard and Oxford with a medical degree from Vienna. The Rives were anonymous major donors to Satterlee's enterprises, beginning with the Galilee Mission and ending with the Peace Cross on the Cathedral grounds. His wife, Mary, was the sister of Philip and Frederick Rhinelander, members of a family that had made its fortune in the sugar trade in colonial New York and was considered the "crème de la crème" of New York society in the 1880s.

Among Satterlee's strongest supporters was Percy Rivington Pyne, whose father had made a fortune as protégé of Moses Taylor, a legendary merchant-financier in New York in the 1840s. Pyne served on the Calvary vestry and on other parish committees. His wife, Albertina, was one of the most active members of the parish and represented the parish on important diocesan committees. She maintained a close friendship with the Satterlees after her husband's death and was a major contributor to the cathedral project in Washington.[22] Other members of the Satterlee family were also active in the parish, including his cousins Walter Satterlee, an accomplished artist in New York, and F. LeRoy Satterlee, a prominent physician. These and other lay leaders at Calvary were the nucleus of the group of the wealthy, upper-class elite in New York that would provide Satterlee with the financial base he would need a decade later in Washington.

England and the Social Gospel

Beyond these parochial concerns Satterlee was trying to define for himself the proper place of the Church in the social and economic revolution that was sweeping the industrialized world, but whose impact seemed most severe in large cities like London and New York. On the one hand, he counted himself among the hundreds of church leaders who asserted that the Christian Church had to respond to the horrible working and living conditions of the urban poor, to the appalling lack of medical and educational services, to political corruption at all levels of society, to the decline of moral standards, and to the mindless, vicious exploitation of people by laissez-faire capitalists. Satterlee's ministry at Calvary did in fact address on the parish level many of the social and economic problems that were the target of the Social Gospel movement.

On the other hand, Satterlee could not accept the underlying assumptions of the Social Gospel, which was in vogue among church reformers, namely, that the problems of modern society had become too complex for the Church to solve by the traditional methods of promoting personal salvation. Instead, what was needed was a new theological approach that confronted issues at the social rather than the individual level. What troubled Satterlee about the Social Gospel was that to him it implied that the new "science" of sociology, rather than religion, would solve the problems of the modern world. Such a perspective was completely incompatible with his high-church vision of the Christian community, in which salvation was achieved through loving relationships among individuals and with their immanent God. Satterlee firmly believed that the Incarnation, in which God chose to take on a human existence in Jesus Christ, demonstrated that God was not a distant and passive observer of human affairs but participated directly in the work of the faithful. It was God, not mere mortals, who would direct the social ministry at Calvary and ultimately build the cathedral in Washington. Satterlee's entire ministry had been centered on creating such sacramental communities at Zion Church and Calvary. He was not about to change course in order to keep in step with the current fads of Social Christianity.[23]

As part of a family trip to Europe in the summer of 1890, Satterlee stopped in London for a few days to visit Toynbee Hall and Oxford House, two London settlement houses that were attracting wide attention among social reformers in England and America. Samuel Barnett, a wealthy Anglican clergyman, had established Toynbee Hall in 1884 as a memorial to Arnold Toynbee, the Oxford don whose lectures on Christian responsibility for social reform had sparked interest on both sides of the Atlantic. For years Barnett had tried to encourage philanthropically minded young men from the universities to live and work among the poor of East London. Although called a settlement house, Toynbee Hall did not provide social services to the poor but actually resembled a small version of an academic college that provided a residence for meetings, discussions, lectures, exhibits, concerts, and other activities. Furthermore, Toynbee Hall, unlike Oxford House at Bethel Green, was a purely secular enterprise with no ties to the Church.[24]

Satterlee returned to London in the summer of 1892 to learn more about what English churchmen were calling Social Christianity. With Lord Meath, whom he met on the Atlantic crossing, he visited "one or two dozen places in London where the Association of which he is president has provided open spaces for the poor and especially for the children." From Charles Booth he obtained fascinating statistics on parish mission projects. He and his son, Churchill, spent a week at Keble College, Oxford, where they met several times with Charles Gore, the eminent high-church theologian, who had recently published an article on "The Social Teaching of the Sermon on the Mount." This second visit to London's East End confirmed Satterlee's earlier impression that Toynbee Hall was "of secondary importance" but that Oxford House had succeeded "beyond all expectations." He thought it stood firmly on "the sociological law of the New Testament. . . . Oxford House puts first things first, it takes men as they are and tries to develop their characters in the state of life in which God has placed them."[25]

Always interested in the practical more than the theoretical, Satterlee was captivated by the commitment of P. R. Buchanan, a wealthy tea merchant who had moved from London's

West End to Bethel Green to live among the poor. There he had built for the working classes an arcade of cooperative shops, a pharmacy, and a temperance bar near Oxford House, where church services were held. The workingmen's club above the shops included rooms for meetings, billiards, and cards, all supported by the club members. Satterlee was especially intrigued with the Tee To Tum Clubs that Buchanan and others had opened in seven London locations. Buchanan explained that "Tee" implied that tea rather than liquor was served; "To Tum," he said, was the word used in Ceylon for a club. Before leaving London, Satterlee agreed to write an article on Oxford House for the *Economic Review* and invited Buchanan to come to New York the following summer to set up a workingmen's club at Calvary on the London model.[26]

Satterlee had met Buchanan early in 1892 in New York and invited him to a meeting at the Calvary rectory with Rainsford, who at once saw the advantage of creating a Tee To Tum operation at St. George's. Before the end of the year Rainsford announced the opening of two new missions that would incorporate most of the elements of Buchanan's Bethel Green project. By the time Buchanan arrived in New York in January 1893, Satterlee had purchased two additional buildings on Twenty-third Street next to the Olive Tree Inn. As in the past, the buildings were fully mortgaged so that he and one parishioner personally had to accept title to the property and thus put themselves in financial jeopardy.[27]

Satterlee drew up several floor plans for the new buildings. When completed in March, the Tee To Tum Club had meeting and entertainment rooms on the second floor and also had access to the coffee house, restaurant, and free reading room. There were bowling alleys in the basement while the upper floors contained a circulating library, a boys' clubroom and gymnasium, a mission chapel, entertainment room, and dormitories for 350 men. Like its London counterparts, the Calvary Tee To Tum accepted only men "of good character." For Satterlee, that meant men with sound morals who abstained from alcohol and had some employment. They were required to pay dues (really token amounts), elected their own officers, and controlled the club themselves. Some people in the parish objected when the club decided to open on Sundays, but Satterlee did not intervene; part of the Te To Tum purpose was to instill self-reliance and build character in workingmen.[28]

Calvary's Tee To Tum Club gave the parish more publicity than it had received in years, including a front-page article in the *New York Times* on March 24, 1893. Just a few days earlier the *Times* had reported the failure of Rainsford's attempt to run a workingmen's club that served hard liquor. Robert Graham, head of the church temperance society of the diocese, roundly denounced Rainsford's "church saloon" as "impractical and mischievous." The contrast between the two projects, duly noted in the press, enhanced the standing of the Calvary Tee To Tum.[29]

The press stories did not reveal that Satterlee had already established a strong temperance program concentrating on boys and young men at Calvary. Satterlee considered teenage drinking not only a health problem but a moral one as well. Working closely with Graham, Satterlee's staff had organized a parish branch of the Church Temperance Legion, beginning with the Young Crusaders for boys under fourteen. Legioneers were expected to wear uniforms, attend meetings in the boys' club, participate in devotional rituals and military drill, and take an oath that they would abstain from drinking liquor until they were twenty-one. The success of the program at Calvary gratified Satterlee, who reported in 1895 that five of his Knights of Temperance were preparing to enter the ministry or already had done so. The temperance tradition at Calvary remained strong into the 1930s.[30]

Four months after the Calvary Tee To Tum opened in 1893, financial panic seized the nation. Twenty thousand people became homeless as well as jobless in New York City, and thousands that summer were living in parks and squares, in the Salvation Army Hall, and at Blackwell's Island. Angry socialists and unionists were organizing "hunger demonstrations" within a few blocks of Calvary Church.[31] The parish on its own could do little to stem this enormous tide of misfortune, but Calvary already had in place programs that were on a parochial scale meeting the needs of the dispossessed. The parish regularly provided fifteen women to visit the sick in three hospitals, while others ministered to prisoners at the Tombs and the homeless at Blackwell's Island. One volunteer, Rebecca Foster, worked almost full-time visiting the courts and prisons. She reported that in 1894 alone she and her helpers had spoken to 3,000 persons, were able to have 83 released from prison and 142 women released by the courts, and provided lawyers for 211. These activities caught the attention of Theodore Roosevelt, who later wrote to Satterlee's daughter, Constance: "I had long known your father; I was brought into intimate contact with him first when I was Police Commissioner. . . . I soon discovered that he was one of the clergymen who was a genuine force for civic righteousness and that his deeds made good his words. He was a practical idealist. . . ."[32] The relationship between the two men later blossomed in Washington and gave Satterlee ready access to the White House.

A House of Prayer for All People

Roosevelt's observation that Satterlee was a practical idealist touched a central aspect of his ministry at Calvary. Never able to convince the vestry to abolish the pew rent system, he continued to carry the parish to the very edge of financial collapse, if not occasionally beyond that limit. As a move toward a broader financial base, Satterlee had instituted a "systematic offering system" that encouraged parishioners to pledge annually to support Calvary activities of their choice. He admitted, however, that elimination of the pew rent system would require an endowment of $500,000, which he privately had no hopes of reaching. He expressed his frustration that, in trying to make the parish "the living center of religious life in the neighborhood," there were no seats in the church for new people who did come. In the 1895 Year Book, he wrote, "Private ownership even of a pew in the house of which Christ Himself says, 'My house shall be called a house of prayer for all people,' is felt to be contrary to the Gospel by outsiders, who have come to regard pewed churches in the light of private religious club houses. . . ." "A house of prayer for all people" was a theme he may have acquired from his friend and mentor William Reed Huntington, who had used it effectively in his parish in Worcester, Massachusetts. Satterlee carried the theme to Washington, where it became a mark of the Cathedral in an ecumenical context.[33]

Rainsford's sparkling success at nearby St. George's Church must have added to Satterlee's frustration. Rainsford had insisted as a condition of his accepting the rectorship that the pew system be abolished and that the vestry disband all parish committees. J. Pierpont Morgan, the senior warden, provided the money to replace the pew rent system, gave the rector a free hand in the parish, and financed the purchase or construction of buildings to house the ever-growing mission program. The contrast between the two rectors, however, was more than a matter of financial resources. Personality, churchmanship, and theology were also factors. Satterlee was restrained and methodical, a strong leader working behind the scenes; Rainsford was a charismatic, unpredictable extrovert. Satterlee's high-church principles made him a conservative in matters of liturgy and in strict adherence to the *Book of Common Prayer*; Rainsford was an evangelical who put more stress on preaching than on liturgy and was open to ties with other denominations. Satterlee's theology kept him focused inward on the parish as a sacramental community; Rainsford saw Christian response to the social needs of the community as more important than the inner life of the parish.[34]

THE INSTITUTIONAL CHURCH

By 1895 Satterlee had reached most of the goals he had set for himself in 1882, despite the never-ending financial worries. The Tee To Tum and all the other mission projects on East Twenty-third Street were now firmly established and growing. Annual statistics in the *Year Books* were increasingly impressive: more than 30,000 people had come to the Galilee Mission since it was established; attendance at the boys' club was almost as high. The Year Book for 1895 contained reports from sixty-one organizations and committees. The parish, including the church, Calvary Chapel, and the Galilee Mission, served almost 1,000 families with nearly 2,000 communicants, 87 Sunday school teachers, and 712 students. By any standards Calvary would appear to be in the forefront of the Social Gospel movement in New York City and a perfect example of what came to be called the "institutional church." In fact, however, historians have never recognized Satterlee's Calvary in either category.

This lack of recognition was in large part Satterlee's own choosing. He found that he could not embrace the tenets of the Social Gospel, which he considered a secular movement based more on sociology than on the Christian religion. The 500-page book *A Creedless Gospel and the Gospel Creed*, which he published in 1895, explored, in greater depths than most of his readers required, the philosophical and theological basis of his ministry. In his book Satterlee never mentioned the Social Gospel, but he revealed the source of his reservations about it. "It is one thing to welcome and assimilate the truths that science has discovered in the natural world; it is another thing to adopt and push the scientific method of research into the spiritual world. The danger of error comes not from the science itself, but from a Christianity which would form a partnership with science."[35]

Just as he had earlier avoided taking a public stand in the debates over churchmanship, Satterlee kept his reservations about the Social Gospel to himself. The term "Social Gospel" never appears in any of his writings, public or private. His work contributed to the Social Gospel movement, but he would not be a part of it.

For essentially the same reasons, Calvary failed to make the historians' roster of the many institutional churches that flourished in New York City at the turn of the century. It was true that the scope and magnitude of Calvary's social outreach were comparable to what Rainsford was able to establish at St. George's, but the underlying motivations of the two men were quite different. Satterlee saw the social services offered by Calvary as a direct extension of the sacramental ministry of a Christian community. He explicitly rejected the term "institutional church" as implying a secular rather than a sacred purpose. It is likely that Satterlee was reacting against the administrative techniques used at St. George's to manage its far-flung enterprises. He would have been appalled by the opening sentences of a book published a decade later on the institutional church as it evolved at St. George's: "An institutional church is like a business house in its use of two essential elements of executive success. The first of these is the centralization, and the second is the distribution of authority."[36] This analogy would have been anathema to Satterlee in 1895.

Diocesan and World Missions

When Henry Potter became assistant bishop in 1884, he gave his first priority to revitalizing the mission work of the diocese and appointed Satterlee to a special committee to come up with recommendations. The report in 1885 urged the diocese to extend its mission work beyond the city to the rural parishes, which had neither the resources nor the leadership to launch efforts to reach the unchurched. The report also recommended that the City Missionary Society, which was actually an independent corporation, be reorganized under the authority of the bishop. The first proposal was set in motion when Satterlee and

Irving Grinnell were appointed to the diocesan board of missions and continued to serve in that capacity until Satterlee left for Washington in 1896. The second proposal—to bring the City Missionary Society into control by the diocese—was never adopted in Satterlee's time.[37]

During the closing decade of the nineteenth century the Episcopal Church was still heavily involved in supporting missionaries overseas, and Satterlee was very much a part of that activity. He was in fact living at the control center for all the Church's work in the foreign mission field, with the headquarters of the Domestic and Foreign Mission Society just a few steps from Calvary Church. Calvary itself had been active in supporting missionaries abroad even before Satterlee's arrival. Washburn had organized the parish's Foreign Mission Society in 1875 and concentrated its mission work in Mexico and China. Satterlee continued to promote the parish's foreign mission projects in both of these countries.[38]

Satterlee's support of foreign missions went well beyond the parish. As an active member of the Domestic and Foreign Mission Society, he had a role in setting policy for the national church. In the 1880s a dispute arose over whether the Episcopal Church could establish a mission in Mexico without intruding improperly into the domain of another Christian church with episcopal polity (that is, the Roman Catholic Church). The Clerical Club took up the intrusion issue in 1885 in a meeting in the Calvary rectory with two seminary professors chosen to oppose the Mexican project in a debate with Satterlee and one of his friends on the Board of Missions. Satterlee and his colleague won the debate, but when the General Convention in 1886 refused to fund the Mexican mission, Satterlee still gave countless hours to this project and ended up paying the missioner's salary himself. He was also a leader in the Missionary Council, which encouraged missionary work throughout the Church, and was active in the national conferences in St. Louis in 1892 and 1899.[39]

Satterlee's commitment to the mission field did not end with his ministry at Calvary but remained high on his agenda as a bishop. Despite his growing responsibilities in Washington, he made it a point to attend the monthly meetings of the Missionary Board in New York up to the last week of his life. For Satterlee, mission was a prime function of the Christian Church, second only to worship. From that conviction he declared the Washington Cathedral to be "the Chief Mission Church of the Diocese," a precept that challenges the Cathedral to the present day.

TOWARD A NATIONAL CHURCH

Missions would always be a passionate concern for Satterlee, but he was not immune to the controversies that were sweeping through the Episcopal Church in the last decade of the nineteenth century. There were hotly contested proposals to revise the Prayer Book;

create a truly national church to replace the loose confederation of dioceses; define the basis for Christian reunion with other Protestant denominations; and fix the place of the Episcopal Church and a national cathedral in such a union. These issues demanded attention as the Church struggled to keep up with the rapidly changing landscape of a growing industrialized nation.

During Satterlee's last years in New York, influential liberals like William Reed Huntington were attempting to strengthen and reform the Episcopal Church. Coming out of the broad-church movement, Huntington and others were looking for ways to heal the deep wounds inflicted on the body of the Church by almost a century of strife over matters of liturgy, theology, and governance. Huntington had played a major role in the 1880s on a commission that proposed revisions in the *Book of Common Prayer* to add prayers for industrial workers and provide for greater flexibility in worship. Huntington was also part of a group emerging from the Church Congress that was convinced that only a Christian Church national in scope could respond effectively to the complex social and economic problems of an industrialized, urban nation. Many Episcopalians believed that the episcopacy offered a logical form of leadership for a national church. Another member of the broad-church group, William Montgomery Brown, wrote a best-seller in church circles that observed "that the Episcopal Church was more fit for leadership in a national church than was the Roman Catholic Church because it had a representative government and was not tied to any foreign power."[40]

The General Conventions from 1886 to 1892 rejected Huntington's proposal for *Prayer Book* revision as too radical, but he was successful in convincing the House of Bishops in 1886 to adopt what came to be known as the Chicago Quadrilateral. The statement, largely the work of Huntington, set forth the four basic elements the Episcopal Church would expect to be a part of any national church it would help to create: the Holy Scriptures, the Nicene Creed, the sacraments of Baptism and the Eucharist, and the historic episcopate adapted to local circumstances. Two years later the third Lambeth Conference of Anglican bishops meeting in London adopted Huntington's four principles "as the basis on which approach may be by God's blessing made toward Home Reunion."[41]

Satterlee was not a leader in Huntington's national church movement, but he was a strong supporter behind the scenes. A close associate of Huntington's in the Clerical Club and in New York diocesan affairs, Satterlee saw unity among Christians as a mandate set forth by Jesus and the apostles, but as a conservative high churchman he would not accept unity at any price. For him, Huntington's Quadrilateral, as adopted in Chicago and at Lambeth, offered sufficient conditions for an acceptable proposal for church union. He had reservations, however, about the statement in the Chicago document "that This Church does not seek to absorb other Communions, but rather, in co-operating with them on the basis of a common Faith and Order . . . to heal the wounds of the Body of Christ." In the first place, his strong prejudices against the Roman Catholic Church made it impossible for him to consider union with that communion. Secondly, he would never give up his hope that the American Protestant churches would be ultimately united under the aegis of the Anglican Church. In his last message to the people of Calvary Church before he left for Washington he wrote:

> Now, I believe the Anglican Church comes nearest to this ideal of any Church in Christendom. I believe not only that one hundred years from this time the Anglican Church will be larger and more important than the Church of Rome, but that the more one understands the "genius" of the Anglican Church, the better he will understand the New Testament itself.[42]

In championing Anglicanism, Satterlee was trying to make at least the Protestant Church in the United States a house of prayer for all people. Reunion with the Roman Catholic Church seemed out of the question as long as that communion insisted upon maintaining practices that Satterlee considered corruptions of the structure and governance of the "primitive" fourth-century church as he understood it. Chief among these distortions Satterlee cited the power and authority of the Papacy. The gulf between the Protestant churches and the Roman Catholics loomed even wider in 1896 when Leo XIII issued the papal bull *Apostolicae Curae*, declaring that the clerical orders of the Anglican Communion were invalid.

Satterlee saw a greater chance for a national church among Protestant denominations that could accept the Chicago-Lambeth Quadrilateral. There was no thought in his proposal that the Anglican Church (or the Episcopal Church in the United States) was in any sense superior morally to other denominations. Nor in advocating a national church was he proposing a state church or an official religion in America. Both he and Huntington strongly supported the separation of church and state. It was the liturgical beauty and theological purity of the Anglican tradition, as he saw it, that made it a firm basis for Christian unity.

When delegates to the General Convention of the Episcopal Church arrived in Minneapolis in October 1895, the air was full of speculation about the fate of a dozen proposals to amend the constitution that would, if adopted, make significant changes in the character of the Church. Attracting most attention was a proposal to drop the name "Protestant Episcopal Church" in favor of a more generic title. Undaunted by earlier defeats, Huntington had returned to the convention in another attempt to secure adoption of the Lambeth Quadrilateral. In the interest of creating a truly national church, some delegates favored election of the presiding bishop and giving him the title of primate. Others proposed the grouping of dioceses in twelve provinces, and a few advocated the election of archbishops to head each province. Some saw in the petition to create a new diocese in Washington,

Legation Authorization

D.C., the possibility of making that the see of the presiding bishop as well as the site of a national cathedral.[43]

While the convention delegates debated these issues, Satterlee was at work in New York leading a committee, probably originating in the Domestic and Foreign Mission Society, to draft a resolution calling attention to the persecution of the Armenian Church, "involving the wholesale slaughter of men and the violation of women" by the Turkish army. As adopted by the convention, the resolution called upon clergy and laity to collect funds to be sent to relief committees in Constantinople. As the principal author of the resolution, Satterlee was looked upon by senior bishops as the spokesman for the Episcopal Church on the Armenian crisis. [44]

Six months later Satterlee would be drafted to carry an appeal from the Anglican churches in Great Britain and America to Czar Nicholas II, urging him to use his influence "to

Sitting (left to right): George Zabriskie; Father John of Cronstadt; Metropolitan of Silesi; Bishop Satterlee; Archimandrite of the Greek Church at St. Petersburg. Standing (left to right): Christopher Christobasiles, Interpreter to the Metropolitan; N.A. Gripari, Greek Consul at Sebastopol; Prince Michael Comnene Andronikoff; Prince Constantine Alexandrovich Beboutoff.

secure, in combination with other Christian Powers, safety of property, life, and honor to those [Armenians] who still survive." Unlike Anglican bishops who were officials of the state, Satterlee could go to St. Petersburg without any appearance that he was on a diplomatic mission to the Russian government. It was also considered essential that Satterlee's meeting with the Czar be kept secret even from American embassy officials in St. Petersburg. After waiting in Russia almost three weeks for an audience, Satterlee met with the Czar and Czarina on August 5, 1896. When the press breached the secrecy of the mission in November, newspapers and church journals carried stories about "the American Bishop and the Czar." Satterlee now had national recognition outside the church on both sides of the Atlantic.[45]

A New Diocese and a New Bishop

As it turned out, the General Convention in 1895 did not adopt any of the proposals for revising the constitution of the Church, but it did accept the petition from the Bishop of Maryland creating the new Diocese of Washington. There was a common belief that its presence in the nation's capital would make the new diocese the most important in the

Episcopal Church, and that assumption called for the election of a highly qualified man as the first bishop. Those who quickly came to mind were rectors of the largest and most prestigious parishes in New York, Washington, and Boston, but Satterlee was not among the likely candidates. Perhaps his reluctance to seek high office at the diocesan and national level seemed to remove him from consideration. After all, he had declined election as a bishop twice, first as assistant Bishop of Ohio in 1887 and then as Bishop of Michigan in 1889. It seemed that Satterlee was too closely committed to parochial work at Calvary to seek wider responsibilities.

It was not surprising, then, that when the convention of the new diocese met for the first time in Washington on December 4, 1895, Satterlee's name was not among those nominated. As expected, prominent rectors from large city parishes dominated the list. On the first three ballots on December 5, however, no candidate received the necessary two-thirds vote of the clergy, as required by the canons of the Diocese of Maryland, under which the convention was operating. The wide distribution of votes among the candidates made an early successful election improbable. Even more discouraging, the convention was locked in a bitter and frustrating battle between the high- and low-church parties. Recognizing these circumstances, the convention voted that, if no election occurred in five ballots the following day, a second convention would be called at a later date, probably in May 1896. On the first ballots on December 6, most of the votes were divided between candidates representing the high-church and evangelical factions.

Realizing that the situation was hopeless, Alexander Mackay-Smith, rector of St. John's Church on Lafayette Square, began gathering votes for Satterlee. Mackay-Smith, for some years Archdeacon of New York, had come to know and respect Satterlee for his work at Calvary. Satterlee's accomplishments at Calvary were certainly impressive, but equally important was his lack of identity with any church party. Suddenly the whole mood of the convention changed as the delegates saw a promising way out of their frustration. Satterlee was elected unanimously on the fourth ballot on the second day of the convention.[46]

Even observers who had no part in the convention saw Satterlee's election as an extraordinary turn of events, which led many to see the moment as the work of the Holy Spirit. For Satterlee, however, his course was far from clear. When a New York reporter informed him of his election that evening, "he expressed great surprise as he had not considered himself a candidate, . . . and had no intimation that his name would be proposed." When the *New York Herald* reported that Satterlee might not accept the nomination, he was besieged with letters from Washington urging him to come. He would need time, he replied, to give his decision prayerful consideration.[47]

Satterlee's correspondence and his own notes at the time show clearly that his reluctance to accept the call to Washington was not an attempt to feign modesty but rather a

43

heart-rending decision on his part. As he had always done in times of critical decisions, he compiled lists of the reasons for accepting or rejecting the call. For Calvary, he found nine reasons for staying and eighteen against; for Washington, thirty-seven reasons for going, eight against. Leaving Calvary would mean the loss of old friends and the chance to realize in the parish the many dreams that were still unfulfilled. Most interesting, however, were his reasons for going to Washington. Beyond the promise of laying aside the burdens and frustrations of parish leadership, he looked forward to a ministry to the large "colored" population of Washington; to directing the future of the Cathedral; to having, as a bishop, far-reaching contacts with priests both in the city and the country, with the rich and poor both North and South; and to having greater influence in advancing his interests in the Mexican mission, parochial missions, catholic unity, and the prospective national church under the Episcopal aegis. He saw his election as an opportunity he would never have again to bring men and women of all races, all social classes, and all regions in the United States together in a unified Christian community, for which the new cathedral in Washington would be a house of prayer for all people. Much as the decision pained him and his family, he saw that the lists gave him no choice but to accept the nomination.[48]

Because the Diocese of Washington existed only on paper, Satterlee thought it appropriate that his consecration should take place in Calvary Church. He chose March 25, the Feast of the Assumption, as the date. On that morning a huge congregation that spilled out onto Fourth Avenue assembled for the event. Bishop Coxe, Satterlee's first mentor in the Church, represented the presiding bishop, John Williams of Connecticut, who was too feeble to attend. Among the ten other bishops present were Potter of New York and William Paret of Maryland, who had led the way in creating the new diocese. The procession of nearly five hundred persons included representatives of the national church, the students of General Theological Seminary, delegations from the Board of Missions and the Colored Missions, and clergy from the Diocese of Washington, followed by the bishops and Satterlee with his son Churchill as his chaplain. Frederick D. Huntington, Bishop of Central New York and a member of the Clerical Club, preached the sermon on "the Power of the Church in National Life." Calvary was again crowded that evening as the new bishop confirmed one hundred fifty candidates from Calvary Church and Calvary Chapel.[49]

That same day Satterlee wrote to the people of the Diocese of Washington:

> The first words which, as your Bishop, I write unto you are words of deep
> gratitude for the unity of spirit which so manifestly pervades the diocese. . . .
> May this unity of the spirit in the bond of peace become the ruling influence
> of the Diocese of Washington. Through all coming days and years let us
> guard and treasure it, and then hand it down to our successors as a pearl

of great price; for upon us is resting the God-given responsibility of forming now, in the beginning of our history, the tradition of the future.[50]

Here Satterlee sounded the note of conciliation rather than confrontation that would define his leadership in building the new diocese and the Cathedral. The new bishop was ready to move to Washington.

Washington Cathedral in Renaissance style, as proposed by Ernest Flagg, the New York architect.

3. A Checkered Inheritance

The cathedral project in Washington had its beginnings six years before Henry Satterlee arrived in Washington as bishop in April 1896. During those six years a group of lay and clerical leaders under the Episcopal Bishop of Maryland took the first critical steps to establish a cathedral foundation as a legal entity, organize the foundation, raise money, acquire a site for the cathedral, and determine the architectural style for the Cathedral and all the buildings to be erected on the site. These accomplishments were significant, but they came at high cost. By 1896 the finances, leadership, and planning for the project were in disarray. Satterlee was indeed receiving a checkered inheritance.

A Novel Proposal

The first steps toward a cathedral in Washington came in a roundabout way. In the autumn of 1890 the rectors of two of the largest elite parishes in the city were concerned that the pew-rent system was excluding many people who came to attend Sunday services, especially when Congress was in session. The best solution was to find a site for a new church, preferably near Dupont Circle, where wealthy aristocrats were building large residences. This strategy was intended to attract the newly minted upper class that had made fortunes during and after the Civil War, not members of the more sedate and cultured families that the Satterlees represented.

George William Douglas had been rector of St. John's Church, Lafayette Square, since the fall of 1889. At thirty-nine, Douglas seemed young and relatively inexperienced to be called as rector of one of the largest and richest parishes in the diocese, but he did have some impressive credentials. A native of New York City and a

George William Douglas

47

Randolph Harrison McKim

graduate of Trinity College, Hartford, in 1871, and General Theological Seminary in 1874, Douglas had pursued graduate studies at Oxford and Bonn for two years before returning to New York to serve as an assistant at Calvary and then at Trinity Church, Wall Street. Independently wealthy, Douglas had married the daughter of a prominent Newport family and enjoyed entrée to New York society.[1]

Douglas's partner in the search for property was Randolph Harrison McKim, rector of the Church of the Epiphany in downtown Washington. Like Douglas, McKim was a man of exceptional talents and background. Born in Baltimore in 1842 the son of a merchant, McKim was attending the University of Virginia in 1861 when he enlisted in the Confederate Army. He became aide-de-camp to General "Stonewall" Jackson, decided on the ministry while in the army, and after the war served as rector of prominent parishes in Alexandria, Virginia; New York City; and New Orleans. An outstanding preacher, prolific writer, and able administrator, McKim became, in the estimation of one historian, "the most outspoken Low Churchman of his day."[2]

The two men soon realized that building a large church on prime urban property would be hard to finance. They considered a cooperative effort between the two parishes, but such an arrangement posed complications. Then several laymen in Washington came up with a novel suggestion, that the new church "should take the form of a cathedral foundation."[3] This approach opened the possibility of drawing on financial resources outside the two parishes, perhaps at the diocesan or even national level. However, it also required the approval of William Paret, the Bishop of Maryland, in whose diocese the Washington churches were located.

Bishop William Paret

THE CATHEDRAL IDEA

The very idea of a diocese having a cathedral, to say nothing of one on the national level, was a relatively new trend in the Episcopal Church. Not until the Oxford movement came to the United States in the 1830s did Episcopalians begin to consider the desirability of designating or building large churches as cathedrals for their diocesan bishops. Even then, only high churchmen in the East and Anglo-Catholics in the Midwest promoted the cathedral idea. William R. Whittingham, a high-church cleric, proposed building a cathedral in New York as early as 1839, and soon after he became Bishop of Maryland he considered buying a large Unitarian church in Baltimore to serve as the cathedral of his diocese. In 1852 he expressed his hope that a cathedral could be built in Washington.[4]

Whittingham knew that a Washington cathedral was unlikely as long as the nation's capital was part of the Diocese of Maryland. Despite his appeals to several diocesan conventions in the decades after the Civil War, he was unable to convince the clerical and lay delegates to divide the diocese. After the 1871 convention adopted a resolution "That this Convention is not in favor of any further division of the Diocese or of bringing any proposition before the next General Convention bearing on the matter," the Washington delegation abandoned its efforts to create a separate diocese for the Washington parishes.[5]

Against this background Paret's reservations about cathedrals was understandable. And it was a striking proposal to make to a bishop whose seat was in Baltimore and who had expressed little interest in a cathedral in Baltimore or Washington. Douglas and McKim surely knew that they had to be careful in approaching Bishop Paret. In Washington the bishop had earned the reputation of being a strict disciplinarian, an effective administrator, conservative in churchmanship, and hardheaded on financial matters. Douglas must have written the October 27 letter with these considerations in mind. The letter was brief and to the point, but carefully avoided any mention of possible division of the diocese. A "cathedral foundation" suggested that the enterprise entailed something more than a diocesan institution, but that point was left to the bishop's interpretation. The letter was vague enough to arouse Paret's curiosity but not his anxiety. The bishop replied that he would consider the proposal as long as it did not lead to division of the diocese while assuring Baltimore and Washington equal place as a diocesan center.[6]

FINDING A SITE

The bishop's conditional assent gave Douglas and McKim enough freedom to pursue their true intent—to create a national cathedral in the nation's capital rather than just an edifice for the Diocese of Maryland. In 1891 they pushed ahead to find a suitable site and the money to purchase it. Even if Douglas could obtain the land by gift, he would still need substantial funds to launch the cathedral project. Late in April 1891 he was encouraged when Mary Elizabeth Mann, a member of his parish, offered to leave eight valuable city lots in her will for the cathedral. The estimated value of the property was

$80,000. Douglas drafted a brief statement describing the project for the bishop to present at the diocesan convention in May and then left for Switzerland, where he spent the summer reading the many books and articles he had collected on the history and organization of English cathedrals.[7]   He wrote Paret that his study convinced him of "the importance and present practical utility of Cathedrals" and "the wisdom of seizing hold of the primitive Cathedral idea and moulding it to modern needs." Douglas proposed that the cathedral chapter should be completely independent of the diocese and that "all the schools and institutions connected with the cathedral should be near by it, and the residences of the cathedral chapter should be adjacent to the cathedral."[8]   While avoiding the thorny issue of dividing the diocese, Douglas now felt it safe to reveal his larger intentions to the bishop.

Charles C. Glover

When Douglas returned to Washington in the fall of 1891 he found that a group of laymen, led by Charles C. Glover, the head of Riggs Bank and a civic leader, had already found four possible sites for the cathedral. Douglas was able to convince Paret that it would be safe for him to present his vision to the Washington group without risking loss of control of the project. At the meeting on November 9, Paret raised so many reservations about the project that Glover and his associates were profoundly discouraged. Only after Douglas convinced Glover that the bishop was committed to the project did Glover call a second meeting. This time, probably with Douglas's urging, Paret approved appointment of a committee to select a site, and before the end of December 1891 there was unanimous agreement on fourteen acres offered free by Francis G. Newlands, whose Chevy Chase Land Company was subdividing lots along Connecticut Avenue from Rock Creek Park all the way to the District line. The site Newlands was donating to the cathedral was hardly ideal; it sloped sharply toward the north away from the city, with only a small wedge of land on the avenue at Klingle Road. The entrance to the site would have to be from Cathedral Avenue, which had not yet been laid out in the subdivision.[9]

The Quest for a Charter

Announcement of the Newlands gift seemed at last to put the cathedral project in motion, but it was only a first step and a faltering one at that. The intention to acquire the site was not the same as actual acquisition. Until legal documents of conveyance could be drawn up, there was always the danger that Newlands might think twice about his generous offer and sell it at a good profit. Until the cathedral foundation was incorporated, there was no legal entity to receive the property. Because the District of Columbia did not charter charitable institutions at that time, Douglas, Glover and their associates had no choice but to seek a charter from Congress. They also realized that a congressional charter would enhance the image of the cathedral as a national institution and would convey a sense of prestige that District incorporation could not match.

During the spring of 1892 Douglas, Glover, Mary Elizabeth Mann, and George Truesdell, a prominent Washington realtor and District commissioner, drafted a short one-paragraph charter that would grant broad authority to the incorporators. The list of incorporators included Bishop Paret and two clergymen from Maryland; Douglas, McKim, Glover, and ten other prominent men in Washington; and nine men from other states who were obviously selected as potential major donors to the project. The selection of a woman to serve on the drafting committee was a signal honor for Miss Mann at a time when women rarely engaged in such activities, but Douglas recognized her ability, interest, and knowledge of the ways of Washington and accepted her offer of assistance. The absence of her name from the list of incorporators reflected the protocol of the times.

By late June, Douglas and the charter committee had a draft ready for the bishop's review. His prompt approval enabled the committee to send the draft to the District committees of the Senate and House of Representatives, thus setting in motion the deliberative process of the legislature. As the summer wore on, however, Paret began to have second thoughts about the charter. He was concerned that the draft seemed to give full powers to the incorporators and thus infringed upon his authority as bishop. Furthermore, he was unhappy to discover that two of the incorporators were not Episcopalians. In a letter to Miss Mann, the bishop announced that he had decided to withdraw the draft charter and rewrite it. Outraged, Miss Mann denounced the bishop in a stinging letter and promptly resigned from the committee.[10] Douglas then had to rally the committee members and others to convince the bishop that withdrawal would delay congressional action for another year and that, once adopted, the charter could be easily amended. Paret finally relented, and both houses of Congress adopted the bill late in December 1892. President Benjamin Harrison signed the bill on January 6, 1893.[11] This was neither the first nor the last time that Douglas had to assuage hard feelings engendered by Paret's sudden lapses of confidence in his advisors in times of stress.

CRAFTING AN ORGANIZATION

The charter gave the cathedral foundation legal standing, but it by no means cleared the way for the future. Until a workable board of trustees could be selected and appointed, Bishop Paret would have to deal with the unwieldy group of twenty-five incorporators, many of whom had been selected as potential big donors and who knew little about the project. In turn, it was inadvisable to appoint the trustees until some organizational structure had been adopted for the foundation.

The task of organization became much more difficult when Douglas announced his resignation as rector of St. John's in June 1892. He had reluctantly accepted the advice of physicians that his wife's illness would require him to move away from the Washington area.[12] This was a bitter blow both to Douglas, who considered the cathedral project the crowning point of his career, and to Paret, who had come to rely on Douglas's advice on every matter, large or small, concerning the cathedral.

There was some consolation for both men in the fact that most of the work in drafting of the constitution could be done by mail. From his temporary residence in southern California, Douglas took on that task with the help of George Edmunds, a former United States senator from Vermont, and several other incorporators who lived in Washington. Drawing on his earlier studies of English cathedrals, Douglas proposed a complex organization that defined the authorities and responsibilities of the bishop, dean, chapter, and canons.[13]

Months of correspondence with the bishop and several of the incorporators were required to clarify the emerging patterns of organization. Behind the lengthy correspondence and heavily annotated drafts lay fundamental issues about the nature and role of the cathedral. Was it to stand alone or to be the first church of the diocese? If part of the diocese, was it to be primarily a diocesan cathedral, as Paret still tended to prefer, or was it to be also the great national church that McKim and Douglas advocated? Would Washington or even Baltimore parishes be represented on the board of trustees, as the bishop proposed, or would prominent churchmen outside the diocese and even other bishops be on the board? If the cathedral was indeed to be national, what place would the diocese have in its governance? Would the university proposed for the cathedral site be an independent institution or subject to the bishop and trustees?[14] Not until the spring of 1894 was the constitution in anything like final form.

Even after a year of redrafting, the constitution was still clearly Douglas's creation, both in concept and language. The cathedral described in the draft was to be much more than a diocesan church—it was to be national in its scope and mission. Because Douglas saw his creation as both a diocesan and a national institution, he devised a complex structure of two governing bodies, a larger and smaller chapter, each with its own membership and authority. Judged by some from the beginning to be unnecessarily complicated, Douglas's structure has not survived, but his conception of the cathedral has never been abandoned. His most enduring contribution was in naming the cathedral. In a letter to the bishop on December 7, 1893, Douglas wrote:

There is another important matter that may be settled now by you and released to the incorporators in connection with the cathedral statutes, viz., the name of the Cathedral. I have thought much about it & prefer "The Cathedral of St. Peter and St. Paul." The next best wd. be "St. Paul's." But I want to proclaim to the Romanists that we allow them no monopoly of S. Peter, while at the same time it wd. be striking to have also proclaimed our kindred with the English Church whose London Cathedral is St. Paul's. What do you think?

The bishop replied, "I like the title of St. Peter and St. Paul and will try to have it adopted."[15] So it seems the cathedral was named and probably will be known as such as long as it exists.

Growing Disillusionment

By the spring of 1894 the cathedral project was weighing heavily on Bishop Paret. The constitution had not yet been adopted, nor the trustees appointed. Some criticism had arisen over the selection of the Newlands site on the grounds that it was too far from the center of the city. Connecticut Avenue north of Rock Creek was at that time nothing but a dirt road and would be virtually inaccessible until the planned trolley line was constructed. Several prospective donors had withdrawn their pledges when they decided that the public would never support construction on that site. To make matters worse, Glover and Truesdell had been unable to come to final agreement with the owner of the Newlands site, and the magnanimous offer of 14.5 acres of free land seemed to be evaporating. In fact, the foundation was in serious financial straits. In May, McKim reported that the treasury was overdrawn by $2,000 and there was another $1,000 in unpaid bills. It was essential to keep this information private, but doing so would hamper efforts to secure large pledges and would also force the bishop to delay activation of the organization.[16]

Equally discouraging to Paret was Douglas's continuing absence. Since the summer of 1892 Douglas had been spending summers with his wife in Switzerland and the rest of the year in southern California. Although Douglas wrote that his wife's health was improving, he gave the bishop no hope that he might return to Washington to direct the development of the cathedral. On several occasions Paret urged Douglas to accept the position of sub-dean, who under the proposed constitution would be the chief operating officer of the cathedral. Douglas respectfully rejected the bishop's intimation that the offer might be a divine calling by suggesting that he had a higher calling to protect his wife's health, but he did admit that he might be able to serve as sub-dean in the preconstruction years, when his presence in Washington would not be required full-time.[17]

A New Diocese for Washington

It was now clear to Paret that the new institution would not be the cathedral for Maryland but rather for a new diocese centered in Washington. He recognized that division of the diocese became inevitable when Congress adopted the charter in January 1893. His failure to entice Douglas back to Washington destroyed any hope that Douglas could lead the campaign for the new cathedral. Paret also knew that many in the Diocese of Maryland would oppose division because it would deprive the diocese of many of its most prosperous and fastest growing parishes. But he now accepted McKim's frequent observation that the cathedral movement was almost entirely centered in Washington with virtually no support from Baltimore.[18]

Moving cautiously, Paret introduced the subject of division at the diocesan convention in May 1893. It was, he said, "a matter of very grave importance." He had never advocated small dioceses, and he had opposed any suggestion of division when he became bishop in 1884. But he now realized that the rapid growth of both Baltimore and Washington would make division "absolutely necessary before long." One bishop would not be able to meet the needs of the existing diocese. Furthermore, he added, in Washington "God has given us national opportunities and national responsibilities." He was now ready to give his consent to division on two conditions—that there be "a fair division of the territory and work, as should equalize their burdens, and such honorable provision for the support of two Bishops as should forbid their becoming by serious annual taxation a burden on the Parishes and the People." Paret requested that a special committee be appointed to present a plan for division at the 1894 convention so that the proposal could be adopted and presented to the General Convention for approval in 1895.[19]

While Douglas would continue for another year to speak for the bishop on all matters relating to the cathedral, Paret counted on McKim to coordinate the Washington campaign for the new diocese. As the time for the convention approached, the Washington churches were buzzing with excitement. McKim used the occasion of his Sunday sermon at Epiphany on May 26 to present a lengthy exposition of the case for division. "God is calling the churchmen of Maryland as, I believe, by the plainest Invocations of His providence, to go forward and establish this new diocese, in the interest of the progress, prestige, the power of this branch of Christ's Holy Catholic Church."[20]

McKim repeated the familiar argument that the rapid growth of the area required a second diocese and a second bishop, but he placed his greatest emphasis on the need to meet the challenge of other denominations in the District of Columbia and the promise of the cathedral. The Methodists, Roman Catholics, Baptists, and Congregationalists all had established national universities in the city. "Shall this church," he asked, "primitive, catholic, as we believe her to be—possessing such peculiar qualifications to minister to the American people so scriptural, so reasonable, so broad, so tolerant, so practical in its genius, lag behind in recognizing such a vantage ground as this?" As for the cathedral, McKim saw it "not merely as a splendid architectural structure for the greater glory of God," but also as a center for the work of the diocese. "Now if this great enterprise is to be prosecuted with vigor, there must be a Bishop of Washington, who will have the strength to devote to the care of it." The sermon, published the following morning in full in *The Washington Post*, was a rallying cry for the new diocese. McKim's skillful leadership at the convention held the Washington delegation together and overcame persistent parliamentary maneuvers to reject division of the diocese.[21] Late on the evening of May 29 the convention overwhelmingly voted for division.[22]

Now, after the decades of frustration and disappointment, the nation's capital was to have its own diocese and its own cathedral. On October 8, 1895, the General Convention of the Episcopal Church, meeting in Minneapolis, consented to the erection of a new diocese within the limits of the existing Diocese of Maryland.[23]

In the broadest sense, the new Diocese of Washington, as it emerged from the legislative labyrinths of General Convention in 1895, stood as evidence of the prominence and importance that the nation's capital had achieved in the closing years of the nineteenth century. In terms of population, Washington was only half the size of Baltimore, but it had lost most of the provincial atmosphere that the Maryland city still retained. By 1895 the city had achieved a measure of permanence and respectability that laid to rest once and for all the proposal to move the nation's capital to the Midwest.[24]

Most important of all, by the end of the century the United States had emerged as one nation with a national purpose, and that new sense of nationhood was focused on Washington, the nation's capital. Every public debate over the question of division in one way or another had invoked the national character of Washington. Other arguments, such as the size of the old diocese and the workload on the bishops, had been raised in the 1850s, but it was the stature of Washington and its national prominence that made the difference in 1895.

THE HEARST SCHOOL

In the spring of 1894 Douglas let it be known in church circles that he was close to persuading a wealthy woman in California to make a large gift to the cathedral, news he thought would bolster sagging support for the project. Phoebe A. Hearst could be taken seriously as the widow of millionaire and former U.S. senator from California, George Hearst. She could easily afford her offer of $100,000 to build a school for girls on the cathedral grounds, and her interests in education were genuine. As a teacher she had set up one of the first kindergartens in the nation in San Francisco and training schools for kindergarten teachers in California and Washington, D.C. She had also been instrumental in founding the Parent-Teachers Association.

Douglas did not wish to present Mrs. Hearst's proposal to the ungainly group of incorporators, who had been called to meet only twice since the charter became effective more than a year earlier. In October he succeeded in obtaining a congressional amendment of the charter to extend the powers of the incorporators to a board of trustees. The new board met for the first time on December 5, and Douglas presented Mrs. Hearst's proposal to the board five days later.[25]

Mrs. Phoebe Hearst

Appointment of the board of trustees gave Douglas for the first time a decision-making body of talented advisors, most of whom had been deeply involved in the project for years. He now pushed forward quickly to secure the foundation's hold on the Newlands site and to begin its development. The board appointed a committee on buildings and grounds, which Douglas chaired with John M. Wilson, a distinguished military officer soon to be promoted to brigadier general as chief of the Army Corps of Engineers, and Alexander T. Britton, head of a major Washington law firm and corporate director of banks and railroads. The committee then selected Ernest Flagg, a prominent New York architect, who had designed the original Corcoran Gallery of Art in Washington, to prepare two sets of architectural drawings for the cathedral, the Hearst school, and other buildings on the Newlands site, one set in Renaissance style, the other Gothic. By the time the board met to consider the two sets of plans in April 1895, Mrs. Hearst had signed an agreement to pay $175,000 for the school.

The agreement removed a major obstacle in the path of the cathedral project, and the trustees were well aware that it had largely been the result of Douglas's sure but careful touch in dealing with Mrs. Hearst. Before Flagg's presentation on April 25, the board approved Bishop Paret's nomination of Douglas to be dean of the cathedral. Now Douglas could feel even more confident than ever that he could win the board's approval of the Renaissance style favored by Mrs. Hearst. He was even more encouraged by Flagg's arguments, when the architect began by describing the obsolescence of Gothic. Flagg noted that Gothic had been developed in an earlier age, when limitations in construction techniques required a multiplicity of structural supports and a nave of restricted width, which was compensated for by exaggerated height and length. In medieval times Gothic churches were not expected to accommodate large numbers of worshipers in view and hearing range of the service. "At the time of the Renaissance," Flagg argued, "men cast off gothic art just as they cast off gothic superstition. The Renaissance style is emblematic of modern times and liberal ideas, just as gothic art is emblematic of medieval thought and superstition. . . . The grandeur of the interior of a church no longer depended upon extreme length and a great disproportion of the height to the width but all three proportions might be used simultaneously."[26] Flagg had clearly attracted the attention of the board, and Douglas now felt certain that the board would accept Flagg as the architect and the Renaissance style for the buildings.

Britton did not share Douglas's optimism. He was worried that McKim and Alexander Mackay-Smith, who had succeeded Douglas as rector of St. John's Church on Lafayette Square, were determined to undermine the preference of the board and Mrs. Hearst for the Renaissance style. As he put it in a note to Douglas, the potential trouble lay in "the jealousy of two rectors and the vacillation of the Bishop."[27] Britton was relieved when the board of trustees the following week rejected McKim's attempt to postpone a decision on architecture. Then the board formally adopted the Renaissance style "for the Cathedral and all other buildings to be erected by the Corporation" and confirmed Flagg's appointment as architect.[28]

Britton was soon to learn that the board's decision was anything but final. Bishop Paret informed him by letter that he had visited the Newlands site with McKim, Mackay-Smith, and three other trustees, who decided that the Hearst School should be moved to

Flagg's proposed design for the Close, with the boys' and girls' schools on either side of the Cathedral.

the rear of the property where it would be less conspicuous. In taking this action without consulting the members of the building and grounds committee, the bishop left Britton and Wilson no choice but to resign from the board of trustees.[29]

To make matters worse, Paret learned that Mackay-Smith had attempted to convince Flagg to abandon his recommendation for the Renaissance style. Even more alarming, McKim, without the bishop's knowledge or consent, had written to Mrs. Hearst asking her whether she considered "that there was any obligation on the part of the Trustees to erect [the school] where it was located on the architect's drawing and whether you understood that the rest of the plan, viz., the Cathedral itself, would necessarily be carried out." Mrs. Hearst replied that "there was a positive understanding that the whole of Mr. Flagg's Renaissance plan for the Cathedral and schools had been adopted. . . . I do consider that the Trustees are under obligation to carry out the above mentioned plans and I wish it to be emphatically understood that if they break faith with me, I shall feel at liberty to withdraw my gift."[30]

Once again Paret had allowed himself to be lured away in a disastrous unilateral diversion that contradicted a decision he had reached with his advisors. This time his action threatened the loss of Mrs. Hearst's gift, and he did not have Douglas, who was in Switzerland, on hand to save the situation. As it happened, the majority of the trustees in Washington rose to the occasion. They reconfirmed their decision on architecture, reassured Mrs. Hearst that the school would be built on the site and in the architectural style she had approved, and sent two members to persuade Britton and Wilson to withdraw their resignations.

In this effort to save the cathedral project, the majority trustees were successful, but not all the damage of the bitter dispute could be repaired. Douglas, now fully exasperated with the bishop's continuing failure to support him, resigned as dean of the cathedral and trustee to accept the rectorship of Trinity Church in New Haven, Connecticut. Douglas's decision devastated Britton and Wilson, and they implored him to reconsider. They gently suggested to Douglas that he was breaking his commitment to the project and abandoning his chosen life-work for an elite New England parish. Douglas was adamant in his decision. Paret rejected Douglas's resignation and refused even to respond to his letter. Paret had already announced at the diocesan convention in May 1895 that he had decided to remain as Bishop of Maryland rather than move to the new diocese in Washington. It now seemed that the cathedral project would be leaderless until the first Bishop of Washington was elected and consecrated. The final blow fell when the construction costs for Flagg's plans for the Hearst school came in at $315,000, far above the ceiling of $175,000 that the trustees had set for the entire project.[31] In the eyes of the board, both Flagg and his plans had been discredited. It would take months to find a new architect and develop a new set of plans. The delay raised the specter that Mrs. Hearst might lose patience and withdraw her offer for the girls' school or, even if she stayed the course, would she accept a new design and placement on the Newlands site? The future of the cathedral project now lay in the hands of the new bishop. Satterlee was ready to accept his checkered inheritance.

Tenleytown Road Trolley, 1890s

4. A Great Church for National Purposes

I n April 1896 Satterlee arrived in the nation's capital to take up his responsibilities as the first Bishop of the new Episcopal Diocese of Washington. At the age of fifty-three, six feet two inches in height with an erect military bearing, he towered over most men of his day. There was about him an air of determination, serious intent, and moral rectitude that made him the epitome of a Victorian cleric. His impeccable credentials as a member of the social elite in New York gave him easy access to the lay and clerical leaders on whom he had to depend to create a new diocese in Washington and to carry forward the steps already taken to create the Cathedral.

The next twelve years ending with his death in February 1908 were to be the most tumultuous and challenging of his life. On the diocesan side he had to find ways to reconcile the cultural, social, and historical differences that separated the city parishes from the remote rural churches scattered over the four counties surrounding the District of Columbia. Drawing on his New York experience, he assumed direct responsibility for the mission congregations, many of which were languishing with insufficient financial support and leadership. He sparked new interest in Christian education in the parishes, especially the Sunday school movement, and supported seminaries to train more blacks to serve as clergy in black parishes. In January 1907 he held a conference of Southern bishops in Washington to find ways to bring more blacks into the Episcopal Church. In adopting the Supreme Court's separate-but-equal doctrine, Satterlee was considered a liberal in his approach to racial segregation in the Episcopal Church of that day.[1]

Satterlee as Bishop of Washington

Providing effective leadership for the diocese was essential, but the task was similar to that faced by most bishops in urban dioceses in the Northeast. The real challenge was the cathedral project. From his days at seminary through his years in New York, Satterlee had been exposed to the high-church enthusiasm for cathedrals. Many of his mentors and close associates in New York were leaders in the cathedral movement. Arthur Cleveland Coxe designated a large church in Buffalo as his cathedral when he became Bishop of Western New York. William Croswell Doane had built one of the first cathedrals designed for that purpose when he became Bishop of Albany. Henry Codman Potter had already launched his efforts to build a cathedral in New York City while Satterlee was still at Calvary. William Reed Huntington as a New York high churchman supported the cathedral idea. It was no surprise, then, that Satterlee brought enthusiasm for the cathedral with him when he moved to Washington.

One of his first decisions was to designate St. Mark's Church on Capitol Hill as his pro-cathedral until the new structure could be built. The Cathedral became the very center of his ministry in Washington. He saw it as an extraordinary opportunity, not just to build a great church but also to have a lasting impact on the Christian Church in America.

Satterlee's sense of this larger vision for the Cathedral led him to record his experiences in what he called his "private record." It seems likely that he gathered notes and letters from his voluminous correspondence and perhaps from time to time drafted narrative sections of the *Record,* which for the most part follows a chronological order. Since he intended his entries to be private, he could set down his unrestrained feelings of elation, anxiety, or frustration as they came to him in the heat of decision-making. Also, as he explains in the opening paragraphs, he wanted to protect the privacy of the many individuals whom he solicited for financial support. He did not wish to embarrass those who, in response to his fervent appeals, later found it impossible to give what they had promised. After a century, all the persons mentioned in the record have long since died, and the record can be used as a historical document of great value.

The *Private Record,* reproduced in full in Chapter 5, is an extraordinary document describing events recorded nowhere else in Satterlee's personal papers or official records. It does not begin, however, to constitute a complete record of the cathedral project. As he points out in the first pages of the *Record,* Satterlee wisely excludes recollections of events that he did not witness firsthand. Moreover, he is careful to avoid critical judgments of other people even though he intends his account to be private. In some instances, particularly the decision to select the Gothic style of architecture, Satterlee considered the issues so sensitive that he excluded them entirely.

Thus, this chapter does not attempt to tell the full story of the creation of the Cathedral but is limited to covering events that Satterlee omitted in his record and providing a larger context for his account. The *Private Record* still carries the burden of history.

New Leadership

Satterlee came to Washington with the kinds of talent and experience needed to lead the Cathedral enterprise. At both Zion Church and Calvary he had honed his natural ability to lead people through contentious issues in ways that would leave them with the impression that they, not he, deserved credit for what was accomplished. He was a master at achieving his goals without alienating those who disagreed with him. He was willing to take risks for a good cause, and he knew how to raise money and recruit talented men and women to help him. Satterlee's elite upper-class credentials opened doors to people and institutions that were essential to his success. In terms of practical experience, he had learned how to manage building projects both at Wappingers Falls and in New York. Through his father he had developed a good taste for the fine arts, and over the years he had spent months in England and Europe studying cathedral architecture. Now, for the first time in his life, Satterlee could see how five decades of living and working in New York had prepared him for the challenge he faced in Washington.

Although Satterlee had never lived in Washington or spent much time there, he personally knew some of the cathedral trustees and clergy in the new diocese. Both McKim

Satterlee with his diocesan advisors

First row, (left to right): Caleb C. Stetson, Philip M. Rhinelander, Satterlee, William L. DeVries, G. Freeland Peter; Second row: E.D. Johnson, F.J.A. Bennett, unidentified, Deaconness Mary E. Libby, and unidentified.

and Mackay-Smith, who were men to be reckoned with on the board of trustees, had served in New York City parishes while Satterlee was at Calvary. Henry Pellew, one of the stalwarts on the board, had a summer estate near Wappingers Falls on the Hudson. Close associates in New York also followed him to Washington: Philip M. Rhinelander, who had grown up at Calvary before deciding to enter the ministry; William L. DeVries, whom Satterlee had tried to recruit for his Calvary staff; George C. F. Bratenahl, whom Satterlee lured into the ministry in New York; and William C. Rives, a wealthy patron and devoted supporter at Calvary, who actually moved to Washington as a close advisor to the bishop.

Satterlee also had the advantage that he was now living and working in Washington, unlike Bishop Paret, who had to spend most of his time in Baltimore leading the Diocese of Maryland. The new bishop's residence on Thomas Circle N.W., then a fashionable neighborhood in the city, served as his headquarters. Meetings of the trustees were held there, at St. John's parish hall, or at Riggs Bank, at Glover's invitation. Trips to the Newlands site by horse and carriage were still time-consuming, with only one bridge across the Rock Creek gorge on a roundabout route through city streets to what was to become Connecticut Avenue. All the land north and west of Rock Creek was still open country or forested, with residential development only beginning. But the cathedral project now had a leader on the scene of action. He could deal with his associates face-to-face rather than by letter, as Paret was forced to do. And he could act quickly when necessary.

THE HEARST GAMBIT

Satterlee makes clear in the opening pages of the *Private Record* that he saw Mrs. Hearst as the key to getting the cathedral project back on track. If he could satisfy her and secure her financial commitment to the school, all else would fall into place. His contact with her was direct, not by letters from the board. He met her in Washington, took her to the Newlands site, and carefully led her to the conclusion that the site was unacceptable. He then had her meet with the board so that she, not he, could explain to the trustees that the Newlands site would have to be abandoned. There was no need to reopen the controversy over architectural design because he had seen Flagg's plans while he was still at Calvary. He had already accepted the Renaissance style for the school "with the express understanding that I do not thereby commit myself to the adoption of the Renaissance order of architecture for the Cathedral itself or the plans regarding any other buildings on the Cathedral grounds."[2] That letter saved the Hearst school and left him a free hand on the style of all the other buildings on the site. The touchy issue of architectural style would not appear in the minutes of board meetings or in other board correspondence until 1905, when Satterlee was prepared to act upon it.

Acquiring Mount St. Alban

With these problems laid to rest, Satterlee turned promptly to finding a new architect for the Hearst School, abandoning the Newlands site, and acquiring the Barber property on Mount St. Alban. The *Private Record* provides a graphic account of the bishop's prolonged and often frustrating negotiations with Amzi Barber, the owner of the property Satterlee wanted for the Cathedral. Barber, a Washington college professor turned industrial tycoon, had created a national corporation that enjoyed a virtual monopoly of asphalt paving in the United States. A hardheaded businessman, Barber was no easy match for Satterlee, but the bishop was unshakable in his determination to bring Barber to terms, even to the point of signing a personal note to meet Barber's final offer. Once again, as he had done at Wappingers Falls and at Calvary, Satterlee was willing to take full responsibility for paying off a mortgage, this time to the tune of $145,000 should the trustees fail to raise the money from donors. Satterlee's commitment obviously set an example for others and probably was calculated to put pressure on others to rescue him from his predicament. However, the risk he was taking was real, as he had learned in his parishes in New York when he alone was left with the full burden of paying off the debt.[3]

Building a National Image

Satterlee knew that the financial resources available in Washington would never be sufficient to build a cathedral that would realize his breathtaking vision of a great church with a national and even world mission. The hard fact was that the project had not yet caught the attention of most Episcopalians in the Washington parishes, to say nothing of church leaders in other dioceses. With good reason he complained privately in the *Record* that the Episcopal Church was still hopelessly parochial. Bishops had little authority over the operation of the parishes in their dioceses, and it would be another quarter-century before the presiding bishop would actually be a chief executive officer and would have anything resembling a full-time administrative staff at the national level.

If Satterlee had no hope of transforming the Church into a national institution, he was determined to give the new Cathedral in Washington a national image around which the Episcopal Church and other Christian churches could unite in one national and worldwide mission. Over the next twelve years he never missed an opportunity to foster that image.

His first opportunity came in 1898, when the General Convention of the Episcopal Church was scheduled to meet in Washington. Satterlee explored the possibility of laying the cornerstone for the Hearst school in October when the bishops of the Church and the clerical and lay deputies were in Washington. Disappointed that the architectural plans for

The Peace Cross

the school would not be completed in time, he then fixed on the idea of erecting a peace cross to mark the end of the Spanish-American War, thus establishing the Cathedral for the first time with a role in national events, or as a place of worship in times of trouble or celebration. Embedded in this idea was his great admiration for Admiral George Dewey, the popular hero of Manila Bay, but it also opened the way for the Cathedral to respond to a secular event that had significance in the life of the nation. In the *Private Record* he relates the intense effort that was necessary to have the limestone quarried in Indiana, shipped to Washington, and carved and inscribed, all in a matter of weeks, in time for the unveiling on October 23.

Having the members of the General Convention present provided a way to tie the new Cathedral to the national Church. Two days later the House of Bishops adopted a resolution that gave formal recognition to the existence of the Washington project.[4] Equally important was evidence of ties to the federal government, clearly achieved by Satterlee's success in convincing President McKinley to attend the ceremony and even, at the last minute, to speak to the large gathering on Mount St. Alban overlooking the White House and the national capital. The presence of the Marine Band, in full-dress uniforms, marked a tie between church and state that would become a tradition in ceremonies at the Cathedral throughout the twentieth century.

Satterlee found more ways to capitalize on the Peace Cross celebration. The day following the ceremony a conversation with two prominent bishops led them to propose that the remains of Thomas John Claggett and his wife be transferred to grave sites on the Cathedral Close. As the first bishop in the American Church to be consecrated on American soil, Claggett was revered as one of the founding fathers of the new church, and the physical presence of his grave on the Close tied the new Cathedral to the earliest history of the Episcopal Church.[5] Satterlee also tied the Cathedral to the Anglican Communion by inviting the Bishop of London to take part in the Peace Cross ceremony.

To assure that the ceremony received maximum print coverage throughout the Church, Satterlee asked Thomas Nelson Page, a former ambassador and author of books and novels on the Civil War, to write the *Peace Cross Book*, which was sent to the church press and all the bishops and clergy of the Church. Satterlee also arranged to have printed two hundred copies of an article in the *New York Sun* describing the impressive plans announced by the Roman Catholics to build a national university in Washington. The article, sent to all the bishops of the Church, was intended to challenge church leaders across the nation to respond to this sort of competition by supporting the cathedral project.[6]

In describing these endeavors in the *Private Record*, Satterlee made it a practice to attribute original ideas to others. Perhaps he thought it proper to show modesty even in his private accounts, but this device also reflected his technique of leading others to believe that they were the source of his ideas. He always chose to appear merely as the implementer of ideas proposed by others.

THE SCHOOLS

The plans of the Roman Catholics were not the only competition Satterlee thought he faced from other denominations. Both the Methodists and Baptists were establishing national universities in Washington, later to be The American University and The George Washington University. His only available response to this competition lay in the Hearst school, to which he gave a large share of his personal attention, beginning in 1897. With an additional $25,000 from Mrs. Hearst, Satterlee convinced the trustees to set up a blind competition to select a new architect. He was pleased when the architect of the winning plan turned out to be Robert W. Gibson, whom he had known as designer of the Albany

The Hearst School

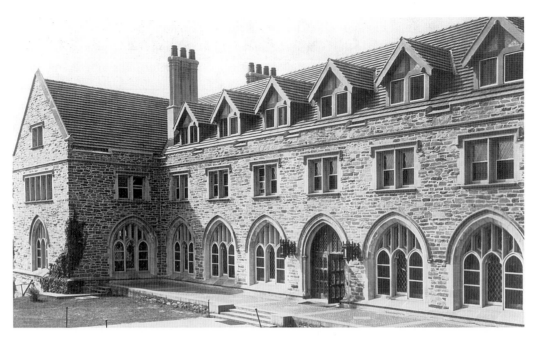

The Boys' School

Cathedral and the Church Mission House next to Calvary Church in New York. In the *Private Record* Satterlee describes how he arranged the ceremony for laying the cornerstone of the school, recruited the principal and vice principal, and won Mrs. Hearst's agreement to name it the National Cathedral School. When the school finally opened in the fall of 1900, after long construction delays, the bishop tracked school activities almost daily, even to the point of deciding how individual students were disciplined.[7]

Hopes for a boys' school seemed remote until July 1903, when the Foundation received $300,000 from the estate of Harriet Lane Johnston for construction of a boys' school, which would provide education and lodging for members of the Cathedral boys' choir. Satterlee sent Bratenahl and DeVries to visit the elite boys' schools in New England and the choir schools at several English cathedrals. Architects, using the reports of these visits and Satterlee's own ideas, completed drawings for the school early in 1905, and the cornerstone of the school was laid in May. Apparently, he saw no need to use this occasion as a special event that would garner wide publicity. The boys' school opened for classes in September 1910.

THE QUEST FOR FUNDING

Satterlee's efforts to lift the heavy burden of debt that fell on the trustees' and his own shoulders occupy more pages in the *Private Record* than does any other subject. The size of the debt was enough to shake his confidence, but even more challenging was finding effective ways to raise such a large sum. His initial appeals to his fellow bishops produced little. He then decided to send books of "Founders Certificates" to the rectors of large parishes nationwide. The certificates were to be sold to individuals for one dollar, each presumably covering the cost of one square foot of ground on the Close. Few of the clergy responded, and the returns did not cover the cost of printing and distributing the certificates. Advertising in church papers and periodicals produced equally poor results.

Satterlee now decided that he would have to take his appeal directly to potential donors. He made a series of trips to Philadelphia, New York, Boston, and Baltimore in the spring of 1899. With the permission of the bishop in each diocese, he found wealthy individuals who were willing to convene "parlor meetings" in the homes of potential donors. At each meeting Satterlee presented his vision of the Cathedral, with emphasis on the national role it would play in the life of the Church at large.[8]

The parlor meetings did produce some pledges, but not nearly in the amounts Satterlee needed. Seeking new sources, he returned to New York in January 1900 to call on J. Pierpont Morgan to ask him for a list of wealthy men whom he could invite to a fund-raising meeting. Through diocesan affairs in New York he had known Morgan for years and had appealed to him unsuccessfully for funds at Calvary when Morgan was helping to rebuild his own parish, St. George's. Morgan thought that a meeting with businessmen would not prove effective, but other men Satterlee called on that day liked the idea. Somewhat taken aback, Satterlee presented his dilemma to several friends after dinner with Dr. and

Mrs. Rives that evening. Skipwith Wilmer, who was raising funds in Baltimore for the Cathedral, mentioned that Senator George Wharton Pepper was planning to form a committee in Philadelphia to invite prospective donors to meetings to promote the Cathedral. Wilmer urged the bishop to create similar committees in other cities. Satterlee seized on the suggestion and that spring succeeded in establishing committees in Philadelphia, New York, and Boston, as he describes that effort in the *Private Record*. The committees not only raised money but also gave the Cathedral project a continuing presence.[9] In time the committees would become the base for the National Cathedral Association.

Senator George Wharton Pepper

The *Private Record* describes these efforts in detail, but it does not explain the reason for Satterlee's success in raising money outside his own diocese in what he lamented as a most discouragingly parochial church. His own impressive personality and his obvious total commitment to his task were important factors in his success. But equally essential was his social standing as a member of the upper-class elite in New York. His status gave him entrée to individuals who could appreciate his religious and artistic vision of the Cathedral. What he was proposing was not just another church but an extraordinary symbol of Christianity that would endure throughout the ages to come.

It was typical of the times that the membership of formal bodies such as the board of trustees and committees in other cities was restricted almost entirely to men. Likewise, men dominated the lists of donors in the *Private Record*. However, in the text of the *Private Record* it is clear that women were more likely than men to come to the bishop's aid when needs for money were most urgent. Albertina T. Pyne, Matilda W. Bruce, Bessie Kibbey, Margaret F. Buckingham, Isabel Freeman, Mary M. Ballinger, Mary R. Rives, and Cassie M. Julian James were among those Satterlee called his "holy women." Independently wealthy, they could respond quickly and in some cases even found projects of their own that they offered to support. It was Mrs. Julian James who offered $50,000 to pay off the last of the debt on the cathedral property in October 1905. Satterlee wrote in his *Record* that "no one can ever appreciate what it is to be delivered from this burden. I feel like one released from prison, after having been in confinement seven years, from 1898 to 1905."

ASSEMBLING THE CATHEDRAL FABRIC

During these same years Satterlee set about gathering stones from what he considered sacred sites in the Holy Land and in England to be fabricated into liturgical furnishing for the Cathedral: the Jerusalem high altar, the Canterbury Pulpit, the baptismal font, and the Glastonbury cathedra (bishop's throne). His many visits to England and the Middle East had given him firsthand knowledge of sites that had special biblical or Anglican significance. Over the years he had also established contacts with bishops and others in England who could help him in acquiring stones from historic Anglican buildings. Herbert Clark, an agent whom he had known for years in Palestine, arranged the shipment of selected stones to Washington. Once the stones arrived, Satterlee personally directed the design for the carving of each piece. For the Canterbury Pulpit, which was carved in England, he gave the designer detailed instructions in a series of letters.[10]

The font was for Satterlee an equally important furnishing for the Cathedral, not only in terms of design but also in its use. The font was designed to be large enough to accommodate full immersion of the person being baptized. He hoped that the immersion font would attract other Christian denominations to perform baptisms there and thus advance his vision that the Cathedral would be the locus of an ecumenical movement centering in the Episcopal Church.

Satterlee knew that he would never see the Cathedral himself, but by fixing the design of these key furnishings he would irrevocably set the architectural style of the completed church. It would be Gothic, which was, as he put it, "God's style." Nothing pleased him more than to be the creator of these furnishings that would have a central place in the Cathedral. A century later visitors and worshipers could not help but see his creation carved in stone.

Until the Cathedral could be built, Satterlee needed some space sheltered from the weather to store these large artifacts. He decided to build a temporary chapel south of the cathedral site near what would become St. Albans School. Again using a blind competition to select an architect, he was pleased when the winning design turned out to be the work of his nephew, Edward Lansing Satterlee, who also designed All Hallows Gate, leading from Wisconsin Avenue to the Little Sanctuary. The altar, pulpit, and cathedra were out of scale in the little chapel, but they were in a place of worship, where they would remind worshipers of their ultimate destination. To house the font, Satterlee decided to build a temporary building close to what would be the southwest corner of the Cathedral. The baptistry was rarely used after Satterlee's death and became the Herb Cottage after World War II.

The Question of Style

In the original typescript of his *Private Record*, Satterlee devotes more than ninety pages to his efforts to purchase the site on Mount St. Alban, build the Hearst school, give the project a national image, and assemble the principal liturgical furnishings for the Cathedral. In all these pages covering the years 1896 through 1905, there is not one mention of architectural style, the subject that consumed Bishop Paret and the board of trustees in 1894 and 1895. Was it that the subject was too explosive even for inclusion in the *Private Record*? If this were true, we would expect to find at least some hints of controversy in Satterlee's correspondence or in the board's minutes during those years. In fact, there is not a single word on architectural style in any of the records in the Cathedral archives. The only reasonable explanation is that Satterlee deliberately avoided the subject from the day he became bishop until December 1905, when the last of the debt on the land was paid off. Looking back over Satterlee's career, we can recall other instances in which he refused to declare himself in a controversy. In his ministry in New York he had never committed himself on the question of churchmanship, even though by his words and actions he could safely be called a high churchman. His refusal to declare himself on this, the most divisive issue in the Episcopal Church at that time, was a critical factor in his election as bishop. It is not surprising, then, that a few months later he was careful not to declare himself on the subject of architectural style. When he reviewed Flagg's plans he had little choice but to accept the board's and Mrs. Hearst's decision adopting the Renaissance style for the school. In the same letter, however, he declared that he did not commit himself to that style for the Cathedral itself or for other buildings on the Close.

Once the land was debt-free, Satterlee abruptly turned the attention of the board to obtaining plans for the Cathedral in Gothic style. Clearly by this time the decision on style had already been made that the Cathedral and all the other buildings on the Close, except the girls' school, would be Gothic in design. Presumably, Satterlee had achieved this decision in informal discussions with board members but never put that decision in writing. The closest he came to acknowledging the trustees' action was his statement in the *Private Record* that "we were rid of all plans for the school and the Cathedral" when the cost estimates for Flagg's plans were rejected.[11]

Satterlee already had in mind a plan to establish a committee of outside experts to advise the board of trustees on how to proceed. Within days after the debt was paid, Satterlee wrote to two of his fellow bishops whom he had long regarded as mentors. Bishop William Lawrence of Massachusetts recommended Henry Vaughan for the advisory committee as the best Gothic architect in Boston. Lawrence admitted that Ralph Adams Cram was widely recognized for his knowledge of Gothic architecture, but he, in Lawrence's words, "enjoys making an effort at originality, and is so self-confident that I am not so sure of him as an advisor." Bishop William Croswell Doane of Albany, drawing on his own experience, was emphatic that no architects should be on the committee. Doane claimed that in Albany the architects on the committee had ended up rejecting for procedural reasons the plan that he considered the best. The best Gothic architects in America, in Doane's opinion, were Vaughan and Robert W. Gibson.[12]

THE MERITS OF COMPETITION

In launching the Cathedral project Satterlee encountered many perplexing alternatives, but on the selection of the architect he had no qualms. The architect should be selected in an open competition. This was not the first time Satterlee had taken this position. In February 1891, when he was still at Calvary, he had urged this procedure on the committee that was planning the New York cathedral, and he had employed the same method in selecting the architects for the Hearst school and the Little Sanctuary.[13]

After consulting many persons in Washington, he was convinced more than ever that competition would produce the best results. He reasoned that an open invitation would attract hundreds of plans from young or unknown architects "who will come forward with a plan superior to that sent in to any limited competition by experienced architects." He cited the selection of a man in his twenties to design the cathedral in Liverpool, England.[14]

Satterlee had worked out a schedule in detail. The initial competition would be closed after three months and the plans exhibited in some public place like the Corcoran Gallery of Art or the Library of Congress to attract public interest in the Cathedral project. Citing a chapter in Lord Bryce's book, *The American Commonwealth,* on the formation of public opinion, Satterlee wrote: "If we want the people of Washington and Church people at large to be interested in the Washington Cathedral, we must so to speak take them into our confidence, let them know what we are doing and give them the opportunity of so far cooperating with us as to criticise [sic] the designs for the Cathedral, and thus gain the benefit of public opinion which forms very slowly. . . ." The public display could then be followed by a paid competition among the architects of the four best plans. He proposed that the open competition be announced in February 1906 and the four best plans selected in October. Plans for the closed competition would be submitted in March or April 1907, with the final selection by Ascension Day 1907. Satterlee admitted this was an ambitious schedule, but he was determined to move quickly before public interest in the project was lost.[15]

Siting the Cathedral

Satterlee was equally confident that he had reached the right decision about the site of the Cathedral on the Close. The Cathedral, he was convinced, should overlook the intersection of Massachusetts Avenue, "destined to be the street whereon the residences of the wealthy, are and will be erected," and Wisconsin Avenue, "already being built up with houses which, until it comes to the neighborhood of the Cathedral and Cleveland Park, are of an humbler class; and, here as elsewhere, electric tram-car lines are a new force in modern civilization. . . ." The Cathedral would be on the very spot where "two tides of population" would be trending toward it.[16]

There were, however, practical reasons for choosing this site. As Satterlee had often done in the past when he faced critical decisions, he chose to compile lists of the advantages and disadvantages of this location and of another at the northern side of the Close, near the National Cathedral School. The first location would leave room for "a great open square before the West Facade and for a Gothic colonnade or cloister around it (St. Peter's)." The whole northern half of the Close would be left for academic quadrangles near Hearst Hall. There would be an open view of the Cathedral, from the approach on Massachusetts Avenue, all the way from the Capitol. The major disadvantage was that the Cathedral would not be built on level ground and would require retaining walls that would be architecturally difficult and costly. Conversely, the northern site would place the Cathedral at the highest elevation on the Close and avoid the cost of retaining walls. The disadvantages included leaving no room for the schools, providing only a partial view of the Cathedral from the city, and raising the possibility that the Cathedral would eventually be obscured by buildings on the east side of Thirty-fifth Street, the eastern boundary of the Close at that time. There was no doubt in Satterlee's mind that the southern site was the best.[17]

The Time for Decision

With these opinions in hand, Satterlee prepared for a critical meeting with the board of trustees on December 29, 1905. The day before the meeting he sent the trustees a letter labeled "Strictly confidential," in which he pointed out the supreme importance of the meeting. "We can afford to make no mistake in so vital a matter as the choice of a plan for the Cathedral of our Church which is to stand for coming centuries in the Capital of the Country as a witness for Christ and as an inspiration for worship." Any error at this point, he warned, would be "irretrievable." If the plans awakened the interest of the people at large, the funds for the building would "undoubtedly flow in as they are needed for the work." Otherwise, the work would be postponed for years.

Now, at last, the bishop was prepared to declare himself on the matter of style. "I am sure," he wrote, "from many indications in past years that the Gothic style of architecture appeals most strongly to the people at large for a Church building. . . . Nothing is so strong as the power of a lasting public sentiment like this, and therefore we may be most thankful that the Cathedral Board have already decided in favor of the Gothic style. . ."[18] Because Satterlee never took this question to the board of trustees in a formal meeting, we can only assume that he obtained approval from individual members in personal conversations.

At the board meeting on December 29, Satterlee obtained the appointment of his old friend William C. Rives as a member and appointed a board committee to review the draft of a new constitution, which he describes in the *Private Record*. Following Bishop Doane's advice, Satterlee proposed to exclude architects from the five-member committee that would advise the board on how to proceed. On the recommendation of Bishop Lawrence, he quickly settled on Charles F. Moore, a distinguished professor of Gothic architecture at Harvard. He knew he could rely on Casper Purdon Clarke, his father's English friend, who had recently been appointed director of the Metropolitan Museum of Art in New York.[19]

William C. Rives

For the remaining three positions, however, Satterlee had trouble finding qualified members who were not architects. Several members of the board thought he should appoint the two architects who had served in 1902 on the Park Commission that developed a master plan to carry forward L'Enfant's original concept for the District of Columbia. Out of the commission's plan would come, among other things, the clearing of the railroad tracks and station from the Mall and the dedication of the area south of the Mall to parks and recreation fields.[20] Following the board's advice, Satterlee accepted Daniel H. Burnham, the chief architect of the famous White City built at the Columbian Exposition of 1893 in Chicago, and Charles F. McKim, an equally well-known architect in New York. The fifth member of the advisory board was Bernard S. Green, a civil engineer, who had supervised the construction of the Washington Monument and many of the federal buildings on the Mall. It seems unlikely that Satterlee could have found five men better qualified to serve as his advisors, whatever their views on architectural style.

The Advisory Committee

Satterlee took four members of the advisory committee out to the site in February 1906. Despite the snow, they were able to get a general idea of the contours of the Close, particularly the southern portion, where the land sloped down to Massachusetts Avenue. Then the committee decided not to meet again until May, when Burnham would return from three months in Europe. Satterlee wrote to Burnham that he had asked Professor Moore to write a paper setting forth the fundamental principles of Gothic architecture. This note was a clear signal to Burnham that the question of architectural style was already settled, at least in Satterlee's mind.[21]

On May 5 Burnham and the other committee members met with Satterlee at the site. In a private conversation with Satterlee, Burnham revealed the committee's conclusions. In every respect the committee rejected the principles of architectural design that Satterlee had cherished for years. On the question of the location of the Cathedral, the committee unanimously recommended the highest part of the Close, near Hearst Hall. On selection of the architect, the committee unanimously rejected Satterlee's idea of an open competition. On the question of architectural style, the committee was divided. Burnham and McKim favored the classic Renaissance style, while Moore and Clarke favored Gothic.

The Commitment to Gothic

After this stunning reversal, Satterlee had several weeks to lay out a new course before he formally reported to the trustees at their regular meeting on May 21. In the *Private*

Record Satterlee devotes only two sentences to the committee's report and says nothing about the trustees' reaction. It was clear that he was prepared to accept the committee's recommendations on the first two points, but not on the question of style. At the May 21 meeting he presented a resolution that the trustees adopted unanimously: "That the Board heard with deep interest the report of the Bishop of the Diocese in reference to the architectural style of the new Cathedral and while fully recognizing the beauties of the classic style, sees no reason why it should change its views as originally enunciated, and therefore adheres to its decision that the Gothic style shall be adopted."[22]

Choosing once again to push the question of style aside, Satterlee asked the board to appoint a committee of three to help him move quickly to select the architect, now that the time-consuming procedure of an open competition would not be used. The three men he selected to join him on the committee were among his most trusted colleagues on the board, the ever-dependable Alfred Harding, who would later succeed him as Bishop of Washington; William C. Rives, a devoted supporter for more than twenty years; and Daniel C. Gilman, the wise and well-connected retired president of Johns Hopkins University.

The one sentence in the official minutes of the meeting and Satterlee's two sentences in the *Private Record* represent the sum total of all that he reveals to the reader about the

Satterlee and the Board of Trustees

decision on style. He chose not to mention that Burnham did not drop the issue but responded a few weeks later. Neither contentious nor argumentative, Burnham merely examined the basis of Satterlee's preference for Gothic. "It is perhaps true that most people love Gothic work, but that does not seem to be reason enough for a choice. . . . In this country we need correction of our tendency to settle things on the basis of our own private feeling." Could we not, he asked, use the Cathedral as an object lesson in placing public duty ahead of our private leanings? Burnham felt certain that Satterlee would not have selected the Gothic style for the government buildings in Washington and would agree that the Park Commission was correct in specifying the classic style for that purpose.[23]

It appears that when Burnham wrote this letter, Satterlee had not yet conveyed the trustees' decision of May 21 to the advisory committee. Burnham could reasonably conclude that the question of style was still open to debate. He must have been perplexed when he received a letter, dated August 21, from the bishop that mentioned only the trustees' decision to accept the advisory committee's recommendations on the site of the Cathedral and against an open competition in selecting the architect. Satterlee wrote: "Though the giving up of an architectural competition is in the face of what I, myself have persistently held over twenty years, I feel so strongly the cogency of the reasons you adduced, that a new perspective has been opened up before me, and I am most grateful to you and the other members of the Advisory Committee for the very great help you have afforded us."[24] The letter contained not one word about style.

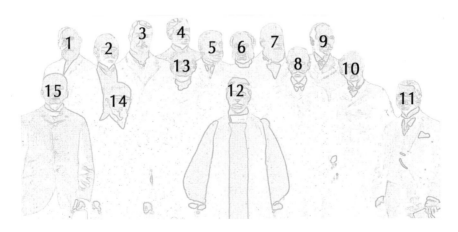

Legend to photo on left: Satterlee and the Board of Trustees, circa May 1906

1 - William C. Rives; 2- Wayne MacVeagh; 3 - Alexander Mackay-Smith; 4- George Truesdell; 5 - George Dewey; 6 - Randolph H. McKim; 7 - Daniel C. Gilman; 8 - Thomas Hyde; 9 - Charles J. Bell; 10 - John A. Kasson; 11 - Charles C. Glover; 12 - Bishop Satterlee; 13 - John H. Elliott; 14 - John M. Wilson; 15 - James Lowndes

Six days later Satterlee wrote an apologetic letter explaining that he had only just received Burnham's letter, which had been diverted to a board of trustees' committee while he was in Europe. "I have read with deepest interest," Satterlee wrote, "and thank you for your courtesy in setting forth so clearly and forcibly the reasons for building the Cathedral in the Style of Classic Renaissance." He assured Burnham that the trustees had set aside the "great weight" of the architects' opinions only because the subject of style had been before the board continuously since 1895. Satterlee admitted the wisdom of the Park Commission in selecting the Renaissance style for the government buildings in Washington. "But," he added, "in the building of a Cathedral there is another Consideration surpassing even that of Monumental Unity. First, last, and always, the Cathedral is 'A House of Prayer for All People' that was Our Lord's own description of the Church. . . . And experience has plainly shown that the Gothic is the distinctively Religious and Christian Style of Architecture which excels all others in inspiring prayer and devotional feeling among all sorts and conditions of men." He added that a cathedral in Gothic style would create positive contrast "between it and the magnificent classic buildings in Washington."[25] This was Satterlee's final declaration on the subject.

Selecting an Architect

In contrast to his brief reference to the advisory committee's recommendations and the question of style, Satterlee describes in The *Private Record* the exhilarating but exhausting chain of events during the summer of 1906 leading to the selection of George F. Bodley and Henry Vaughan to prepare preliminary plans for the Cathedral. In the *Record* Satterlee describes his whirlwind tour of England and the continent and his meetings with bishops, deans, and architects. He came home virtually convinced that Bodley was the best Gothic architect in England, but there remained in his mind the proposition that the architect of an American cathedral should be an American. He was convinced, however, that few American architects really understood Gothic architecture or had any experience in designing buildings in that style. Americans, Satterlee believed, tried too hard to be original and thus were incapable of capturing the essence of Gothic design.[26]

In further discussions with the trustees and others, Satterlee moved toward the conclusion that the team of Bodley and Vaughan was the best choice. He still had concerns about Bodley's advanced age and whether Vaughan's participation would be an asset. These matters were laid to rest by George S. Walpole, an English cleric whom Satterlee had known at General Theological Seminary in New York. Walpole, later Bishop of Edinburgh, wrote Satterlee that the consensus in England was that "Bodley's physical powers are quite equal to the task . . . I learned that there was no drawback from his age that could be noted . . . "

George F. Bodley

On the second question Walpole added: "It seems to me in any case you are better off with him than without him. Without him you will have only Vaughan, Gibson, or __ __ , but you double Vaughan's powers by adding Bodley to it." Walpole concluded: "I am convinced that you are right and I should have no doubt that with Bodley & Vaughan you would not only have by far the best Cathedral in America, but one that would satisfy you & American Churchmen."[27]

Both Bodley and Vaughan had independently mentioned each other to Satterlee as possible partners in the Washington project. That fact gave the bishop reason to believe that the two would work well together. Born in England, Vaughan had worked under Bodley for several years before moving to Boston, but he had been active long enough in America to serve as a valid representative of American architecture.

In The *Private Record* Satterlee describes events leading up to the trustees' acceptance of Bodley and Vaughan on October 8, 1906, and the meeting with the two architects in Washington on December 1.[28] Within weeks both architects were soliciting Satterlee's views on architectural details, perhaps to gain some sense of what features might be possible in the preliminary design. In his initial response the bishop focused not on design details but on what he saw as the mission of the Cathedral as a guide to design. The structure, he noted, would be "the representative Cathedral of our

Henry Vaughan

own church in the Capital of the country" and of "the Anglican Communion in America." The Cathedral would help the cause of Church unity by offering a home for those American Protestant denominations that only a few centuries earlier had broken away from the Church of England. He suggested that the statuary and stained glass could include portraits of great Protestant leaders like John Bunyan, George Fox, and John Wesley. And because the Cathedral "would not only be religious, but also National," the stained glass could depict events in American history. Windows in the choir could be devoted to scriptural scenes, while the portico could represent the Bible. As for the central tower, Satterlee reminded the architects that "the first carol ever sung was sung by herald angels from Heaven. Thus the tower, with its bells, might well be named the Gloria in Excelsis Tower . . . while the Chancel stands for the Ascension of Christ, and the triumph of the Christian faith."[29]

In March 1907 Bodley reported that Vaughan had been in England and had accepted the design decisions already made. Both the architects found the work too fascinating to set aside. They thought the bishop would like the design because Satterlee "had [given] or *transmitted* the inspiration." The report describing the design was already written, and Vaughan would bring it to Washington. Bodley wondered whether the bishop should see the report before it was printed. In any case, he thought Satterlee should not yet show it to the board of trustees. In the meantime, Bodley was reading the bishop's book, *The Building of a Cathedral,*" with much interest and edification."[30]

Satterlee welcomed the news that the report was complete, but he was waiting eagerly for the drawings so that the board could review them before the members scattered for the summer. He was also hoping to lay the cornerstone for the Cathedral on St. Michael's Day, the last Sunday in September, the week when the Bishop of London and most of the bishops of the American church could be in Washington on their way to the General Convention in Richmond. Satterlee reminded Bodley that no funds had been raised since the debt on the land was paid. Without the design, gifts to the project would be small. "After the design, however, has been adopted, I expect to begin a propaganda work."[31]

With the report in hand, Satterlee conveyed his reactions to Bodley in a nine-page letter. He and the trustees were "delighted with it," because the architects, bishop, and trustees were all united in hope that the Cathedral "would breathe the atmosphere of the triumph of the Christian faith." The architects had "taken every possible means to give the Cathedral this uplifting power." It is striking to see how many architectural features of the Cathedral as it stands today were endorsed by Satterlee in the report. The large clerestory windows would allow light to come not only from above but would reflect on the ribs of the vaulting. He could hardly wait to see the drawings of the west front with its triune arches flanked by the two west towers. "I think it will have all and more of the effectiveness of the great west porches of Rheims Cathedral." He was pleased that there would not be a great tower opening in the crossing but that the nave roof would continue into the crossing "at the very place where the choir and the congregation are meeting." He welcomed "the broad chancel arch with the soffit of over nine feet wide, to be filled with the figures of angels, and with the exquisite thought of their hovering about the crucifixion, the mystery the angels desired to look into." He assumed that "the open work rood screen would of course be surmounted by the crucifix. . . . This is the proper place for the crucifix. The cross on the altar is without the body of Christ, because it represents the cross from which Christ rose from the dead and ascended into heaven." He endorsed Bodley's decision to keep the Lady Chapel in the apse and place the Virgin's and St. John's chapels on either side of the rood screen, symbolizing their standing on either side of the cross. Satterlee confessed to Bodley that he could find little to criticize in the report. He could add only suggestions on many points that the architects had not yet addressed.[32]

THE COLOR OF THE STONE

While waiting for the drawings to arrive from England, Satterlee turned to Vaughan on two matters that could best be explored in America. Neither of these appears in the *Private Record*. The first was the selection of stone for the Cathedral. From the outset of the design work in the fall of 1906, the architects had recommended a red stone, something somewhat lighter than that used at Liverpool. Both Satterlee and some of the trustees accepted the suggestion, but others preferred white stone as the "color of purity," used in the newer government buildings in Washington. Satterlee found the appearance of white stone in a cathedral "cold and formal," but he strongly objected to a red stone that at some distance would look like brick. Satterlee and the trustees found all the red samples Vaughan produced to be too dark. Vaughan ruled out granite as being too difficult to carve, and the question, overtaken by the arrival of the drawings in June, was put off for the future. The type and color of the stone was still unresolved in 1909.[33]

LOCATING THE CORNERSTONE

A more urgent question for Satterlee was the location of the cornerstone, which he hoped to lay in a grand ceremony in September. Because it would be difficult to place a cornerstone precisely at a western corner of the Cathedral before the plan for the foundations had been determined, Satterlee proposed instead a foundation stone as the first stone to be set for the Cathedral, but there was still the question of the stone's location. Making it part of the foundation of the Cathedral was out of the question, but Vaughan thought it could be placed "under where the altar would probably come, and not to have it form any part of the construction." Vaughan's suggestion led Satterlee to propose building a chapel of the Nativity there, an idea that Vaughan quickly accepted.[34]

But why a Chapel of the Nativity? When Randolph McKim asked this question at a board meeting, Satterlee replied that "it was just a matter of sentiment," which we know from other sources was a profound understatement. Since his days in seminary Satterlee had seen the Incarnation as absolutely essential to understanding that God had actually come into the world as Jesus and was still active in the lives of all people. The Incarnation was a key principle in high-church Anglican theology, a subject that Satterlee explored at length in *A Creedless Gospel and the Gospel Creed*, his magnum opus on Christian theology. In England he had met Charles Gore, the leading advocate of Incarnational theology, and quotes Gore's book, *Lux Mundi*, in *A Creedless Gospel*. Perhaps his statement to McKim was but another example of his strategy of approaching a potentially controversial subject obliquely. The determination Satterlee describes in the *Private Record* to obtain stones from Bethlehem in time for the September ceremony reveals his commitment to a chapel of the Incarnation. As Christopher Row noted in his history of the Cathedral's architecture, the inscription Satterlee selected for the Foundation Stone was hardly conventional for such a purpose: "The Word made flesh and dwelt among us." It was fitting after construction of Bethlehem Chapel that Satterlee's sarcophagus was placed behind the altar, above the Foundation Stone and below the Jerusalem Altar, surrounded by the four pillars representing the Chicago-Lambeth Quadrilateral.[35]

Arrival of the Drawings

At last, on June 5, Bodley's drawings arrived in New York. Satterlee arranged to have a friend contact the express company and asked George B. Cortelyou, the treasury secretary, to clear the drawings through customs so that they could come to Washington by the night train. Within two hours after their arrival in Washington on the morning of June 7, the drawings were before the trustees. The following day Satterlee wrote Bodley that the reaction of the board seemed favorable. For himself, Satterlee thought the plans surpassed his expectations. "Mr. Vaughan will tell you of the subdued serene pleasure with which all the members of the chapter contemplated the two perspective drawings after they had been interpreted by Mr. Vaughan from the architectural plans."

Satterlee noted that the design would bring a flood of light into the chancel and focus on the altar with "a wonderful effect." In contrast he saw that "the roof high up in the obscurity under the broad soffit with the angels bending over it is just in the right place, because without their knowing it, it will act as a suggestion to every beholder that this building is dedicated to Christ; . . . The worshipping congregations will often look up, and realize that they are gathered beneath the cross of Jesus, and then looking toward the bright light that falls upon the altar cross, they cannot help saying that the crucifixion leads up to the resurrection and the Ascension."

But even before he had time to study the plans in detail, the bishop found things to criticize. "The West end towers were too low, and . . . the interior of the choir ought to be more than one step above the floor of the nave." He also reported that the board found the sample of red stone suggested by Vaughan was "entirely too dark." With this letter Satterlee launched an exchange of correspondence that continued through the summer of 1907.[36]

Christopher Row in his detailed description of this exchange of architectural ideas concluded that "this Cathedral (like its medieval predecessors) was very much a collaborative effort between architects and the 'patron.' Satterlee's direction and guidance in the sphere of architectural and decorative iconography clearly influenced the shape of the finished Cathedral."[37]

The last entry in the Private Record is dated in August 1907. The Record stands as an extraordinary account of what Satterlee achieved in his first eleven years as Bishop of Washington. It is a document that deserves close reading.

The West Front of the cathedral as proposed by architects Bodley and Vaughan in June 1907

5. THE *PRIVATE RECORD*

Three years after Satterlee's death in 1908 his wife, Jane Lawrence Satterlee, succeeded in convincing Charles Henry Brent, the Episcopal Bishop of the Philippine Islands, to write a biography of her husband. Much to Jane Satterlee's dismay and disappointment, Brent had twice refused election as Bishop of Washington as her husband's successor, but she considered Brent the ideal choice for a biographer. He had already published at least ten books or articles with Longmans, Green, and his work among the poor in Boston resembled in some ways Henry Satterlee's ministry in New York City. During the winter of 1911 Jane Satterlee began collecting documents, papers, publications, and scrapbooks to send to Brent in Manila for his work on the biography. On May 13 she wrote to Brent: "I have now engaged the best Secretary and typewriter in Washington to transcribe from my dictation such portions of his 'strictly private journal,' never opened before, as will be of use."[1] She sent the completed typescript to Brent and placed several copies in Bishop Satterlee's papers retained by the Cathedral. Satterlee's original manuscript has never been found, and it seems likely that Mrs. Satterlee destroyed it after the typescript was completed. The typescript itself did not come to light until the cathedral archives was established in the 1980s.

Whether Jane Lawrence Satterlee deleted any sections from the bishop's handwritten manuscript is impossible to tell. Because the typescript was obviously not meant for publication, there was no incentive to make

Jane Lawrence Satterlee

---

[1] Jane Lawrence Satterlee to Charles Henry Brent, May 13, 1911, Charles Henry Brent Papers, Box 9, Manuscripts Division, Library of Congress.

deletions. Furthermore, she was careful to mark with her initials the few explanatory notes that she added to the typescript. Her care in doing this suggests that she was scrupulous in seeing that the *Record* was transcribed exactly as the bishop had written it. The few misspellings of proper names were probably the result of the secretary's errors in taking dictation. What seems perfectly clear is that Satterlee wrote all of the text of the typescript except for the few additions by "J.L.S."

The *Private Record*, then, can be accepted as a valid account of Bishop Satterlee's efforts, in his own words, to create Washington National Cathedral. As such, The *Private Record* is the most authoritative single source on the beginnings of the cathedral project between 1895 and 1908.

The entire typescript, as prepared by Jane Lawrence Satterlee, has been included without any deletions. Obvious typographical errors introduced in preparing the typescript have been corrected. In a few instances, proper names were spelled incorrectly in the process of Mrs. Satterlee's dictation, and these have been corrected.

The original typescript consists of straight text with no topical divisions, with the result that the subjects of the narrative often change from paragraph to paragraph. To make the text more readable, I have inserted side headings. In some instances, I have rearranged the order of paragraphs so that those on the same subject appear together.

The *Private Record* contains more than a hundred names, sometimes ten or more on the same page. To avoid extensive, intrusive footnotes to identify individuals, I have added a section on Biographical Notes, which includes brief biographies of all the persons we were able to identify. The notes are arranged alphabetically. The name of the individual as it appears in the *Private Record* is used on the first line of each entry, with the full name on the second line.

HISTORY of the CATHEDRAL of St. PETER and St. PAUL

Private Record of Henry Y. Satterlee.

Introduction

The beginnings of the history of the Cathedral will be different as seen by different eyes and told by different lips. They reach back several years before the date of my consecration. I should only refer to that part which came under my personal notice and observation, and therefore, in a sense, their record will be incomplete, beginning with the time when I became Bishop of Washington. This record must never be published without careful revision. I here utter the solemn charge, if any parts of it are ever given to the public, the selection must be made in that spirit of charity which thinketh no evil, which rejoiceth not in iniquity, but rejoiceth in the truth, and which in the eye of God would hurt no man's reputation.

The four factors of consideration which induced me to accept the Bishopric of Washington were, first, the separation of the Church and State, and the importance of creating the traditions of the diocese at the capital of the United States on this line; second, the solution of the problem how to Christianize the colored people, Washington being the point where North and South meet; third, the desire, if possible, to mold a small diocese like Washington on the lines of the primitive, undivided Church, in such a way that it would promote the cause of American Christian and Church unity by combining all the true elements of Catholic and Protestant life; fourth, the importance of making the Cathedral a center of diocesan life and, if possible, a witness in the Capital for all that the Protestant Episcopal Church in the United States stands for.

Different Bishops, by their counsels, before I was consecrated all deepened these convictions in me. Among those who gave the most valuable suggestions, all following the same general lines of thought I had been pondering, were Bishop Williams, of Connecticut, Bishop Doane, of Albany, Bishop Paret, of Maryland, Bishop Coxe, of Western New York, Bishop Potter, of New York, and last but not least, Dr. Heman Dyer and Dr. W. S. Langford, General Secretary of the Board of Missions.

Early Cathedral Plans

When I began to inquire into the history of the Cathedral of Washington, the following facts came, from time to time, to my attention. I do not give these in the chronological order in which I heard of them, but give them in their own actual chronological order. Major L'Enfant, the architect employed under General Washington to lay out the plan of the Federal City, projected a State Church, to be built on the site of the present Patent Office, as a kind of American Westminster Abbey, yet to belong to no denomination. Of course this was impossible, in a land where Church and State were to be forever separate. The State Church was never built; yet here was the germ of the idea of a Christian cathedral, and it slumbered in the minds of "Episcopalians."

Washington also suggested a university of the United States in the capital of the country. This idea took hold forcibly of other Christian bodies. Just as the Baptists started long ago their Columbian University[2], the Romanists at a much later day their Catholic University of America, the Methodists still later their American University, and the ladies of many Christian bodies are now projecting their great National University of the United States, so the Churchmen of Washington have persistently cherished the ideal, not of a university[3], but of a National Cathedral.

I have recently been told that about 1865, when the creation of the new Diocese of Washington out of the old Diocese of Maryland was warmly discussed in and outside of the Diocesan Convention, there was an informal meeting of the clergymen and laymen at St. Alban's Church, at which the same subject was warmly debated. After the meeting was over, Dr. Charles H. Hall, the celebrated old War Rector of the Church of the Epiphany[4], said: "Gentlemen, sooner or later the Diocese of Washington will be created. It must come, and I am heartily in favor of it." Then, turning to the magnificent view of Washington spread out before him, he added: "I have just been telling Brother Chew that this is the spot for the future Cathedral." This anecdote was told me by William H. Meloy, who was present. Mr. Meloy added that Dr. Hall also said, in his well-known humorous vein: "What more favored site could there be for the See of Washington or the site of the Cathedral?"

About 1893 I heard that Congress had actually granted a charter for a Protestant Episcopal Cathedral Foundation in the District of Columbia. After Easter, 1894, I happened to be riding in the cars from Washington to New York, when I met the Rev. George W. Douglas. He gave me an animated description of

---

[2] Now The George Washington University.

[3] The initial conception of the Cathedral by George William Douglas and others included a university.

[4] 1317 G Street NW, Washington, DC

the exciting meeting of the Board of Trustees of the Cathedral which had recently taken place.[5]

In writing the history of the Cathedral, it is not quite just to omit the name of Miss Mann, who was one of the originators of the Cathedral idea in Washington. Before the division of the diocese, she had donated some property she had acquired, which she rated very high, at $70,000, but which would probably be estimated at $20,000, donating it in trust to the Cathedral Board, the Standing Committee of the diocese, the Diocesan Convention and the Rector of St. John's Church, the Rev. Dr. George William Douglas. But alas the property she had given—or partly given—was so encumbered by back taxes and interest on mortgages that she asked that it might be returned to her to prevent its forced sale for taxes, so that now it has all been transferred back to the original donor, Miss Mann herself, each of the former recipients having executed an individual release to her.

I heard that there were dissensions in the Cathedral Board at Washington, but I was at that time interested more in the recent doings of the Convention and in the opening out of my winter's work at Calvary.[6] Little did I dream how soon I, so far away, was to appear as an actual actor on the scene myself, or that in a few weeks' time I would be elected Bishop of Washington. This is all I can remember that I knew about the Cathedral before I was chosen Bishop.

I was elected Bishop of Washington St. Nicholas' Day, December 6, 1895. I was consecrated March 25, 1896, on the Feast of the Annunciation. In the preceding February three events occurred:

I visited Bishop Paret, at Baltimore, and he told me that there had been some friction in the Board of Trustees. Dr. Douglas resigned his position, both as Dean and as trustee.

The second event was a visit I received, in Calvary Rectory, from Mr. Flagg and Col. Britton, in which they brought plans with them. I was scrupulously non-committal, of course.

The third event was a visit that I paid to the Cathedral grounds about a month before I became Bishop. I was deeply distressed. I saw that of the eighteen acres not more than half could be utilized. Even that half was a side hill, sloping

---

[5]Douglas was no doubt referring to the dispute that had arisen within the Board of Trustees over the architectural style of the proposed Cathedral School for Girls.

[6]Calvary Episcopal Church on Fourth Avenue at Twenty-first Street, New York City, where Satterlee had served as rector.

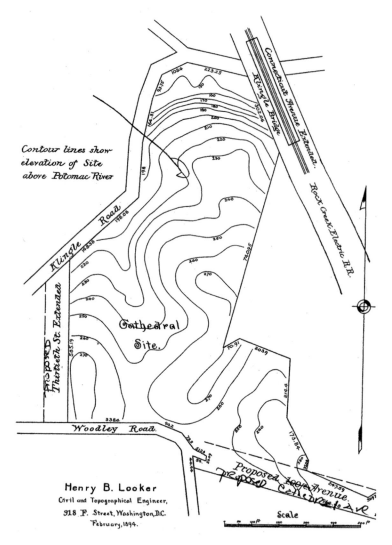

The original Cathedral site near Connecticut Avenue, 1894. Note the sharp drop in the terrain to the north, away from the city.

down 120 feet in 18 acres from Cathedral Avenue, and not towards but away from Washington. Again, the grounds were not situated on a thoroughfare. Then I went to St. Alban's,[7] saw its magnificent view, and felt at once that this land on Massachusetts Avenue was the site for the Cathedral. But alas! the property

---

[7] St. Alban's parish church on the Cathedral Close.

The Connecticut Avenue bridge over Klingle Run looking north in the 1890s. The Cathedral property on the left touched the unpaved avenue at this point. The land to the west of the avenue had been cleared for Cleveland Park homes.

had been bought a fortnight before by Mr. A. L. Barber. So I tried to buy the land owned by Madam Hemert, between the Cathedral ground and Connecticut Avenue, but she asked a prohibitive price, $15,000 an acre.

I saw Bishop Paret before my consecration once more, and asked him if we could consecrate the Cathedral grounds by temporarily using St. Alban's, a quarter of a mile away, for a Cathedral chapel, and at the same time, for the sake of the Cathedral work, take some mission down town for a Pro-Cathedral. The Bishop said the idea was perfectly feasible.

Selection of a Pro-Cathedral

The first visit I had after my consecration was from deputations of the two vestries of St. Mark's, Capitol Hill.[8] In process of time both Trinity[9] and St. Marks Churches were offered to me for a Pro-Cathedral. In the autumn, when I returned

---

[8]St. Mark's Episcopal Church, 118 Third Street SE, Washington, D.C.

[9]Trinity Church, C and Third Street, NW, no longer exists.

from Europe, I selected St. Mark's, first because it was down in an out-of-the-way neighborhood, and down also in finances, and hence would not arouse antagonism or jealousy of other parishes; second because, after the sorrow and trials of heart-burning divisions, they were ready for unity and peace. Then I secured a clergy house and engaged as my chaplains the Reverends Charles H. Hayes, William L. DeVries and Philip M. Rhinelander, to start a post graduate clergy school for deacons, using the Pro-Cathedral as a training school of pastoral experience, somewhat in the same way as hospitals and clinics are for physicians. The clerical school lasted four years. Fifteen deacons were instructed, and it was only closed because we had no further candidates for orders for two years, because, very naturally, bishops of other dioceses wanted to keep their own deacons.

The Cathedral School for Girls

The next step in advance was that relating to the Cathedral School for Girls. A year or two before I came to Washington, Dr. Douglas had asked Mrs. Phoebe A. Hearst, widow of Senator Hearst of California, to be one of five to give a Cathedral School for Girls, costing about $100,000. She said: "Dr. Douglas, one person can do this work better than five. The amount you name is insufficient. I will give $175,000 for the school."

In the summer of 1896, Mr. Flagg, the architect who had drawn the Cathedral plans, sent in plans and specifications for the school. The price was about $155,000. When the estimates were sent out to builders, the lowest price was $294,000, the highest $315,000—that is, the lowest was nearly twice as much as the Board expected to pay. The consequence was that nothing was done; but it brought together those who opposed and those who had approved of tentative plans. We were rid of all plans for the school and the Cathedral.[10]

Selecting a New Site

In the meantime, I had been trying to secure the land adjoining the (Chevy-Chase)[11] Cathedral property, between it and the higher, better ground on Connecticut Avenue, but the owner, Madam von Hemert, in Paris, wrote to me that she would charge $15,000 an acre for these 7 acres, and when her husband came to America afterwards, he said he would not sell even for that price. This

---

[10]Chapter Minute Book, Nov. 23, 1896, Vol. 1, 89-91.

[11]The Chevy-Chase Land Co., owner of the site.

was to me a severe blow. The Cathedral grounds were utterly inadequate for an institution that was to stand and grow for centuries. Shortly after this I met Mrs. Hearst. At that time I felt completely paralyzed as far as the Cathedral was concerned. Nothing could be done, and time was precious. I didn't tell Mrs. Hearst how I felt about that land over which the Cathedral Board was so enthusiastic, but she, of her own accord, expressed her own positive opinion, and said: "Bishop, the first time I saw this ground where they were going to put my school I was sick at heart. I went again the next day and that was enough." I said: "I wish you would attend a meeting of the Cathedral Board and tell the trustees what you have told me." She said: "I will do so gladly." At that time matters were at a pretty low ebb.

At a meeting with two or three of the trustees, who keenly felt my want of enthusiasm about the land, one of them said: "I do not see daylight anywhere"; and another was almost in favor of giving up everything, winding up the business and resigning the Cathedral charter; and the fact that we had to pay a yearly assessment of taxes and interest, amounting to $1,800, with no funds at all in the treasur[y], did not help matters, especially as this payment was a continual drain on the pockets of the trustees themselves.

When, therefore, Mrs. Hearst appeared at the board meeting and expressed emphatically her strong disapproval of the site chosen, the feeling of gloom grew deeper and deeper. This was, as I remember, in the autumn of 1897. Secretly, as the clouds grew darker, I felt brighter and brighter. We were free of any architect of the Cathedral plans, and now, if we could get rid of the land and start, ab ovo, with no obstacles in the way, I felt that the real movement was not at all backward, but forward. Then, when the opportunity came, I said frankly to the Board: "The Chevy-Chase land was chiefly donated. Only eight acres were bought. The donated portion was given under the restriction that $500,000 should be expended in buildings within ten years. The eight acres bought were mortgaged for almost all their value. We have expended about $25,000 on the site in taxes and interest. We owe on mortgages nearly $40,000. The $40,000 is to be raised chiefly by the bishop. Now, I put it to you squarely. How can a bishop raise $40,000 for land that he disapproves of, in which he takes no interest, and which he believes to be utterly unfit for a Cathedral?" This question settled the case. The Board agreed to part with the land if the bishop could raise money for the purchase of another site.

I then asked Senator Edmunds if he would write me a letter that I could publish. He said: "My advice to you is to apply to the Bishops of the Church for help. Let them be the leaders in raising funds for the Cathedral throughout the land." Little did the senator realize how deeply our Church was saturated with the spirit of diocesanism and local jealousy. The Roman Church in the United States is a unit. It will sacrifice local objects for national objects. The Methodist Church, on the other hand, is national rather than local, from its want of local organization. But the Episcopal Church, which makes so much of the parish and the diocese, sees nothing beyond the parish and the diocese. The great want of the Episcopal Church at the present day is a greater spirit of national unity and organization. Still, Senator Edmunds was right. From the moment that he spoke a new light dawned upon me, and I felt that, acting on the Gospel principle of overcoming evil with good, I ought to ignore diocesanism and appeal to the bishops just as though they had a deep interest in the National Cathedral. Afterwards, when I spoke to Bishop Paret about Senator Edmunds' plan, he answered: "Yes, that is the only thing to do; I realized this long ago." When I asked him why, then, he did not appeal to the bishops, he responded: "My courage failed at such an undertaking."

A Building for the Girls' School

In the meantime it was necessary that we should do something about the school building. This was due to Mrs. Hearst. She had behaved most generously and most patiently. At one time some of her friends advised her to withdraw her offer to build the school. I gladly testify here that it was the generous gift of $175,000 of Mrs. Hearst, and her persistence in holding to her offer, which kept the Cathedral Board together in this trying period, 1895 and 1896. In 1897 she increased her gift to $200,000, to pay for an architectural competition. Five firms were singled out. Plans were sent in. All were carefully analyzed and tabulated by Mr. Adolph Cluss, and an architectural superintendent employed on recommendation of General John M. Wilson. This tabulation and plans [were] submitted first to Mrs. Hearst, who told me she preferred the one labeled "Fireproof." Then I called a meeting of the Board.[12] The comparative table of merits of all five were carefully submitted to them; I asked the individual opinion of each trustee separately, and all agreed on "Fireproof." I then expressed the same opinion, and lastly told them that Mrs. Hearst's opinion was exactly the same as ours. The acceptance of Mr. Gibson's plan "Fireproof" was thus unanimous. This was very auspicious, as he was the architect of the Albany Cathedral and of the St. Agnes's School in Albany.

The Barber Property

This meeting of the Board of Trustees took place, if I remember aright, in May, 1897, and it was a great encouragement to us. I then set about raising

---

[12]Chapter Minute Book, Apr. 9, 1897, Vol. 1, 97-106.

the money, and at the same time asked Mr. A. L. Barber what he would sell the St. Alban's property for. He wrote in answer that he would not sell for less than $300,000.

In September, 1897, the War with Spain seemed imminent. When at this time Commodore Dewey was ordered, at his own request, to take charge of the fleet at Japan, the day he left Washington one of the Justices met him on I Street and said: "Commodore, it looks as though the Spanish War were coming." "It certainly does," was Dewey's answer. "I suppose," said the Justice, "that the first battle will be fought at Havana." "No," said the Commodore, "it will be fought at Manila." "What do you mean?" said the Justice; to which Dewey replied: "If I have anything to do with it, I shall sail over in the night and capture Manila before breakfast."

Of course the uncertainty as to war affected the value of property. I told Mrs. Hearst that I wanted to drive with her to St. Alban's. She consented, and I went in her carriage to inspect one or two sites. At last we went to St. Alban's. As I was showing her the view, Mr. James Nourse and one or two others came up and began talking to me. I at once descended from the carriage, as Mrs. Hearst wished to remain incognito. Mr. Nourse said at the carriage wheel: "Mrs. Hearst is reported as being a very generous woman; I wonder if she would not help us." Afterwards I said to her: "Did you hear how you are talked about behind your back?" "Yes," she said, "every word."

She then took me to Kalorama, to the property which I believe is called "Widow's Mite." It was a magnificent site,[13] near Dupont Circle, Massachusetts Avenue, but only six acres; yet so near the city and on such a commanding hill that I went to see Mr. Howell, Rector of St. Margaret's,[14] and we arranged that if this site were bought, St. Margaret's should be the Cathedral Chapel. This was in November, 1897; but the property was so irregular in shape that I found that we should have to buy an additional twenty lots from almost as many owners. I then went to ask the advice of one of the trustees conversant with business matters. The property was to be sold on December 9th. The asking price was $270,000. The other lots would cost at least $100,000 more. The trustee answered: "The site, notwithstanding its small size, is so much nearer the center of Washington that it is preferable for a Cathedral; but unless you have $400,000 cash in hand, you had better not touch it."

As a matter of fact, I had not one dollar in hand; but I am most glad that this site was so carefully considered by us. It was the only available site left for a

---

[13]North of Florida Avenue and S Street NW, and west of the present path of Connecticut Avenue in Kalorama Heights.

[14]St. Margaret's Church, 1820 Connecticut Avenue NW, just east of the proposed site.

cathedral in the whole portion of Washington that is now thickly populated. If in future years people ask why we went so far away, across Rock Creek, for a site out in the country, where there as yet were neither streets nor houses, we can answer that we made every effort to secure the only available piece of land large enough for a cathedral within a mile and a half of the White House, but were prevented from purchasing it by circumstances utterly beyond our control.

Meeting the Barber Option

In December, 1897, Mr. Barber gave us an option for thirty days to buy St. Alban's for $224,000. His reasons for doing this were as follows: First, he had tried to buy St. Alban's Church property, with a promise of removing, or rather, building a stone church on the opposite corner of Woodley Road, and the Nourse family indignantly refused, saying that the Church was consecrated to their sister's memory and built on land set apart to God. Second, the war with Spain was very imminent and all values were insecure. Mrs. Hearst, Mr. Bell and Mr. Glover said it was a very high price, but we could afford to pay for the property an extra $24,000 rather than lose it.

After this, in February and March, 1898, we were in a very embarrassing position. Mr. Barber's option on the St. Alban's property had expired and he would not renew it. On the one hand I had to raise money enough to make them some kind of an offer; on the other hand, I had to appeal for funds for a cathedral, without any fixed sum or option from the owner of the land on which to base an appeal. The whole thing, as some one said, was "up in the air." As a trustee said, "We were checked and paralyzed on both sides." This was a time for earnest prayer, as I told the ladies of the Bishop's Guild at their Lenten meeting. Many of these ladies were wives of city rectors. Others took no interest in the Cathedral. Yet all generously agreed that the corporate communion of the Guild should take place at St. Alban's Church on Easter Monday, April 11, 1898. Now, it so happened that this was the very day when President McKinley was to send in his memorable message to Congress about the blowing up of the "Maine" in the harbor of Havana. That message meant peace or war. On Easter Monday morning, Mrs. William Belden Noble came to me and said, in a manner intensely in earnest: "Why is there no prophet, no Savanarola, today to go to the halls of Congress to stay this war, to prevent bloodshed, to deliver God's own message of peace?" I forget what I answered. I only know that her words kept ringing in my ears, driving out all other thought.

The corporate communion of the Bishop's Guild was to take place at 12 m., at the very hour the President's message was being read to the impatient Senate. I felt that I could speak of but one subject in such an hour. In my Communion address I earnestly exhorted all present to pray for the peace of our beloved country, to pray that those who were at this very moment listening to the message might feel the influence of the Holy Ghost, the Spirit of Peace; and I am sure that this was the one thought uppermost in every mind as all approached the altar to partake of the Sacrament of Christ's body and blood.

[Note by J.L.S. The Bishop's address on this occasion can never be forgotten by those who were present. It was plainly inspired.]

I then made every exertion to secure the money needed to buy the St. Alban's property. From one source I expected, with some reason, to get $200,000, and when I wrote for it and received a "no" in reply, I shall never forget the agony of that sleepless night. I learned a lesson that night that I shall never forget.

Then came other discouragements in answer to letters. I persevered, however, from January to August, making visits and spending my vacation, in the summer of 1898, writing letters. At last I gathered $83,000 together, from Mrs. Percy R. Pyne, Miss Kibbey, Mr. Morgan, Cornelius Vanderbilt, Mrs. Noerishoffer, W. K. Vanderbilt and Miss M. V. Bruce; also $8,000 loaned without interest from Mrs. Hearst. This, with the $17,000 that the Chevy Chase Land Company promised to refund, in return for money advanced by us on the old site, made $100,000.

In the latter part of July, 1898, I wrote to Mr. A. L. Barber, telling him I had raised $100,000 and asking him if he would sell for $200,000. He answered that all the political conditions had changed since January 1st. The battles of Santiago and Manila had been fought. The war was practically over. Money was easier. He could not afford to se[ll] now for $224,000, but would for $250,000. Then he said he would come from New York to Bar Harbor, whither I had gone with my wife, son and daughter for a month, to talk matters over.

About the 20th of August he appeared with his yacht before the Clifton Hotel, Northeast Harbor, where I was staying. He made these propositions: First, he would sell three-quarters of the land for $200,000, reserving the northwest corner for himself. Second, three-quarters of the land reserving the northeast quarter for himself; or the whole for $250,000. I said: "But the property is not worth over $8,000 an acre." He replied: "There have been three booms of land in Washington, each followed by a depression of six years. The last was in 1893. The present depression will end before 1900." I said: "We are the only purchaser." He replied: "Yes; but I don't want to sell to any one." I said: "But it costs you $10,000 a year to keep the property." He replied: "I can afford to pay the interest and wait, can't I? What I propose to do is to build myself a handsome residence costing $150,000, which, mark my words, I shall begin this very autumn. I shall then enjoy the beautiful park as my home in my lifetime, and by-and-by sell it at a great advance in price which will more than cover any expense that I put upon it. Bishop, this is your last chance. If you don't buy the property now, you will never buy it."

I then asked him to put in writing his proposition, and also wrote that I was favorable to a purchase. The next day I wrote an account of the interview to each of the members of the Cathedral Board, asking them to telegraph their answers whether or not they would consent to buy the land before September 10th, the day when the option expired. I received telegrams consenting to the purchase from Messrs. Glover, Lowndes, Edmunds, Dr. McKim, Dr. Mackay-Smith, Col. Britton, General Wilson, Col. Truesdell, General Kasson; negative, Dr. Elliott, Mr. Pellew, General Parke. Affirmative, counting my own vote, 10; negative, 3.

I then asked Mr. Barber to extend the option. He refused.

On September 7th I went to Washington and called a meeting of the Board for that day. Col. Fleming, Mr. Barber's agent, called on me. I asked him if he would not consent to take less than $250,000, as I had only $100,000 to pay, and had not been able to secure a dollar more. He said he would urge Mr. Barber to do so. Mr. Barber telephoned in reply: "If Bishop Satterlee will buy the property for $245,000 before the Board meeting this afternoon, I will sell it to him for that sum; but to the Board the price is $250,000."

I went at once to Col. Britton. He said: "Ten-thirteenths of the Board have consented already to buy for $250,000. If you can save a year's interest by buying now for $245,000, there is no objection." So I consented. I shall never forget the sensations with which, at the Board meeting, it was voted to buy the land. All knew the responsibility of raising the money depended chiefly on me. On the preceding Sunday, at Twilight Park,[15] September 4th, I had walked out into the woods with the feeling that this was the last Sunday I should be free for many years, and that next Sunday my life would be practically mortgaged for $145,000.[16] Then I thought of Admiral Dewey at Manila, and how for the sake of his country he had taken his life in his hands; how, if he had been beaten at Manila, there was absolutely nowhere for his fleet to go; how they would be portless, coalless, homeless, disabled. Then I felt, "If Dewey can do this for country, surely I can take a different kind of risk for God."

Signing the Contract

Fourteen months afterward, when Admiral Dewey was elected a trustee of the Cathedral and he came to see me, accepting the position, I told him about

---

[15] A summer community at Haines Falls, west of Hudson, New York

[16] Equivalent to $2,900,000 in current dollars.

this, and added that in this way, through his influence, he had already helped the Cathedral. He responded: "Did you really think of Manila at that especial time?" When I answered "yes," he said: "I am grateful that it is so. My father helped to build the little church at our home in Vermont. Everything that is good in me I got from him, and if I can help in any way to build the Cathedral of Washington, I am following in his footsteps."

Yet, when at the Board meeting I took up the pen to sign the contract for the purchase of the Cathedral property, it required as much nerve and courage as I have ever put forth. And we paid $50,000 down. Five minutes afterwards I said to Col. Fleming: "How about those fences that separate the church property of St. Alban's from the Barber land?" He responded: "That land is now yours, to do with as you please. You can have the fence removed tomorrow." And it was removed the next day.

After the Cathedral land was bought, the Vestry of St. Alban's informally decided that they would not resign the two and a half acres of land owned by them, upon which the Church and rectory stand, until the Cathedral land itself was freed from debt. As soon as that takes place, the parish will give up its property to the Cathedral Board. It will keep its identity as a parish, with its own vestry and parochial limits, but the advowsen or appointment of a rector will rest with the Bishop and the Board.

Laying the Cornerstone for the Girls' School

Then came the vision of the approaching General Convention at Washington. At once I wrote to Mrs. Hearst and asked her if she would consent to her school being built on land which was mortgaged for three-fifths of its value. She generously consented; and I then contemplated the laying of the cornerstone of the Hearst school during the General Convention, but soon discovered that this was utterly impossible in the short time before us.

The Peace Cross

Then all suddenly, on the Sunday after the purchase was made—that is, Sunday, September 11th—while I was in the little Church in Twilight Park, the remembrance came back to my mind of the Communion service on Easter Monday of the Bishop's Guild, in which we had prayed so earnestly for peace. On that day the war with Spain was practically begun. Now it was practically over. Then came the remembrance of another service at Northeast Harbor on August 11th, when the news came to us regarding the suspension of hostilities, and when Bishop Doane called us all to the little Church there, Dr. Nelson, my son Churchill and I ringing the bell, Drs. Huntington, Mackay-Smith[,] Cornelius Smith, President Gilman of Johns Hopkins, being present, and we held a short thanksgiving service for the restoration of peace.

This suggested the erection of a Cross of Peace as the first monument on the new Cathedral grounds, with the inscription: "That it may please Thee to give to all nations unity, peace and concord; we beseech Thee to hear us, Good Lord!"[17] At once I told the thought to my wife and daughter, also to Dr. and Mrs. Rives; and Dr. Rives said at once he would give the Cross. We all agreed that no more beautiful beginning could be made of the National American Cathedral of the Prince of Peace. But no time was to be lost. The next day I wrote to Mr. Gibson, the architect of the Hearst School, to prepare a sketch and get estimates for a monolithic cross like that erected by Bishop Doane to his daughter behind the chancel of the chapel at Northeast Harbor. Mr. Gibson wrote back that we needed a larger cross, at least 20 feet high.

After this there was great delay in getting estimates. After several failures, a Mr. Flannery, on Capitol Hill, said, on Sunday, September 23rd, that he would make the cross for $400, and start at once for Bloomington, Indiana, to get the stone. But on Tuesday, three days later, he excused himself from going, saying that he had telegraphed his instructions instead. At the end of that week they had not begun to cut the stone from the quarries.

In the meantime, I had gone to President McKinley, and he promised to be present at the unveiling of the Cross, fixing Sunday, October 23rd, as the date; but he refused to speak. Through continuous importunity, I finally arranged for the stones to be cut and shipped on the freight-cars. In the meantime the General Convention met in Washington on Wednesday, October 7th, and continued its daily sessions at the Church of the Epiphany.

On October 9th, only 14 days before the Peace Cross service, I heard that the car on which the stone had been sent was lost and could not be found. Mr. Fitzgerald, superintendent of the B. & O. Railroad, promised that the moment the car came on his line he would have it attached to an express train and hurried to Washington. On October 10th I determined to send Rev. Mr. Bratenahl to trace the whereabouts of the freight-car. An hour after he returned, saying it had arrived that very morning in Washington, Mr. Flannery at once set his stone-cutters at work on it. Rev. Dr. DeVries gave me some valuable suggestions regarding the inscription, and also at my request, set about the arrangement of the Peace Cross

---

[17] From the Litany, *Book of Common Prayer,* 1893 ed., 30-36.

service, as I was constantly in attendance upon the General Convention. On Friday morning, October 21st, Flannery called, showed me the stones on the wagon before my door, and said that the Cross would be erected that very day.

In the meantime, the pilgrimage of the General Convention to Jamestown, under the auspices of the Churchmen's League, had taken place. This was very successful and full of historic associations. It made a profound impression, and really prepared all minds for the Peace Cross service.

The Peace Cross Ceremony

At last October 23rd dawned, bright and beautiful. Everything was arranged most admirably. Col. Truesdell had erected a platform, secured free tickets and extra service of electric cars, had arranged for the police, etc. The Churchmen's League attended to the ushering, Rev. Mr. Hayes to the 250 choristers, the military band, the tents for robing, etc. It is estimated that from eight to ten thousand persons attended. There were seats on the platform only for the members of the General Convention. The clerical members came in surplices, and Bishops in their robes.

Peace Cross ceremony

101

President McKinley

[See diagram made by the Bishop in his personal journal as to the platform arrangement.] [18]

I called at the White House, with Churchill as my chaplain, for the President. On the way out I said to him: "I wish I could venture to ask the President to speak, notwithstanding his refusal." He responded: "I should not venture, Bishop, for he might refuse again." But, said I: "This Cathedral is to last through coming centuries. One word from the President, if it were only a 'God bless this undertaking,' would make the occasion historic." He was silent a moment and then said: "After your own speech is over you may appeal to me if you wish, and I will then decide whether or not to speak."

When the President, with the Bishops, were gathered together in St. Alban's Church, at once the band began to play the processional hymn, the choristers to move before the door, and Bishop Doane, his face all glowing, said: "This is Glastonbury over again"—referring to the closing Services of the Lambeth Conference [19] of 1897. But the President's brow was dark as a thundercloud. He did not as yet understand it, until he started, preceded by the lay members of the Board of Trustees, and walked between Bishop Doane and myself to the platform only 200 feet away.

The scene was indescribably beautiful, with the whole city of Washington spread out beneath us in the golden sunshine of the October afternoon. Bishop Dudley took the first part of the Service. Dr. Dix read the lesson. Bishop McLaren took the Creed and prayers. All this was arranged at the last moment, for Bishops Paret and Potter were absent. Then I spoke and made the appeal to the President. He rose and made a beautiful little address, which we have since utilized as an exhortation before all the Cathedral services.

Then I gave the signal. The American flag that enveloped the Cross floated down, giving the effect of a white Iona cross shooting up out of its folds and then

[18]The diagram has not been found.

[19]Meetings of all the bishops of the Anglican Communion, held in England every ten years.

from red clouds of glory. The whole choir of 250 voices, with the band, burst out with the hymn, "In the Cross of Christ I glory, towering o'er the wrecks of time." As Dr. Battershall described it, "It was the sensational moment." I felt instinctively that a profound impression had somehow been made upon the vast assembled multitude. The President turned to me, exclaiming: "Beautiful! It is wondrous in its beauty!" Then came the conclusion of the service and the benediction, pronounced by Bishop Whipple.

I drove the President home, with Rev. P. M. Rhinelander as my chaplain, and when I landed him on the steps of the White House safely, without accident, a mingled feeling of thankfulness and relief came to me. The load hanging over my spirit since September 4th was lifted. The first Service of the Cathedral was historic. The presence of the President of the United States and of our General Convention had nationalized the Cathedral of Washington. Henceforth it could not fail!

The Claggett Reinterment

The next day, Monday, both houses of the General Convention passed resolutions which practically commended the Cathedral to the Church at large. On the last day of the Convention, Bishop Johnson of Los Angeles, suggested that Bishop Claggett's remains should be transferred to the Cathedral Close, and to my great surprise Bishop Dudley, instigated by him, moved that a committee of five Bishops be appointed to prepare a proper monument. Then the Convention adjourned.

Knowing that the remains of Bishop Claggett ought to be translated at once, before differences of opinion could arise, I consulted Dr. Chew and his family, who own the farm where the remains were interred, and gained their consent. Then Mr. Bratenahl suggested that the day of all others for the translation was All Saints, less than a week off. I engaged the undertaker, and appointed two Deacons, Rev. Messrs. Johnson and Thompson, to superintend the removal as witnesses for the Church. Then, when I went to the Health Officer for a permit, the greatest obstacle of all developed itself. He said it was positively against the law to have any interments save in an incorporated cemetery. I told him that the remains were that very Monday morning being exhumed and brought to Washington; that the vault in St. Alban's churchyard, behind the chancel, was nearly built, and that the whole service had been arranged. He remained firm. It was against the law. Then Mr. Glover and I pointed out to him that he had liberty to give a permit for a temporary interment. He acquiesced in this and gave a permit to December 31st.

At 11 o'clock that night the Rev. Edward Johnson telephoned me that the remains had arrived in Washington. I at once telegraphed Bishop Paret and the whole Chew family that the Service would take place the next afternoon, All Saints' Day, at three o'clock. Twelve clergy were present. The remains were deposited in sealed metallic boxes and these were enclosed in antique coffins, with large crosses on the lids, for both Bishop and Mrs. Claggett. Both were before the chancel. The Service was the Pro anaphora[20] of the burial service of King Edward the Sixth's first Prayer book, with the beatitudes instead of the Commandments, and the service at the grave was an adaptation of our burial service. Over fifty of Bishop Claggett's descendants were present, and all of them signed the parish register. Afterwards the burial permit was extended to December 31, 1899. Then a bill was drawn up by Ex-Senator Edmunds and presented to Congress, permitting four interments a year in the Cathedral grounds.

[Note by J.L.S. There was some personal opposition made, which, however, fe[l]l to the ground.]

Then I went with Mr. Glover to see the Health Officer and District Commissioner, to whom Congress had referred the bill. We explained its nature, and I wrote a letter stating that we only would ask permission to use the Cathedral as the English use Westminster Abbey. The Commissioners readily gave consent, and the bill was passed in the early part of the year 1900.[21]

The Peace Cross Book

Immediately after the General Convention of 1898, Miss Bessie Kibbey sent me a strange publication in the *New York Sun* regarding the immense "plant" that the Romanists were establishing at their National University of Washington. I at once felt that this ought to be sent to the Bishops of our Church, and accordingly purchased 200 copies of the New York Sun of October 30, 1900, one week after the Peace Cross Service, and sent it in a letter to all the Bishops of our Church, with a typewritten letter of my own, explaining the situation and asking their co-operation in the Washington Cathedral.

Shortly after this, Mr. Thomas Nelson Page, the author, proposed that we should issue a Peace Cross book, and at my request he not only wrote one of the articles, but supervised the whole publication. The book was issued by February, and sent to all the Bishops and Clergy of our Church.

---

[20]The Pro anaphora, now called Ante Communion, included all that part of the Communion service that precedes the Sursum Corda, "Lift up your hearts."

[21]Public Law 104, 56th Cong., 2nd session.

About January, 1899, I also devised the founder's certificate, which was to be given to every one who contributed one dollar, representing the purchase of five square feet of land, to the Cathedral. These were sent first to the Clergy of our Church. Then the Churchmen's League of Washington sent other copies to the members of the Diocesan Convention and Church clubs in the various States of the Union.

The Bishop's Guild of Washington has manifested a helpful and increasing interest ever since the corporate communion of Easter Monday, 1898. My wife, Mrs. H. Y. Satterlee, as the head of the Guild, has enlisted the sympathies of the members, and more. It is chiefly through the efforts of the Guild that I have been able to pay the semi-annual interest on the $145,000 in March, 1899, September, 1899 and March, 1900. In addition to this, the Chevy Chase Land Company have not redeemed as yet their verbal promise, made through Mr. Francis J. Newlands to Mr. Glover and myself, to pay back the $17,000 we had advanced on the old site, and in consequence I have had to pay five per cent interest on that sum. This makes considerably over $8,000 a year which I have had to pay in interest and taxes.

Site Planning

Plans and specifications for the Hearst School were given out about November, 1898. At that time the successful competing Architect, Mr. Robert W. Gibson, and also a young lady who had been named to me as the most skillful landscape gardener in America, Miss Beatrix Jones, were employed by the Cathedral Board to consider and report upon the best site for the Girls' School with reference to the proximate position of the Cathedral. They both brought in a report as follows:

First, the best site for the Cathedral was on the southern portion of the grounds, with the axis or transepts in a line with Thirty-sixth Street and the nave with Harford Street. This position would leave the whole east front to be seen with unobstructed view from all points. The chancel and towers will be visible from every part of Washington, for the ground will slope down from 80 to 120 feet on the east side of the Cathedral. So also is it with the south. The slope of the ground between the south transept and Massachusetts Avenue is beautifully adapted for parking. The west front or facade will be close to the Wisconsin Avenue approach. Thus the east, south and west of the Cathedral will always be free and open, with no buildings intervening to obstruct the view, while the north of the Cathedral will (as it should be) be covered by "quads" of educational buildings. As the beginning of these quads, the Cathedral School was placed at the northwest corner of the

Cathedral grounds, about fifty feet back from the roads on either side, Woodley Road and Wisconsin Avenue. This report of Miss Beatrix Jones was handed in and unanimously accepted.

In March Miss Beatrix Jones gave a lecture upon landscape gardening to about fifteen young ladies in the Bishop's House, and then was formed by those ladies who attended this meeting a young ladies' association for the care of the Cathedral grounds, called the "Cathedral Park Board." This Board, under the presidency of my daughter, Constance Satterlee, Miss Kane treasurer, divided itself into sub-committees, under Miss Chandler, Miss Wetmore, Miss Boardman and others, with Miss Beatrix Jones as landscape gardener, to care for the roads, fences, trees and shrubs of the Cathedral Close, and it is to have branches in different cities.

Building the Girls' School

To return to the school: The plans were given out. The contractors accepted were the Moulton-Starrett Company of Chicago. Col. Britton was most efficient in arranging all details and finally the ground was broken for the school in April, 1899. On Ascension Day, May 9th, 1899, we had the service of the laying of the cornerstone. It rained so hard that at the last moment we were obliged to have the service in Trinity Church, where the Diocesan Convention was holding its sessions. The Marine Band led the hymns. The addresses were delivered by Bishop Paret and the Rev. Dr. George William Douglas. After the service was over, carriages were in waiting, which took Bishop Paret, myself and a few others to the Cathedral grounds. We then deposited the documents in the cornerstone: Convention Journal of Washington, Church Almanac, portrait of Mrs. Hearst, daily papers, signatures of Board of Trustees, etc. I used the new silver trowel that is to be used at every future cornerstone-laying. About 1,500 people were present on the ground, notwithstanding the rain.

Two months after this Col. A. T. Britton died very suddenly. The week before I had been with Mrs. Hearst and him to the School, and then was suddenly summoned back to Washington to his funeral. He was the Chairman of the Building Committee and his loss to us is simply irreparable.

From this time the school building rapidly went up, though the constant succession of strikes this year caused innumerable delays. The architect tells me that this is no unusual occurrence. He says that no large building can be built nowadays without such a succession of strikes. The workmen now are the tyrants. They not only feel and use their power, but they abuse it, as all tyrants do. It is a very strange condition of affairs. Of course it cannot last.

The faculty of the National Cathedral School, 1901, with Bishop Satterlee and George Bratenahl, school chaplain and later dean of the Cathedral.

Selecting a Principal

In December 1899 I went to Philadelphia to see Miss Sophie Irwin regarding the position of Principal of the School. Then I had an interview with Mrs. Hearst before her departure for California, in which she said that she did not think it expedient or best to call the school the "Hearst School." I told her that out of loyalty to her I had never thought of the subject definitely, but always banished it from my mind. Now, however, that she had mentioned it, I would give it my serious consideration and report to her. Accordingly, two days after, I went to see her and said that if she was going to call the school the "Hearst School," she ought to endow it, for the name would prevent any one else from endowing it. She said: "I never dreamed of endowing it, and your point is well taken; I fully agree with you." I then suggested it might be called the "St. Phoebe School," but she objected strongly to this name, saying: "Call it simply 'The Cathedral School'"; and we then and there agreed it should not be the "Hearst School." When Mrs. Hearst asked me about the principal and I told her I had been thinking of Misses Agnes and Sophie Irwin, she said: "If you can secure either of the Irwins as head you will instantly place the school in the forefront of American educational institutions."

All through the winter the Board of Trustees seriously considered the question of the principal of the school. I went to see personally Miss Agnes Irwin, Dean of Radcliffe College, Cambridge, and Miss Sophie Irwin, of Philadelphia, both of whom came to Washington and met members of the Board and inspected the school. We afterwards unanimously offered the place to them, but after a week's consideration they refused it. Then I went to see Miss Carter, at St. Timothy's School, though I did not offer the place to her. She and her sister came down voluntarily to see the school, without any thought of the principalship.

Then I went to see Miss Bangs, the head of the academic classes in New York. Dr. Huntington, of Grace Church, recommended her most strongly. So did Dr. Croswell, of the Brearly School, New York, Dr. Nicholas Murray Butler, Dean of the Philosophical School, Columbia University, Presidents Lowe and Raymond, and many others. Miss Bangs and Miss Whiton then came down, at my request, to inspect the school and also to see the members of the Board, and shortly after Easter we engaged them as principal and vice-principal.

Promoting the Girls' School

It was then so late that we saw the necessity of advertising the school at a very early day. But we had no money wherewith to open it, so I asked Senator McMillan to introduce me to Senator Clark, of Montana. Senator Clark listened most kindly, and finally promised to join with one other in pledging a guarantee fund of $10,000 a year for two years, provided the sum were regarded as a loan. In the meantime, I had written to Miss M. V. Bruce, and she generously pledged the whole amount, so that we did not need Mr. Clark's loan, and I wrote to him and told him so, with, of course, many thanks.

The next step was to advertise the school and the plan I adopted was as follows: Owing to the strikes, the building was still in a most unfinished condition, and a formal opening, with set services, is of course impossible. So I arranged for a garden party, with the Marine Band, on Ascension Day, which is to be Cathedral Day, and in the course of the afternoon we were to have a short dedicatory service of the school, which would sufficiently advertise it as to notify the public at large that it was open for pupils. I was to be the only speaker and was to write a short address, the greater part of which could be used as a "quotation from the Bishop's address at the opening service" in advertising. Ascension Day this year at last dawned, dark and rainy. Of course there could be no garden party, and the Marine Band was brought into the school building. The assembly hall was dressed with flags. The service, half an hour long, was printed. The rain came pouring down. Only about 250 persons were present. Eight members of the Cathedral Board sat with me on the stage.

After our service was over, I felt the necessity of some cheering exercises to kindle enthusiasm. I accordingly called on Miss Bangs, who, in a neat little speech, presented a large American flag, 20 x 16, which the girls of her school presented to the Cathedral School. The flag, with a touch, was then unfurled at the back of the stage. The audience arose and there was great applause. I then mentioned the fact that this happened to be the birthday of a woman who had been an "illustrious example to the women of the Nineteenth Century in the purity and the nobility of her life, the Queen of England." Once more the audience arose, this time with most enthusiastic demonstration of applause, while the band played a verse of "God save the Queen." Then, feeling that something more was needed, I asked Miss Bangs to give in a few words her ideal of the school, which she did in an impressive way which at once captured all hearts.

The National Cathedral School

We then had in the school a meeting of the Cathedral Board, at which several important matters were settled, and when it was unanimously Resolved, That the name of the school should be the "National Cathedral School." I thought at the time that the rain-storm was a great help to our small but enthusiastic gathering, and that the service was as great a success as the Peace Cross service, though in an entirely different way.

Mrs. Hearst about this time came to Washington, and could not see her way clear to allowing any of the $2,000 of accrued interest of $6,000 that we had been so carefully saving and counting upon, to be appropriated for the furniture of our school. This left me two days before my departure for Europe—whither I am going by the doctor's advice for a much-needed rest until August—in a position of great awkwardness. I have to raise from $8,000 to $10,000 at once for the furniture of the school. I wrote instantly to Mrs. Westinghouse and also to Pierpont Morgan, asking them each to give the whole amount. Mrs. Westinghouse had had time to reply before I left. Mr. Morgan will receive my letter on his arrival home (we cross each other on the ocean). I know that the furniture fund will in some way be contributed, and if it is not given before I come back, I shall write letters from Europe. I went abroad early on purpose to return early in August for the school affairs.

The Fund-Raising Tours

In 1899 I took the first real rest I had had for four years, since I have been a Bishop. The first summer I went to Russia with a petition for the Armenians.[22]

---

[22]Brent described Satterlee's trip to Russia in detail. Brent, *A Master Builder* 190-206.

The Founders Certificate

The second summer I went to the Lambeth Conference. The third summer I spent in raising money to buy the St. Alban's property. In the Autumn, after I had paid $8,000 interest and taxes on the Cathedral property, it was brought home to me that I must do something to secure the principal. Every plan for this object heretofore has been a slight advance, but a failure on the whole. The Founder's certificates, upon which we built such strong hopes, have brought in thus far but $500 all told.

[Note by J.L.S. Later they became more successful.]

So I concluded to go about and tell my story in person in the various cities of America, and thus evoke an interest in a National Cathedral.

Bishop Whittaker most kindly consented that I should speak in Philadelphia, and presided at a meeting in the house of George C. Thomas, at which Senator Edmunds and I spoke. There were about twenty-four gentlemen present, and a Philadelphia Committee on a National Cathedral was then and there formed of which Mr. Thomas became president and Mr. George Wharton Pepper, Secretary. These pledged themselves to raise one-fifth of the $7,500 interest on the Cathedral land until the whole debt was paid.

I also preached about a National Cathedral in the Church of the Holy Trinity, at the request of my dear friend and former Assistant, Rev. Floyd W. Tompkins.

In the next month, December, 1899, I paid 51 calls in Philadelphia regarding the Cathedral.

I then went to Boston, where I preached in Trinity Church, at Dr. Donald's request, my sermon on a National Cathedral, and afterwards delivered the same sermon at the Church of the Advent in Boston (Rev. Dr. Frisby).

I paid many calls in Boston, but was able to form no committee as I had done in Philadelphia; but about three months afterwards Mrs. Hamlin (Miss Pruyn) wrote to me of her own accord, offering to form such a committee. I sent her the papers and believe she will make a success of whatever she undertakes.

In February I preached in New York, first at Dr. Grosvenor's request in the Church of the Incarnation, and second at the request of Dr. Dix, in Trinity Church. Then we had a very successful parlor meeting at the house of Governor and Mrs. Levi P. Morton, at which Bishop Doane presided. Dr. Dix, in Bishop Potter's absence, represented the consenting ecclesiastical authority of the diocese, and Dr. Huntington and Dr. Grosvenor made very effective speeches regarding the Cathedral. Mrs. W. A. Street thereupon formed a New York Committee on the National Cathedral, of which Mrs. Levi P. Morton, Mr. Alexander Hadden and Mr. George W. Bowdoin, Mr. Irving Grinnell and some other of my friends were members. This committee has already sent me $500 and up to this time has collected over $1,200 more, as Mr. Nourse, the Secretary, tells me. The New York Committee has taken hold with great vigor and I am hoping great things of them. At first there was a feeling on the part of a few that the Cathedral of Washington would injure that of New York. I told them that the reverse would be true, that the two cathedrals would stimulate one another; and so it has already proved.

In February, 1900, on the invitation of Mr. William Kaiser of Baltimore, a parlor meeting was held in his house, at which Bishop Paret presided. About nineteen were present. In March I held another parlor meeting there at the house of Mrs. Robert Garrett, at which Dr. Hodges presided. He had previously asked me to preach at St. Paul's Church on the Washington Cathedral, which I did, to a crowded congregation. At Mrs. Garrett's house about forty ladies and gentlemen were present. Dr. Hodges and Dr. Powell of Baltimore, Dr. Elliott and Dr. McKim of Washington, and Mr. Skipworth Wilmer of Baltimore, all spoke, and most effectively. Of course I made the principal address, and governed by experience, made it much more pictorial than before. A week after Mrs. Garrett wrote to me that she would form a Baltimore committee next autumn.

So far, therefore, the following committees have been formed this winter: First, the Philadelphia Committee on the National Cathedral, all gentlemen, fifteen members, with a chairman and secretary, pledged to raise $1,500 a year for the payment of one-fifth of the interest. Second, a Washington committee of ladies, the Bishop's Guild, pledged to raise $1,500 a year for one-fifth of the interest. Third, a New York Committee of ladies and gentlemen, Mrs. Street, Chairman, Mr. Charles J. Nourse, Treasurer, to raise one-fifth of the interest, at least. Fourth, a Baltimore committee, Mrs. Garrett, Chairman, to be formed in the Autumn. Fifth, a Boston Committee, Mrs. Hamlin, Chairman.

In the meantime I had been making strenuous efforts to secure forty persons to assume forty notes of $2,500 each that cover the $100,000 of first mortgage. I have been successful in securing $30,000.00 as follows:

Mr. C.C. Glover	2,500
Mr. Thomas Hyde	2,500
Mrs. Joseph White, of New York	2,500
General Parke	2,500
Miss Freeman and Mrs. Buckingham . .	2,500
Mr. Kasson	1,500
Messrs. Woodward & Lothrop	1,000
Mr. James Lowndes	1,000
Dr. Mackay-Smith	1,000
Mr. Stevens	2,500
Mr. W. E. Dodge of New York	2,500
Mr. Green	1,000
Mr. Hunniwell of Boston	1,000
Mr. Bowdoin, New York	1,000
Mr. Knower, New York	1,000
Mr. Goodwin, New York	1,000
Smaller subscriptions	3,000
Total paid to date $30,000	

This reduces the first mortgage from $100,000 to $70,000. I have, in addition, pledges:

Col. Truesdell	$2,500
Mr. Wm. J. Boardman	2,500
Mr. Newbold of Philadelphia	2,500
Mr. Francis L. Stetson of New York . .	1,000
Mr. James Johnson of Riggs Bank	1,000
Mr. Hunniwell	1,000
Mr. Kauffman (paid)	1,000
Total $11,500	

These pledges are all to be paid before March, 1901, reducing the first mortgage $11,500 more—or $58,500 in all. At the present time the whole debt stands at $162,000, less amount paid this year, $30,000: $132,000

          Pledges for coming year   11,500

          Total $120,500

If the Chevy Chase Land Company fulfill their pledge to pay back $17,000, this will reduce the total indebtedness to $103,500.

The Glastonbury Cathedra

Before the meeting of the General Convention, while I was arranging for the Peace Cross, I wrote to the Bishop of Bath and Wells, asking him if he could induce Mr. Austin, the owner of Glastonbury Abbey of St. Peter and St. Paul, to donate a window, or sufficient stones to form a cathedra for the Cathedral of Saints Peter and Paul in Washington. I then asked Miss Jones to take a letter of introduction from me to Mr. Austin himself. This she did. Mr. and Mrs. Austin received her most kindly and promised to give the stones. We have had some correspondence on the subject and the stones are at this very moment on the way to America, June 11, 1900, while I am going to Europe.

When I reached England, in June, 1900, I wrote to Mr. Austin of Glastonbury. He answered that three boxes of Glastonbury stones were now on the way to Washington, and invited me to come to the Abbey in August. At the S. P. G.[23] anniversary meeting—200th—in Exeter Hall, I sat next to the Bishop of Bristol, who had made the address at Glastonbury Abbey after the Lambeth Conference, and asked him to name the Glastonbury Bishop's seat for us. In answer I received the following letter.

The Athenaeum, Pall Mall,
June 20, 1900.

My dear Brother:

You were good enough to ask me yesterday if I had any suggestion as to a title for the stone seat which you are to build in the Cathedral of Washington, of material from the ruins of Glastonbury Abbey. You asked me on the score of my having given the address at Glastonbury

---

[23]The Society for the Propagation of the Gospel.

when we all met there at the conclusion of the Lambeth Conference in 1897. The purpose of our meeting there was to emphasize the existence of the British Church in this land long before the coming of Augustine from Rome, the thirteen hundredth anniversary of which we had been keeping. The key-note of the whole was the word and the idea "British." If you do not think that "British" is in these modern times regarded as meaning, among other things, "non-American," I should be induced to recommend the use of the word in some such phrase as the "British Cathedra." If you think that "British" has in these last times come to mean that, then I should face the fact that a "Glastonbury chair" is a very common thing, and 'go one better,' as the slang phrase has it, by boldly naming your treasure 'The Glastonbury Throne.' Yesterday I leaned to the 'British Cathedra'; today I incline to hope that when Britannia and America have ruled the waves sufficiently straight I may come over and see you seated on the 'Glastonbury Throne.' Only bear in mind, metathesis will turn your seat into the 'Glastonbury thorn' of world-wide celebrity. Sitting upon thorns is I hope not so much your function of Bishops on your side as it is on this.

Yours with all warmth of regard,

G. F. Bristol.

I answered the Bishop of Bristol, thanking him for his kind and graceful letter, and saying it would be itself one of our treasures in the annals of the beginning of the Cathedral of Washington.

Mr. Austin, in answer to my letter requesting some suggestions as to the inscription to be placed on the chair, most graciously said he did not wish his own name to appear, but wished the inscription to read, "From the Churchmen of Glastonbury to the Churchmen of America."

I have this day (June 25, 1900) received from my secretary, Mr. Warner, word that the Glastonbury stones have arrived in Washington.

The Jerusalem Altar

At Paris, France, I unexpectedly met my old drayoman of the Holy Land, Herbert Edgar Clark, whom I had not seen for twenty years. He was staying at the same hotel, "Tremoille." In the course of our interview I asked him if he could procure us stones from the Jordan for a Cathedral baptismal font. He said he could only procure boulders and pebbles from there; and then I suggested, "Why not take stone from the quarries of Solomon, the best white limestone called 'Melekee' or 'Royal'?" This suggested to me in turn another idea, namely, that of a stone altar for the Cathedral. I thought the matter over after I saw him, and finally, on shipboard, as I was on the way from Cherbourg to New York, I wrote him, asking him if he could procure stones from the quarries of Solomon for this

Stones for the Jerusalem Altar

purpose. These would form an altar for the Cathedral than which none could be more sacredly appropriate, for the "Quarries of Solomon" are situated at the base of that which is now supposed to be the hill just outside of the Damascus Gate of Jerusalem, Mount Calvary; i.e. the place where Christ was Crucified, where Joseph of Arimathaea's new-hewn sepulcher was, and where Christ rose from the dead. In the Roman Church the association between an altar and a tomb is preserved by placing relics and bones of the Saints beneath that altar. In the Cathedral of Washington (if this plan is carried out) the stones of the altar will be taken from that selfsame hill in which was cut Joseph's new-hewn sepulcher, where Christ Himself was buried and from which He arose in the power of His resurrection life. Thus, while the ancient associations of the altar are preserved, they will be freed from superstition and will come from the most sacred spot of all the earth. Besides this, the first stone of the Cathedral will be its stone altar.

The National Cathedral School

On my return home, I conferred immediately with Miss Bangs and went to the Cathedral School, which was far from completion, owing to the insecurity of the Moulton-Starrett Company. When we found last March that this firm had been using up our money to pay their bills in other cities, at once (March 15th) Col. Truesdell took measures that the sub-contractors should be protected by receiving all funds hereafter paid out from our treasury, and that the work should go on, if possible, under the Moulton-Starrett Company; but as under the circumstances we could not, on the one hand, bring this firm to bankruptcy, nor, on the other, dismiss them without hurting the school, the whole work was in a very unsatisfactory condition. It was a very difficult matter to get the school, the grounds about it and the equipment in working order before October 1st. We had to borrow $8,000 for the furniture, and Miss Bangs and Miss Whiton worked all summer. However, the school opened October 1st with a full corps of teachers, and by October 20th had over thirty boarders and twenty day scholars. The income from these will probably be $25,000, and enough to pay all current expenses. If so we do not want the school at present to be any larger, because the educational standard is very high, and we want to create a school prestige.

December 28, 1900. The school has been now running for three months, with the following results: First, the principals have been meeting with considerable opposition on account of their strictness. Miss Bangs was told by three college presidents in New York, "You will never succeed in making a first-class educational institution out of a church school." When she asked why, the answer was: "Because the Bishop and clergy will thwart your efforts to be strict. They are so used by their clerical life to govern solely by love that they will mitigate punishments, interfere with strict rules, break down the discipline, forgive offenders and take sides with parents against teachers."

The opposition to the school has almost died out. In fashionable circles, two months ago, the school was the theme of conversation at all the ladies luncheons. It was said by some that when a girl did not know her lessons she was shut up four days and fed on bread and water; that girls could not write home to their parents; that parents' letters were opened by the principal; that visitors were told they were not properly dressed to call on the young ladies, etc. etc. The school has now about 55 boarders and day pupils and is probably paying expenses. It has already begun to make its mark, not only in its general educational standard, but in music. So far the girls have been kept in unusual health.

Cleveland Park

February 18, 1901. I have this day returned from one of my lectures to the girls of the school in sacred studies. I observed on the road (I went in my coupe) that Mr. Waggaman had leveled many acres on the west side of Connecticut Avenue for building purposes. Mr. Glover says that this cost him $400,000. There are now three iron bridges spanning Rock Creek, one in the neighborhood of Connecticut Avenue, crossed by the Chevy Chase electric cars. The real Massachusetts Avenue bridge, which is to be sixty feet wide, is in the process of construction, but is not yet above the foundations. There is only one house besides the Naval Observatory between the Creek and the Cathedral grounds. The land is covered with thick forest trees and the ridges are 100 feet at least above two valleys which yawn between them. I don't see how these differences are ever to be leveled for houses, but I know it will be done and done very soon. Further up toward Connecticut Avenue there are two heights, each crowned by a single house. There are no others.

On Woodley Road, between the Cathedral grounds and Connecticut Avenue, there are only the following houses: Nearest the Cathedral, "Beauvoir," the residence of Admiral Dewey; next, "Twin Oaks," the residence of Mrs. Gardiner Hubbard; next, Mr. Charles J. Bell's House. Then comes a wide gap of a quarter of a mile, when we come to Woodley House, which President Cleveland occupied. Then, opposite the old Cathedral site, Mr. Buckey's cottage. Then a house at the corner of Woodley Avenue and Connecticut Avenue in a very dilapidated condition and on ground forty feet above the level of Connecticut Avenue. It is on Madam von Hemert's land. There are no other houses; but on Wisconsin Avenue there is a continuous line of wooden cottages from Georgetown to Cleveland Park.

Fund Raising

Last week Miss Bessie Kibbey contributed $500 for the Glastonbury Cathedra. Mr. Gibson has furnished drawings, and Flannery, the stonecutter, is doing the work. It is to be done by Ascension Day, and all the stones sent from Glastonbury, twenty-three in number, each a cube of about 18 or 20 inches, are to be used.

This week I went to visit Mrs. Hamlin (Miss Pruyn) in Boston. She has taken great interest in the formation of a Boston Committee on the National Cathedral. We never could have formed it without her and her husband, Mr. Charles S. Hamlin. Mrs. Van Rensaler Thayer, nee Miss Alice Robeson, kindly consented to have a parlor meeting in her house. Dr. Donald, rector of Trinity Church, (Phillips Brooks' successor) presided. About forty were present. I spoke about three-quarters of an hour and showed location by my map of Washington, and a committee was formed, with Mrs. Thayer for chairman and Mrs. Hamlin as secretary.

On my way back I stopped at Providence. I saw Bishop Clark, also Bishop McVickar, who consented to preside at a Rhode Island parlor meeting. I also called on Mrs. Henry Russell and Mrs. Coster about the same object. In New York I saw Mrs. Street, Mrs. George Bowdoin, and Mr. and Mrs. Irving Grinnell, of the New York Committee. They reported great progress.

I have omitted to state that a month ago, in January, I had in Philadelphia a parlor meeting at the house of my cousin, Mrs. Charles Platt. About seventeen were present. Senator Edmunds spoke and so did I. Mrs. Lewis consented to act as the secretary of the Philadelphia committee. I hope to give a fuller account of these committees further on. They ought well to be historic, for they are assisting more than all others to nationalize the Cathedral.

July 9th [1901]. This day I attended a meeting of the Newport committee. Mrs. George P. Wetmore most kindly had a parlor meeting in her house, which Bishop Clark, the Presiding Bishop of the Church, opened with a most helpful address. A Rhode Island Committee was formed.

The Jerusalem Altar

On my return to Washington, on February 9th, 1901, I received the following letter from Mr. Herbert E. Clark:

Jerusalem, Palestine,
12 January, 1901.

Rt. Rev. Bishop Satterlee,

Dear Sir:

I trust you will excuse the long delay in answering your private letter of August 13th, in regard to getting the stones for the altar. The fact is I had only a few days at home before I was called away to Beirut to meet a party of six, Mrs. Charles Pratt, whom perhaps you know, and had to conduct them through Assyria and Palestine for a long camping tour, so that I could not do anything until the last month. After consulting a friend of mine, Mr. Paul Palmer, an architect here, who suggested that we should send you first specimen of stones of the old quarry and of the neighborhood, which would give you a better idea than any description, and the very thing that he had done with the building stones of Palestine several years ago when the German Emperor was deciding of what material the Church was to be built, which church he came to dedicate two years ago. Which suggestion I thought very good and that is what delayed my answer. I have only been able to send you today the specimens in four separate boxes, by German parcels post. You will please find there are five specimens. First, Melekee, the white soft stone from Solomon's Quarries. Second, Mizzi Helu or Muzzi, soft also, from that part of the Quarries called Jeremiah's Grotto, the no doubt site of our Lord's crucifixion. Third, Mizzi fahudi or hard Jewish mizzi, which is the most common used for building, it being the most plentiful stone. These stones are for you to choose from the material for the altar. I shall think the Mizzi Helu would be about the kind to be chosen, if you conclude the Melekee to be too soft, although this hardens to a certain extent in time, after being exposed to the air. In sending the stones, six according to his estimate, he says he would have to send them roughly dressed, as they might get damaged in transport and fall short of the required size. You will see that his estimate for their freight included to New York. The mention of the backsheesh is for the Government caretakers of the Quarries of Solomon and the old shiek in possession of Jeremiah's Grotto, which would have to be considerable as the stones to be of equal size would necessitate a considerable amount of quarrying.

4th and 5th specimens. One is black, of bituminous limestone, only obtained from the locality near the Mohammedan traditional tomb of Moses, not far from the coast of the Dead Sea. The red is from near the city, and Mr. Palmer suggested sending you these two colors, as they would do, especially the black, to inlay the inscriptions which you propose putting on the sides and the ends of the altar. Of course you had better before deciding upon this give the two slabs to a good sculptor and see what he can do in cutting and letters for the inscriptions, and thus find how many pieces are necessary, should you conclude to use the material for the purpose.

Here attached please find Mr. Palmer's estimate and small bill for specimens, etc. Also my account, including the same and cost of boxes and freight, in all frcs. 48.60, which amount please remit with the bill to my brother, 111 Broadway, New York, at your convenience, which will save you the trouble of sending it here. He, my brother, will return you the bill receipted.

Mr. Palmer, who has had charge of building the German church and orphanage at Bethlehem, and was second architect in full charge of building the German church here, also of the Church at Salb, etc. etc., is thoroughly reliable. So should you wish to get the stones to America at an early date you can communicate direct with them, as I shall be away from now until the end of April nearly all the time, and it is quite possible that I will leave in May for New York. But I can in March just give a little attention to the quarrying of the stones, to see if it is being done at the place desired. But at the same time if we go to quarrying stones I could get Dr. Selah Merrill, our Consul here, to see the stones get out of the quarries should I not be able to be present. I cannot think of any other suggestion to make in furtherance of the object in view and believing that the black stone for the lettering will prove just the thing, as it takes a high polish and seems appropriate, as it comes only from that neighborhood of the Dead Sea. Trusting again that you will excuse this long delay and that you may find the specimens all that you desire, and that I may be of further use to you. Thanking you for your most kind invitation and with kindest regards and respects to you, Mrs. and Miss Satterlee, I remain,

Yours very faithfully,

(signed) Herbert E. Clark

P.S. Mr. Palmer's estimate is the outside cost to New York and with regard to my own services for this or any future service, I do not wish for any remuneration, and shall be only too glad to be of any use to you and such an object.

(copy)   Paul Palmer, Architect, Jerusalem.

Estimate of the stones to be provided for an altar.

Stones: Melekee, Mizzi Helu, Mizzi Fahudi, according to choice; very roughly dressed. 10 feet long, 4 feet wide, 3 feet high (in 6 pieces) total weight, 10,000 kilograms, equals 20,000 pounds.

Post: Stones, including backsheesh and fr. 1000, freight Jerusalem to Jaffa, fr. 500, and Jaffa to New York 750 fr.

Total, fr. 2250, equals $450.00

Stones for inlaid letters: Slabs as enclosed samples, black from Nebi Monsa, red from Jerusalem, according to choice.

Stones and freight 5 francs, equals $1.00 each piece.

N.B. The Melekee and the Mizzi Helu from Jeremiah's Grotto or from Bethlehem, and the Mizzi Fahudi from the neighborhood of Jerusalem.

Jerusalem, Jan. 11, 1901.   (signed) P. Palmer.

On February 21st I wrote to Herbert Clark, Mr. Paul Palmer and Dr. Selah Merrill, ordering the altar to be made exclusively of Mizzi Helu stones taken from the Grotto of Jeremiah. I enclosed two diagrams of an altar 11 feet by 4 feet high, and 3 feet deep, to be made of 3 or 8 or 12 or 16 stones, to be sent at once. In the meantime I asked Mr. John E. Buck, of Gorham Manufacturing Company, to prepare the diagram altar, and he came to Washington and went with me to the Cathedral grounds. I also gave him a specimen of the Mizzi Helu stone about the size of a firebrick, which had been sent by German parcels post from Jerusalem, and made all possible arrangements for the altar to be shipped from Palestine to New York as soon as possible. When it arrives in New York, I propose to send the stones at once to the Gorham Manufacturing Company, to be cut and shaped, and I shall write to every Bishop of the American Church asking a contribution of from

$5 to $100 for the altar from every diocese and missionary jurisdiction. I am now anxiously awaiting the news that the altar has been cut and shipped from Jaffa to New York.

June 29, 1901. Received a telegram on this, the ancient St. Peter's and St. Paul's Day, stating that the Jerusalem stones had arrived in New York by the Hamburg Line steamer. This is a memorable day for the Cathedral. These Jerusalem stones were brought to the Cathedral grounds afterwards, in the middle of July, and placed under a corrugated iron fire-proof shed until they would be needed.

The Glastonbury Cathedra

March 26, 1901. I have this day been to the stoneyard of Mr. L. Flannery, to see the Glastonbury Cathedra. The subsequent history of the Cathedra is as follows: Twenty-three stones of the characteristic ornamentation of the Abbey were sent by Mr. Stanley Austin and arrived in Washington in the last of June, 1900. Then Mr. R. W. Gibson, Architect, New York, sent a sketch of the Cathedra. This was shown to Miss Bessie Kibbey, of 2025 Massachusetts Avenue, Washington, who generously gave the total cost, $500, on condition that her name is not mentioned, but a place left blank on the left side of the Cathedra for her name as the donor, after her death, to be inscribed upon it. Mr. Gibson then gave the work to Mr. Flannery, who had carved the Peace Cross. He is to complete it so that it can be unveiled on Ascension Day, 1901. The whole lower part of the Cathedra, saving the sculptured tops of the two arms and the slab of the seat, is to be made of the old Glastonbury stones. The old carving is to be used everywhere it is possible, on the lower part of the chair and also for the four pillars which arise, two on each side of the back. Everywhere else about the seat, the slabs on the sides, the arms and the back are to be cut out of the old Glastonbury stones. The rest of the Cathedra, that is the back exclusive of the pillars, will be cut out of a single stone from the Indiana limestone quarries.

Missionary Plans

At the present time of writing, March 28th, 1901, there is another matter of deepest interest engaging my attention. I regard the St. Alban's parish as perhaps the most important in all America. It extends from U Street, Georgetown, to the District line, and from Rock Creek to the Potomac, a region at least of nine square miles. By and by this will be the residential portion of Washington, for it is on the northwest. It is several hundred feet above the city in most parts, and after the Massachusetts and Connecticut Avenue bridges are built, population will flow thitherward quickly. If we found mission stations and cottage lecture stations now at, say Palisades of the Potomac, Tenley, Reno, Broad Branch and Wesley Heights, these will probably be self-supporting parishes in the best part of the city fifty years hence, and are all in the neighborhood of the Cathedral. If we occupy this field now, we shall have the prestige of being the first Christian body in the field. In the meantime, I have long felt that we should put something else in the forefront of our Cathedral work than mere dollars and cents. A Cathedral is a great educational institution, and therefore we have done right in making such strenuous efforts to place our Girls' School on a strong foundation as a first-class educational institution. Our Cathedral will be likewise a historical witness for the Primitive Church, and therefore I feel a deep interest in the Jerusalem altar, which will be the first stone of our Cathedral, and in the Glastonbury Cathedra, which will be a witness for the historical continuity of the Anglican Church.

A Cathedral is above all a great missionary church, and therefore I have felt that we ought to have as soon as possible a missionary superintendent attached to the Cathedral Foundation, who will take charge of the missionary work. On looking over the Cathedral statutes, I find that this very office, "Missionary Superintendent," has been provided for under the name of a "Canon Missioner." It was my part to raise an endowment fund of $5,000, yielding an income of $250 a year, for the "Canon Missioner." At last, after one of my Bible lectures at the Bishop's House, Miss Freeman came to me. She said she and her sister had agreed to give the $5,000. I was so bewildered that I could not even thank her; but I called that very afternoon and told Mrs. Buckingham and Miss Freeman that they had lifted a load which had weighed upon me for six months and that I could never express my thankfulness. Then they consented that the fund for the salary of the Canon Missioner should be called the "St. Chrysostom Fund." Mr. Bratenahl had already asked them to loan the money.

On Friday, March 22, 1901, at a meeting of the Board of Cathedral Trustees, I appointed the Rev. Philip M. Rhinelander Canon Missioner of the Cathedral. I felt that this made the position not only secure but a reality. It had an endowment attached to it. The salary indeed was small, but this made the position as secure as that of any rector in the Diocese. Mr. Rhinelander has not yet accepted the place. He is exactly the man for it, but God must call him to it.

Yesterday I received a letter from Mr. W. W. Fraser, of Philadelphia, who will possibly add to the St. Chrysostom Endowment Fund when he returns from Europe.

Site Planning

When Mr. Bratenahl was here last week, we conferred together about Cathedral matters, and went out to the Cathedral grounds and staked out the proximate site of a Cathedral, nave 300 feet, transepts 100 feet, choir 100 feet, x 500 feet long. Width of nave, transepts and choir 100 feet, length of each transept 100 feet. It must surely face the east, not only on account of ecclesiastical traditions, but also on account of city traditions, as all the streets except the diagonal avenues run north and south and east and west. The exact site of the Cathedral is determined for us. It must be on the axis of Harford Street,[24] north and south, and on Thirty-sixth Street, east and west. This leaves it exposed to view toward the east, where the ground slopes down steeply at least for 100 feet, and on the south toward Massachusetts Avenue, where the land is beautifully adapted to landscape gardening. This leaves the whole north side comparatively level land for the buildings of the Cathedral Foundation, arranged in quads. The only difficulty with this site is that a great deal of grading and filling will be needed, say 50,000 cubic yards, but the earth can be taken from the high ground abutting on Thirty-fifth Street, near Woodley Road, which must sooner or later be cut down, and is fully enough for the Cathedral levels and grading.

After mature thought, I have concluded to build the receptacle for the Cathedral altar at or near the west front.

At present I think it might be well to erect two buildings, one for our diocesan and mission libraries, etc., the other as a sort of chapel or Jerusalem Chamber, to contain the Jerusalem Altar and the Glastonbury Cathedra, these two buildings to be connected by a large archway, through which the Peace Cross can be seen. The whole to be erected behind (eastward) the line of trees marking proximately the west front of the Cathedral and to be called "All Hallows Gate." Entering through the gate one would see first the Peace Cross, then the broad gravel path running down the center of the future nave, and the center of the transepts, with the hedge and fence outlining the form of the Cathedral.[25]

April 3, 1901. Saw Mr. H. B. Looker today, Surveyor of the District of Columbia, and engaged him to survey the Cathedral site and have the exact position of the Cathedral at the juncture of Harford and Thirty-sixth Street

---

[24]Now Klingle Road NW

[25]All Hallows Gate and the Little Sanctuary were built on the site Satterlee selected, now south of the Cathedral on Wisconsin Avenue.

marked out and established by twelve granite monuments at the angles, marked thus, as this diagram:[26]

The Little Sanctuary

August 1, 1901. On passing the corner of Twenty-third Street and Fourth Avenue, New York, I happened to see that the cornice of the old Academy of Design was being pulled down. About the same time I saw at Quoque, Long Island, in the train, my nephew, Lansing Satterlee, told him my plans for the All Hallows Gate and Jerusalem Altar, and asked him to secure for me as much of the facade of the Academy of Design as was possible. He saw Seagust, the contractor, and secured all the smaller carvings of the exterior, the railing and balluster capitals and columns, pointed arches, iron window girds, etc., for $300. The cost of sending them to Washington was about $50 or $60 additional.

The Jerusalem Altar in the Little Sanctuary

On this day I was at Twilight Park, and heard that President McKinley had been shot. On September 14th he died, and that Saturday I telegraphed a special collect to be used in the churches of the Diocese of Washington tomorrow, and

---

[26]No diagram has been found.

The Little Sanctuary

after the memorial service in the Church of All Angels at Twilight Park, I started immediately for Washington. On the way down I stopped to see Mr. Alexander McIntosh, Architect, and asked him, also, having asked Lansing Satterlee, to draw designs for All Hallows Gate. We have now three architects preparing designs— Mr. Mullett of Washington, and Messrs. McIntosh and Lansing Satterlee, of New York.

About December 1st the last plans for the Little Sanctuary and All Hallows Gate were sent in, and those of Lansing Satterlee were at once approved as by far the most tasteful and satisfactory.

[Note by J.L.S. These plans were sent in anonymously.]

Lansing Satterlee was chosen architect, and at once the order was given by me to Mr. Jardine, of the Washington Monumental Granite Company, for the carving of the stones of the altar from a design sent by Mr. John H. Buck, of the Gorham Manufacturing Company. The Mizzi Helu stone, sent from Jerusalem, turned out to be a beautiful, dove-colored marble, capable of receiving a fine polish. The texts on three sides are the events of Christ's life, the crucifixion, entombment and resurrection. Those on the front set forth the great doctrines of the Resurrection, Ascension and institution of the Eucharist in Bible words. The center of the altar is a solid block of granite, on the top of which are graven the same words that are inscribed on every brick of the Church of St. Sophia at

Constantinople, built by Justinian: "God is in the midst of her; therefore shall she not be removed." (Psalm, A.V.) In the forefront of the granite are the words that God spake to Moses at the burning bush, as paraphrased in psalm _____, A.V., and the words are: "Thy Name, Oh Lord, endures forever, and so doth Thy Memorial, Oh Lord, through all generations."[27] These words derive additional significance from the fact that the memorial of the Lord is now the Holy Eucharist.

Fund Raising

October [1901]. At the General Convention in San Francisco I preached in behalf of the Cathedral of Washington and also had a small parlor meeting at the house of Mrs. Taylor, which some day may be the nucleus of starting a Cathedral committee there.

In November Mrs. Victor C. Barringer died in Washington leaving the greater part of her estate, some $40,000, as the Victor C. Barringer Fund, the income for the support of clergymen and candidates for Holy Orders. Mrs. Barringer took the deepest interest in the new diocese and its Cathedral, and should always be gratefully remembered.

I omitted to state that the book "The Building of a Cathedral," was written by me in the autumn and the early winter of 1901-'2, and finished on Christmas Eve, 1901. It gives a short history of the Cathedral and was distributed for the first time at the meeting of the Washington Committee.

On Christmas Eve a Christmas card was sent out to all interested in the Cathedral, upon which there was a view of Washington City with the Capitol seen from the Peace Cross, and also an etching by Mrs. William C. Rives of All Hallows Gate and the Little Sanctuary, from [a] drawing of Lansing Satterlee.

In the winter of 1901 and '02, several Cathedral committees were formed. First came the Advent meeting of the Bishop's Guild. A Washington Cathedral committee was formed at the residence of Mrs. Buckingham, 1525 H Street, which was largely attended. Over $6,000 was subscribed through the efforts of this Committee, and the new Cathedral book, written by the Bishop, was for the first time distributed. Over 200 were present.

In March, 1902, a "Connecticut Committee" was formed at the house of Mrs. Samuel Colt, who had a successful parlor meeting, at which Bishop Brewster and Rev. George Williamson Smith spoke. Shortly afterwards, in March, a Chicago Committee was formed at the house of Mrs. Arthur Ryerson, at which Bishop Anderson presided and spoke.

---

[27]Psalm 135.

First Buildings

Ground was broken for the Little Sanctuary in February [1902]. The first estimates were $6,000, but the plans were altered and brought down to a cost of $2,600.

During this winter the committee appointed by Congress brought in their plans in commemoration of the centennial of the city for the improvement of Washington. These plans met with such furore that they will be ultimately adopted, I am sure. This winter, also, the new Massachusetts Avenue bridge is in process of construction, and the work is being pushed so rapidly that it will probably be completed before 1903.

Sometime realization surpasses expectation, and this is now in every way true in the following instance: The Little Sanctuary and All Hallows Gate are finished. The Jerusalem Altar is in its place, and this Ascension Day, 1902, the first celebration at the Cathedral Altar took place at 8 a.m. It was a beautiful spring morning. Mr. and Mrs. Russell, who represented the family of Mrs. Percy R. Pyne, who gave the Little Sanctuary in memory of their mother's interest in the Cathedral, were present; also Mrs. William A. Street, the President of the New York Committee on the Cathedral. The Bishop made a short address, sitting in the Glastonbury Cathedra, recalling the associations of the Altar and Cathedra stones from Melchisedeck and the King's Dale and the Anaforan, and from the Resurrection of Christ to the days of Glastonbury, Richard Coeur de Lion and the Magna Charta. The Little Sanctuary was full to overflowing at the 8 a.m. Celebration, and was well filled at the subsequent Celebrations at 9 a.m. and 11 a.m. Mrs. Satterlee, Mrs. W. C. Rives, Mrs. Bratenahl, Deaconess Libbey and Miss Nina Carroll contributed not a little by their exertions to making the Little Sanctuary ready and beautiful for this first service. At the same time there was a garden party meeting of the Cathedral Park Board, an organization of ladies of which Miss Constance Satterlee is President, for the care of the Cathedral grounds. At this meeting many Washingtonians were present.

The Baptismal Font

In July, 1902, I wrote to Herbert E. Clark, of Jerusalem, asking him if he could procure from the River Jordan ten barrels of pebbles for a lining, either of mosaic or in cement, of the octagonal Cathedral Font, eight or ten feet in diameter, with running water; also if he could procure marble slabs from Bethlehem for the exterior of the Font. On September 3rd I received his answer, stating that he would gladly undertake the work and would do it gratuitously "for love of the Cathedral of Washington." I wrote the same day, giving him the order. Then I wrote to the Lord Bishop of St. Andrew's (Wilkinson), telling him that I hoped this font (large enough for immersion) could be given by the descendants of those sects which had separated from the mother Church of England and separated in America previous to 1776; also to give me his opinion as to the question of "lay baptism" with reference to the question of allowing the ministers of these denominations the use of the Cathedral Font for the baptism of their own people. Personally, I feel that while the Church has allowed lay baptism and received those baptized by schismatics without re-baptism, she has always discountenanced it; but I want to search this question to the bottom before deciding. I want to know what the voice of the Catholic Church is on this subject. If we allow the use of this Font to the ministers of the Protestant denominations, it will help Christian unity among Protestants, but I fear it will retard Church unity among the old historic churches.

Shortly after this, in September, I wrote to Rev. Professor Shields, of Princeton University, asking him if he could give me the names of persons in these above-named denominations who are so favorably disposed to our Church as to be willing to give the Font.

Then, on September 18th, the day of S. D. Babcock's funeral, I went to see the sculptor, W. Ordway Partridge, and told the whole story to him of the Font. He knew Herbert Clark well and said he would do the work. He showed me the beautiful stone fountain of Perugia and other photographs, and was as enthusiastic as I am regarding the Cathedral Font.

In the afternoon of Ascension Day the first of the open air summer services was held, with a large surpliced choir, and at which Bishop Paret preached. The offertory at the Cathedral Altar today was over $2,200 for the Cathedral debt.

A large brass plate has been placed in the Little Sanctuary, upon which are engraved the names of those dioceses which gave the Jerusalem Altar.

A committee of One Hundred has been formed to pledge the payment of the interest and ultimately principal of the Cathedral debt.

Copy of Herbert E. Clark's letter in answer to mine of July 19th, regarding the Jordan Baptismal Font.[28]

The Hilda Stone

I think I have omitted to name the St. Hilda's Stone, or Hildastone, procured for me first by the Rev. Dr. G. H. Somerset Walpole and Rev. Mr. Loxley, of Whitby, through whom the stone was given to the Cathedral of Washington by

[28]Mrs. Satterlee did not include Clark's letter in The *Private Record*.

the owner of Whitby Abbey, where St. Hilda lived, and which was the cradle of all English literature. This stone was the base of an arch in the old Abbey of Whitby, and it is now on the Cathedral grounds. Its shape is so peculiar that we have not as yet determined how it can best be utilized as the Hildastone. This Hildastone was finally used as a cover for a pillar in which a receptable was cut to hold the Book of Remembrance, and it is now at the right of the Jerusalem Altar in the Little Sanctuary.[29]

Reducing the Debt

During the year 1902 we made great efforts to reduce the Cathedral debt, and through the generosity of Mrs. Buckingham, Miss Freeman, her sister, the children of Mrs. Percy R. Pyne, and others, we had actually reduced it to $108,000. At the same time, the necessity pressed hard of squaring the Cathedral lines so as to have streets on all sides of the property. The Busey tract on the Northeast had been offered to us for $8,000 an acre, and the option expired in June, 1902. We therefore bought this property, increasing our debt by $24,000. By this we squared our line on the Northeast to Thirty-sixth street. There now remains a still more important tract on the Southeast needed to square our line to Massachusetts Avenue, Galveston Street[30] and Thirty-fifth Street. This belonged to the John Thompson syndicate. The Cathedral Trustees bought out the share of one of the owners for $13,000, and we shall probably come into possession of it this summer. This will raise the Cathedral debt to $145,000.

All this is absolutely necessary, but as Bishop it depresses me, for I have to raise the money. I am doing all I can for the sake of nationalizing the Cathedral and creating a general interest among our people. I have not only raised money for the land, but also for the Peace Cross, the Glastonbury Cathedra, the equipment of the school, the Jerusalem Altar, the All Hallows Gate, the Cathedral Park Board, the Canon Missioner and the missionary work of the Cathedral. In addition to this I have written a Cathedral book and also many pamphlets, formed Cathedral committees in Boston, Philadelphia, New York, Newport, Connecticut and Chicago, and arranged for Cathedral open-air services and diocesan retreats. Yet our wealthy Churchmen have not come forward, with few exceptions, to assist me with large sums. Nine-tenths of the burden of my work as Bishop in the capital of the country would be lifted if the Cathedral debt were paid, but no one today, with

---

[29]Satterlee later learned that the stone was not authentic, but the legend of the Hilda stone survived at the Cathedral into the 1990s.

[30]Now Garfield Street NW.

such few exceptions as I have suggested, seems to feel any personal responsibility regarding this work of the Church.

The Holy Women

This is characteristic of the times. Our Church is chiefly parochial. I do not complain. Christ knows best and He owns the universe. All power is given to Him in Heaven and on earth. But I mention this lack of a feeling of responsibility in passing, to show how little sympathy with the Cathedral of Washington has been shown up to this year (September, 1902) by those who give hundreds of thousands of dollars to hospitals, libraries, dispensaries, colleges, etc., etc., while they take less interest in the National aspects of our Church or the worship of God. I owe a great debt of gratitude to holy women, to Mrs. Pyne, Miss Matilda W. Bruce, Miss Bessie Kibbey, Mrs. Buckingham, Miss Isabel Freeman, Mrs. Victor Ballinger and Mrs. William C. Rives, without whom the Cathedral work would not have been what it is today. Last but not least, let me not forget the name of Miss Rhoda Rogers, a member of the Washington Committee, who died this summer. She took the deepest interest in the Cathedral, and gave it $750 in her lifetime and left for it $5,000 in her will.

Hope for the Future

New Years Day, 1903, was commemorated by a gift of $20,000 from an anonymous donor, whose name is known to me and not to be published until 1925. It was given on condition that the Board of Trustees, apart from the Bishop, raise $5,000. This whole sum of $25,000 cash was deposited in the Riggs Bank on January 1st, 1903. This brings the Cathedral debt down to $106,000. I tried hard to fulfill the donor's earnest desire to reduce it below $100,000, but could not.

The viaduct is so far completed this winter that one can walk across it. I suppose it will be several months before carriages can drive over it. What a change! A year ago there were two banks 40 feet high on either side of the deep cut of Massachusetts Avenue extended (i.e. on the other side of Rock Creek). Now these have completely disappeared.

On December 2nd (?) a lady who had long ago said she would like to give the Font because [she was] greatly interested, and went with me to Partridge's studio to see the models—for I could not hold the artist back. In February she said she had decided not to give it, but I had gone too far to recede, and now began to raise funds, but only partially succeeded. Providentially, God raised up a friend in this crisis. Mrs. Archibald D. Russell accidentally saw a letter I had written, and sent a note to me suggesting that the children baptized by the Bishop of Washington should donate the Font, and she subsequently guaranteed its whole cost, $15,000.

I then went to see Mr. Spencer Trask, who volunteered to see that the business contracts, etc. were properly drawn. Thus the Font was put in hand. Partridge completed his designs. The Leeland-Hall Company undertook to execute them in Carrara, Italy, and Mr. T. Henry Randall designed the architectural work. I have so far succeeded in securing only about $9,000 for the Font, and part of this is money given to the "Cathedral work, to be disbursed at the Bishop's discretion." I have also only $3,000 in hand for the Baptistry itself.

Ascension Day has come and gone. At this present time there seems to be a decay of interest in the various Cathedral committees who have helped to pay the interest on the debt. Only the New York, Pennsylvania and Boston committees keep up their old vitality. I had hoped to have a great Ascension Day meeting, but for various reasons, which I shall mention afterwards, I feel it wise not to emphasize it.

July, 1903. I told the architect that we had only $3,000 on hand for the Baptistry. Notwithstanding this he drew three sets of plans before contracts could be drawn for a building which would come within our means. Even then I had to appeal for more funds, and received $1,500 plus the $3,000 I had already, making $4,500 towards expenses. Of course it is only a temporary structure of brick and plaster, but will suffice. It is to be erected at a point which will be presumably near the northwest angle of the future Cathedral.

Stones for the Font

Before the ending of July, I received the following interesting letter from Herbert Clark:

Jerusalem, July 14, 1903.

Dear Sir:

At last I have been able to get the stones, and today have packed the twelve barrels and handed them over to the forwarding agent, Mr. Albert Singer, who has them to embark on the first steamer leaving Jaffa. I here enclose his receipt. As soon as he gets them off he will give me the bill of lading, when I will send it to you by the first post after, with all bills and account of expenses on them to arrive in New York. On July 6th I got word that the river was low enough, so the afternoon of the 6th my brother-in-law died. Mr. E. Unger went to Jericho in the afternoon by carriage, sending five donkeys in advance, two for us to use as riding animals and three to load, as I thought it best to send up these three loads first after seeing what could be done. I had arranged with Dr. Selah Merrill, United States Consul, to come down after getting word from me, and if he could not come I had arranged for Mr. Radd to come instead. On Monday the 6th (7th) of July we started early from Jericho from the "Pilgrim Ford" to see what we could do there. Finding we could get nothing there on account of the water and mud, we went to the mouth of the "Cherith," where it comes into the river, but could do nothing there; so we went up to the ford below the bridge, where we heard that there were stones enough uncovered. We arrived there 10:30 a.m., having left Jericho at 5 a.m. As it was so very warm we could not start back until 5 p.m. and got back to Jericho at 7.30. I wrote up to Dr. Merrill and sent up the three loads that night. Remained at Jericho all day Tuesday, July 7th. That evening Mr. Radd, the photographer, came down instead of Dr. Merrill, as he could not leave. On the morning of the 8th we went back to the upper ford by carriage ourselves, taking nine donkeys and one mule, with four men, which we reckoned were enough, as the three donkeys sent up first made something over two barrels. We got to the ford at 7:00 a.m., and just as we began getting out the stones a large caravan of some fifty camels laden with wheat from Moab came down from Moab and began crossing, so Mr. Radd took the first picture or plate and second plate while they were doing so. Mr. Radd sends you today twelve photos, two of each of the six plates taken: First, two plates getting out the stones from the river bed; second, two plates marked No. 2 and 2-A, loading up the animals; third, two plates taken on the plain of Jericho, about half way between the ford and Jericho, with the Mount of Temptation in the background, taking us all as labeled, marked No. 3 and 3-A.

We got back to Jericho at noon and left there at 10 p.m., getting back to Jerusalem on the morning of July 9th. Having only one cooper in Jerusalem, and a Jew, I was only able to get him yesterday and today to pack up the barrels. They are rather small, and I made them so, as the stones are so heavy. I feared the larger barrels would not stand it. I believe you will find them more than you need, and trust you will, and as good as you expected. I got them of all sizes, so they would pack better and also work up the same. By next mail I will send you the R/L and the account of all expenses. In regard to Mr. Radd's account, he charged 80 francs for going down, taking the six plates and sending the twelve copies of them. They may be all you need but I thought perhaps that you might sell some of them at a bazaar at $1 each. I got him to put on the bottom of his bill what he would send them to you for if you ordered five dozen at a time, or ten dozen. He would charge for five dozen 60 francs, for ten dozen, 100 francs. I suppose you have bazaars for the church sometimes, ought to once a year.

Will you polish the stones from the Jordan? Would they not be nice just as they are, natural state, set in cement, all around and on the floor of the Font? The ford from which they came is the direct ford for the East Jordan, the one always used by the present and past. It is just below the ancient bridge and the modern wooden one. Most people believe that John the Baptist was here doing his work when our Lord came down from Galilee. You will have the stones no doubt by the 1st of September or the middle, latest, and trust that it will not be too late. I duly received your kind favor of June 10th by last mail, with the draft of twenty pounds. As our only mail of this week leaves 7 p.m. and it is now 6 o'clock, I close, with kindest regards to you and the ladies, and will write you again next week.

Yours respectfully,

Herbert E. Clark

It ought to be stated here that Mr. Clark has absolutely refused to make any charge for his own services, either for the Jerusalem stones for the Altar or these stones from the Jordan for the Font. He has taken all this trouble gratuitously and freely, out of love for his religion, his native land and the Cathedral of Washington.

December, 1903. About the middle of the month the marble statues from Carrara, Italy, and the Jordan stones arrived, almost the same day, the latter in twelve small barrels, the former in six wagon loads. It took about three weeks for the Leeland-Hall Company to erect the Font. Of course there were disappointments. Notwithstanding all my warnings, the architect failed me; though I told him over and over again what I wanted, he did not take my thought.

God's Work

Thus, to all present appearances, the burden at last is lifted, and one more act of faith in God has been triumphant. I am very, very thankful to God for all He has done in the past five years. The Cathedral is wholly His work, and when I look back its history seems incredible. In 1898, five years ago this month of August, we had unsuitable land, with a debt upon it of $40,000.[31] Not one cent has this ever realized. Then, with only pledges of $83,000 in cash, half of which was paid in, we bought, on September 7, 1898, the Cathedral land, costing $245,000, with a mortgage upon it of $162,000, and interest about $8,000 per annum, every cent of all of which had to be raised from unknown sources.

Then came, first, the Peace Cross; second, the Girls' School, for which Mrs. Hearst had already given $200,000; third, the Jerusalem Altar and Little Sanctuary, costing in all $4,500; fourth, the purchase of ten more acres of land at a cost of $24,000, plus $22,000, equaling $46,000. Though this swelled the price of the land bought $245,000 plus $46,000, to $291,000, every cent of interest has been paid and the debt has been reduced to $128,000. Then came the Font and Baptistry, costing $20,000.

---

[31] $800,000 in current dollars.

I was led into this project. If I could have foreseen the trials it would bring in the winter, spring and summer of 1903, I should never have had the courage to attempt. Now we have money in hand to pay for the Font and Baptistry, though by the failure of those who said they wished to give the cost of the Font (though the wish stopped short of a direct pledge) we had last January not one cent subscribed for it, and the refusals to give have far outnumbered the promises of help.

No one will ever realize the long suspense, continuous strain, the necessity of depending daily on God's help, which the Cathedral debt, the Cathedral School, and then the Cathedral Font has called forth. One must pass through such an experience to know what it means. My only object in writing about it here is to show that God and not man has begun the building of the Cathedral Foundation of Washington, and that the work would not have and could never have reached its present condition of security had not the Cathedral builders tried to obey the New Testament injunction to "walk by faith and not by sight." The whole stress and burden has come from the effort and venture of faith. The risks taken were enormous, but they were not unreasonable, or taken without great caution and incessant prayer. We had the vision. We were obedient to the heavenly vision, but the success that followed has been altogether divine. Man had nothing to do with it except to follow God's lead.

I want to emphasize this fact with all the earnestness I can put into words, in order that future generations may be convinced that the Cathedral Foundation, in its beginnings, was built up by God Himself, and I want those future generations to realize, as strongly as we do in our day, that the work is blessed and hallowed and carried on by Christ Himself, while we have the privilege of being co-laborers with Him as He builds it up, step by step and stone by stone.

New Gifts

The beginning of July Mrs. Harriet Lane Johnston died, leaving $300,000 to the Cathedral Foundation for the erection of a Boys' School in memory of her two deceased sons. It was her wish that the choir boys of the Cathedral School should be educated and maintained at this School gratuitously. She also willed that the building and organization of the school should be conducted under the supervision of the Rev. Philip M. Rhinelander.

A few days later Mrs. Parke died, and in her will devised that the Cathedral Foundation and the Eye and Ear Hospital should jointly divide the residue of General Parke's estate. The latter had previously devised $3,000 to the Cathedral and $3,000 to diocesan missions, under the supervision of the Bishop of Washington. In this same month of July came an unexpected bequest of $5,000 to the Cathedral, also the bequest of Miss Rhoda Rogers was paid at this time, namely, $5,000. All this reduces the Cathedral debt at this time practically to $100,000.

August, 1903

Estimated value of property according to actual amounts paid to date.

The state of property, with the buildings on it, is somewhat as follows:

Cost of land, $245,000, with additional purchase of land, $46,000,= - - - - - - - -	$291,000.
Cost of the Girls' School, - - - - - - - -	206,000.
Equipment and furniture of Girls' Sch.	34,000.
Cost of Peace Cross - - - - - - - - - - - - - -	800.
Cost of Glastonbury Cathedra - - - - - - - - -	600.
Cost of Jerusalem Altar - - - - - - - - - - - -	1,800.
Cost of Little Sanctuary - - - - - - - - - - -	3,000.
Cost of Font, $15,200, and Baptistery $5,000 =	20,700.
Cost of improvement of land - - - - - - - - - -	1,000.
Total - - - - - - - - - - - - -	-$558,900.
Mrs. Harriet Lane Johnston's bequest - -	300,000.
Total - - - - - - - - - - - - -	$858,900.[32]

From this should be subtracted the Cathedral mortgage debt of $100,000, making a total of $758,900.

New Ties to the City

September, 1903. I have just driven out to the Cathedral grounds for the first time over the new Massachusetts Avenue viaduct. A great change has taken place. Two years ago, when one reached the end of Massachusetts Avenue, this side of Rock Creek, there was a yawning gulf before him, two or three hundred yards wide and 100 feet deep, with the creek flowing at the bottom. The opposite bank showed high above one, the cut of Massachusetts Avenue Extended with hills on either side forty feet above it, and surmounted by large trees. Now hills and trees are all gone.

As one stands on the self-same spot he sees a broad causeway, over 100 feet wide, gently ascending to the road house on the grounds of the Naval

---

[32] $17,178,000 in current dollars.

Observatory. This is smooth enough for horses and carriages to trot along, but except for the width of the beaten carriage track it is otherwise rough and uneven all the way to the Cathedral Close. When we reached the latter we found that the District authorities had begun the work so urgently advocated by the Cathedral Trustees of cutting down the "knob" or hill on Wisconsin Avenue, about 500 feet south of Massachusetts Avenue. The earth from this cutting is being used to fill in the 20-foot deep depression on the Cathedral grounds at the junction of Massachusetts and Wisconsin Avenues.

The Baptistry building is almost finished, and is a far more shapely and

The completed Baptistry

attractive building than I expected, even in its rough state, doorless, windowless, floorless, with the scaffolding still around it.

The olive trees set out last spring are flourishing finely, but it is very difficult to keep the Glastonbury thorn in good condition on account of the various kinds of insects which attack this special variety of English hawthorn in our climate.

The open-air services on Sunday afternoons have this season been a remarkable success. Chaplain Pierce, U.S.A., has been so attractive a preacher that his sermons are published every Sunday. The sales, at 10 cents each, have paid the cost, and the attendance has averaged in this latter part of the summer from 1,200 to 1,500, as we know by the seats we have provided. Twelve members of the Marine Band provide the music. The offertory goes to the Canon Missioner Fund. The congregations would be double the size, they say, if the street-car service were only better and more adequate, but there is only one line, that along Wisconsin Avenue to Georgetown. It now takes half an hour at least to come from Dupont Circle by carriage, via the Connecticut Avenue bridge (cars only go as near as Woodley Road and Zoological Garden); 25 minutes' drive via new Massachusetts Avenue viaduct, opened this summer; 20 minutes by electric car (Dupont Circle to Thirty-second Street, change to Georgetown and Rockville cars to Cathedral Close). We are striving to have a siding, large enough for ten cars, in front of St. Alban's.

Building a National Image

October, 1903. The month of October will ever be historical with the Church in Washington. First came the All American Conference of Bishops, which held its sessions in the Pro-Cathedral Church of the Ascension,[33] beginning on October 20th and ending on October 24th, and which was attended by 46 American Bishops, ten Canadian Bishops and the ArchBishop of the West Indies.

On the next day, Saturday, there was a mass meeting at the request of the Presiding Bishop. We had contemplated a children's meeting in connection with the Missionary Council, but the authorities in the Missions House considered this inexpedient, so we found, in this request of the Presiding Bishop, the great opportunity we had desired. After the Bishops had taken a drive in the cold air to see the environment of Washington and the "Catholic University" in carriages provided most generously by Miss Bessie Kibbey, they came to Convention Hall. Half an hour before the service every seat was filled. There were 2,000 Sunday School children, the whole Marine Band in full red uniform, and a vast congregation of 7,000. Most of the seats behind the Bishops were occupied by clergymen of various Christian bodies. All were invited. The five Bishops who spoke, Tucker of Montana, Baldwin of Huron, Hare of South Dakota, Pinkham of Calgary and Nuttall, ArchBishop of the West Indies, each confined himself, at his own request, to a ten-minute address, and the effect of the whole was most inspiring.

Sunday October 25. 20th Sunday after Trinity, 1903. The day broke raw and cold, but fair. I received protests against the afternoon service, but Rev. Dr. Bigelow, from the Weather Bureau, said the day would be a fairly good day for the late autumn and to listen to no protests. In the morning came the closing service of

---

[33] Now the Church of the Ascension and St. Agnes, Massachusetts Avenue and Twelfth Street NW

the All American Conference at the Pro-Cathedral. As I drove with General Wilson, he being in full uniform, to the White House, I realized that the weather was growing warmer. After we had spoken to the President and Mrs. Roosevelt and they had gotten into their carriage, surrounded by Secret Service men, we followed with Secretary Loeb, and when we reached St. Alban's we found, amidst the crowds, that the procession was forming: the boy choirs from all the churches leading, 300 strong; then the Marine Band, in vestments, 60 strong; then the clergy, four abreast, 200; then the 46 Bishops. The Cathedral Trustees met the President near the platform as an escort. Mrs. Roosevelt, with the wives of the Bishops and Trustees, sat between the choir and congregation, and saw the procession as it filed past, each section headed by a Processional Cross.

Here in the hollow it suddenly became as warm as on a summer day. The view from the platform was remarkable. The ravine has wonderful acoustic properties, and as it is about 350 feet square, it affords standing room for 26,000 persons. There must have been at least 16,000 present, for the records of the Tenallytown cars were 12,000, those of the Chevy Chase line 4,000 beyond their usual Sunday traffic, and hundreds walked or came in carriages. As one looked upon this vast congregation every place was filled, and every one whom I have seen said that the whole service and the words of the speakers were heard even by those most distant from them; and when the President, speaking as a Christian man, appealed to the religious leaders regarding their moral responsibilities of leadership, and when, in addition, after he had awakened commingled religious and patriotic associations, the hymn "Nearer, my God, to Thee," so closely associated with the dying moments of President McKinley, was sung, the effect was thrilling. Mr. Walter L. Bogert led with such skill that all the congregation joined in the singing.

We had made the most minute preparations for this service. General Wilson, U.S.A., was head marshal. Rev. Dr. Harding had charge of the chorus. The Churchmen's League and the Brotherhood of St. Andrew were the ushers. Chaplain Pierce and the members of the Marine Band, who had prepared the way through the summer open-air services, and Mr. Bratenahl, Rector of St. Alban's, were most valuable in having an eye to all the lacunae of the preparations. Mr. Goldsborough and Mr. Weaver had arranged a line of herdics[34] from Chevy Chase Railroad to the Cathedral Gate. Before closing this account, I should say that at the open-air service Bishop Dudley read the first part; Bishop Doane the Creed and prayers, and then in a few words made the address of welcome. President Roosevelt then spoke. After his address the ArchBishop of the West Indies said

---

[34]Small, horse-drawn cabs with two wheels, side, seats, and an entrance at the back.

a few words; then the Presiding Bishop said the concluding collects and gave the Benediction.

Our feeling at the moment was that God had taken the whole out of our hands, and wrought an effect which no human effort could possibly have accomplished—in the sudden warm weather, in the Christian address of the President, followed by the McKinley hymn, in the number of Bishops assembled and the crowds who were so unexpectedly present, in the absence of a single complaint and of a single accident among so many thousands. The Archbishop made a most effective address after the President had spoken, and the latter was so much impressed by it that he invited the Archbishop at once to luncheon. When Bishop Doane said: "It is Glastonbury over again," the Archbishop responded: "More than that; Glastonbury was looking backward; this is looking forward. I would have come 10,000 miles just to attend this service and the meeting of yesterday." The Canadian Bishops said that they never had seen or expected to see again such a service. Most of the American Bishops, in bidding me farewell, said that they realized now for the first time the representative character of the Church in the National Capital; and one of the most thoughtful of the trustees said that if we had spent $100,000 in advertising, or if one person had paid the whole Cathedral debt, $100,000, it would not have accomplished so much for the Cathedral as this one service. This is absolutely true; and when, one hour after the service, the chill and cold came back, I realized more than ever that the success of it all we owe to God Himself, and ever since my heart has been full of praise and thanksgiving to Him for His favoring Providence.

After this came the Missionary Council reception at the Corcoran Art Gallery,[35] at which 3,000 were present, and the meeting of the Council on Tuesday. During this week many of the Bishops and Clergy visited the Little Sanctuary and the Cathedral grounds. These are now one mile (less 230 feet) in circumference, indeed more than that, if we take in the property we have dedicated on Massachusetts Avenue and the line (which we own) in the middle of a possible Thirty-fifth Street.

The whole expense of the All American Conference of Bishops and of the Missionary Council, together, was $2,300 to $2,500.

November, 1903. One thought has been brought forcibly to my mind by the events of the past fortnight. People often complain that Washingtonians feel no sense of civil responsibility as citizens because the United States Government cares for everything in a paternal way, or of religious responsibility as Churchmen.

---

[35] At Pennsylvania Avenue and Seventeenth Street NW, now the Renwick Gallery.

This is perfectly true, but the disadvantage may be turned into a great advantage, for if they are in this apathetic and negative state, with no responsibility for Government and no social obligation regarding society, then their sympathies, interest and sense of duty can be enlisted in the building up of the Cathedral, which had nothing to do with Government help or State control. Then this will become an object of civic as well as religious pride. It is a great opportunity.

Promoting the Cathedral Ideal

A.D. 1904. The year opens most auspiciously. Thank God that He has so prospered the work. The accompanying financial statement shows the progress made and tells the whole story. I want to write down my ideal of what this Washington Cathedral should be. Owing to frequent attacks of illness this winter, which somehow followed after the sudden death of my brother-in-law[36] and then my son [37], I was not able to do all that I expected this year. But through God's good help considerable progress was made.

This is a year in which I have spent a great deal of money on advertisements, which brought in less money, by several hundred dollars, than their cost. First, the financial statement was prefaced by a strong editorial article in the Church Standard and then advertised. The same process was gone through with by the New York Churchman and then by the Living Church, Chicago. This cost $150, and advertised the Cathedral far and wide, but brought back not a single dollar. Secondly, we had 100,000 Founder's Certificates. These I had bound in books of 20 and sent to all the rectors of parishes except the very smallest, together with the new Handbook of the Washington Cathedral, the latter costing about $600. Less than one hundred rectors acknowledged the gift. Only a dozen or two sent any money. $150 would cover the whole return. Then I have lost over $600 in advertising the Cathedral among all the parishes in America, of course with the consent of the respective Bishops. Undoubtedly we have gained the sympathy of the clergy and of the parishes. The Washington Cathedral is now everywhere recognized as belonging to the National Church, but the time has not arrived when the Church at large feels any responsibility regarding it.

On Ascension Day, 1904, at the open-air service, there was a dedication of the Font, at which I baptized a child and the Rev. Dr. Packard baptized a young

---

[36]Captain Robert Catlin, husband of Satterlee's sister, Mary, died in the bishop's house in Washington on December 27, 1903.

[37]Satterlee was devastated by his son Churchill's unexpected death, probably the result of a heart attack, in Columbia, South Carolina, on February 16, 1904.

man by immersion. We had after this to increase greatly the supply of water. This was done at considerable cost. The service was most impressive. It can be made much more so, and the Font will be far more beautiful when new windows (with light from above) are placed in the roof.

All through the summer of 1904 I was in bed with typhoid fever and for the rest of the year could do nothing for the Cathedral except that I raised $5,000 for the mortgage debt, and this, in addition to the amount raised in the spring, made $17,000 raised.

The Agnus Dei Cross

During the summer I heard that the ArchBishop of Canterbury was coming to the General Convention. At once, in July, I dictated a letter to him, asking him to come to stay with us in Washington. He answered that the Bishop of Massachusetts and the Bishop of Albany and Mr. Pierpont Morgan were arranging the details of his American trip. I sent two letters to Mr. Morgan, and the latter said that the Archbishop's visit to Washington would probably be the end of September. I then thought that when he came he could consecrate the Glastonbury Cathedra; but that had been consecrated already. Besides, I found that it could not be moved outside the Little Sanctuary. I then went to Bar Harbor, and in August arranged there the details of the Archbishop's visit to Washington with Mr. Morgan, Bishop Doane and Bishop Lawrence.

Dr. Huntington suggested that the Archbishop might plant a St. Augustine's oak on the Cathedral Close. By and by, in September, a fortnight before we went to Washington, Mr. Samuel B. Dean, our next door neighbor, said that he had possessed for many years a Seventeenth Century Altar Cross of Latten brass, which he had long desired to give to some church in memory of his mother, Mrs. Dean of Boston, who was a most devout Christian. The next day he showed me the cross, and I saw instantly that it was exactly what I had been all the summer looking for, an object which the ArchBishop of Canterbury could consecrate, which would for all time historically mark his visit to the capital of the United States. So I called on the Archbishop, and he called on me, at Bar Harbor, when we arranged the details.

The Archbishop's Visit

The Archbishop has come and gone. He came in Pierpont Morgan's private car on Friday night (an accident, which might have been serious, detained him six hours). They came up to the Bishop's House, Washington, for breakfast,

141

The Glastonbury Cathedra

and to stop with us. General Gillespie, Chief of Engineers, took the Archbishop and Mrs. Davidson and his two chaplains, Rev. Mr. Ellison, Vicar of Windsor, and Rev. Mr. Holden, to see Washington. The British Ambassador presented him to the President. Twenty-five persons were present to meet him at the Bishop's luncheon, among them Pierpont Morgan, Sir Mortimer Durand, the British Ambassador,

Bishop and Mrs. Doane, and others. At 4 p.m. there was a public reception at the Corcoran Art Gallery, at which 3,000 were present. In the evening they dined with the President.

On Sunday morning there was early Celebration at the Bishop's Chapel, then the Archbishop celebrated at St. John's,[38] Bishop Brent preaching. In the afternoon, which was warm and beautiful, there was the great Christian Unity service at the Cathedral Close. The Archbishop drove over and quietly planted the St. Augustine's oak. Then he sat in the Glastonbury Cathedra and said the prayer for Christian unity. He consecrated the Altar Cross on the Jerusalem Altar presented by Mr. Dean. Then the procession began to move, 500 choristers, all the clergy of the diocese, visiting Clergy from Baltimore, and Bishops Doane, Paret and Penick.

While sitting in the Cathedra and talking about the Glastonbury stones, the ArchBishop offered to give stones from Canterbury Cathedral to make a faldstool[39] for the Cathedral. This was a delightful surprise. This little faldstool afterwards became a lecturn, given by the Archbishop in memory of Stephen Langston, and illustrating the evolution of the English Bible. The Canterbury Ambon then became a great pulpit, almost all made of stones from the Bell Harry tower of the Cathedral.

The Clergy of various denominations occupied the platform. Bishop Doane preached the sermon. The Archbishop gave the salutation and Benediction, after which all the Clergy of the Church and the ministers of various denominations were presented to him. The papers, basing their calculation on the public and street-car reports, reported 35,000 present. Pierpont Morgan afterwards said that this was the greatest function the Archbishop attended in America, and the Archbishop said it was the most complicated yet best function he had ever attended.

The next morning the Archbishop and party went to Mount Vernon in General Crozier's yacht, after which Pierpont Morgan took him in his private car to New York.

Neither my wife or I were able to go to the President's dinner or to Mount Vernon with the Archbishop, but we were represented by my daughter, Constance. The Rev. Dr. DeVries acted as Chaplain while the Archbishop was here.

---

[38] On Lafayette Square.

[39] A desk at which the Litany is read.

The Boys' Choir School

November, 1905. Competitive plans for the Boys' Choir School by Henry Vaughan and York and Sawyer.[40]   Messrs. Bratenahl and Dr. DeVries were a commission sent by me to the great boys' schools of America, St. Paul's, Concord, New Hampshire, St. Mark's and Groton, Massachusetts. They made a very careful study, helped by the principals of these schools, and a full report, before the architectural plans were adopted. By the terms of Harriet Lane Johnston's will, the building was to be commenced within six months of the time the legacy was paid, so we had to make undue haste in starting the work. We went so far as to have a photograph taken of the foundation of the school six months from the day the legacy was paid.

When I was in Europe, [summer 1905] at Nauheim, taking the cure, I received a telegram from Col. Truesdell saying that the cornerstone of the Choir School was laid on Ascension Day.

While in England, as I could not go about myself, I sent my Chaplains, Rev. Drs. DeVries and Bratenahl, who were in England at the same time, to as many Cathedrals as they could visit, to investigate the choir schools, and also the constitutions of the various Cathedrals, and the reports they brought back were detailed and very satisfactory. As the Archbishop said I would, I gained most valuable information regarding the whole Cathedral system from the Reports of the Royal Commission, which I purchased and brought to America for our Cathedral library.

Reducing the Cathedral Debt

January 1, 1905. The Cathedral debt has been reduced at this date. The Archbishop's service for Christian unity has greatly increased the prestige of Washington Cathedral, and interest is plainly increasing, but funds do not come. This year the Surveyor of the City, Major H. C. Looker, died. We owe a great debt of gratitude to him for his voluntary help in making many surveys of the site for me on different occasions. By April the debt had been again reduced, and I am again making special efforts to further lessen it. No one realizes what a burden it is. When we got below the $100,000 on the debt it seemed as if the goal were in sight,

---

[40]An architectural firm.

and thereafter we have all eagerly watched when it went below $90,000, $80,000, $70,000, etc.

The Canterbury Ambon

This spring [1905] I have been in constant correspondence with Mr. Caroe, the architect in charge of the Canterbury Cathedral, regarding the Canterbury Ambon. I saw him in England this summer, and he is going to make it a beautiful work of art. It is to be made of stones from the Bell Harry Central Tower, and to be given by the Archbishop in memory of Stephen Langton, his sometime predecessor, who led the Barons when they rung the Magna Charta from King John. As the Bible is the Charta of all liberty, it is most appropriate that this Ambon should commemorate the Magna Charta. The Ambon will illustrate the history of the English translations of the Bible. The three bas reliefs will illustrate the death of Bede, the giving of the Magna Charta at Runnymede, and the martyrdom of Tyndal. The four statuettes will be Alfred the Great, Wycliffe, Bishop Andrews (A. V.), and Bishop Westcott (R. V.). The frieze will be of Bibles, each with the date of revision.

Debt Free!

October, 1905. On my return to Washington, Mrs. Julian James came to see me and said she would like to place a memorial to her mother in the Cathedral. I suggested that she should pay the debt and make the memorial a Cathedral Land Mark, with a Sundial, marking not only the hours of the day, but the seasons of the Christian year. The suggestion pleased her. Shortly after I received a letter from her lawyer, Mr. William Allen Butler, of New York, saying Mrs. Julian James would contribute the last $50,000 if the whole debt were reduced to that amount before Thanksgiving Day, and if the proposed Land Mark were erected. The debt at this time was $67,000. At once I set about raising the $17,000. The response was most prompt and generous. On the Monday before Thanksgiving Day, 1905, Mr. Butler met the Cathedral Trustees. In his presence the $67,000 notes were brought out and canceled. The papers were all signed. Then all arose, when I had a short Thanksgiving service in the Board Room of the Riggs Bank, with collects for the Cathedral, for Mrs. Julian James and those present. Then Mr. Butler handed over the check for $50,000 and the Cathedral Close was free! On Thanksgiving Day a letter was read in all the Churches of the Diocese announcing the fact.

(Note. No one can ever appreciate what it is to be delivered from this

The Canterbury Pulpit

burden. I feel like one released from prison, after having been in confinement seven years, from 1898 to 1905. Once more I feel free. I shall ever associate the 37th Psalm with this period of my life. How often have I read it and been encouraged by its promises that if we hope in the Lord we shall possess the land. I wonder now when I look back to the autumn of 1898 how I could ever have had the courage to face the financial problem. I could not have done it without God's Grace. And what wonders God hath wrought in these seven years! We have never failed to meet the interest promptly on the very day of the semi-annual payments, and now the whole debt is paid.)

Plans for the Cathedral

December, 1905. Now that the debt was paid, a work uprose at once which I never expected to do in my lifetime, the building of the Cathedral itself. We could afford to make no mistake.

January, 1906. I called the Board together and they agreed to the appointment of the following advisory committee: (1) Mr. Edwin A. Burnham; (2) Mr. Charles F. McKim; (both of these gentlemen were members of the Park Commission appointed by Congress to report plans for the "lay out" of the future Washington, and who brought in the celebrated report on this subject); (3) Sir Casper Purden Clarke, the Director of the New York Metropolitan Museum; (4) Professor Charles F. Moore, Professor of Gothic Architecture in Harvard University; (5) Mr. Bernard Green, Superintendent of the Congressional Library. This advisory committee had two meetings on the Cathedral grounds, in February and on May 6th, and they reported: (1) that the best site for the Cathedral was not where I had expected, at the corner of Massachusetts and Wisconsin Avenues, but on the highest part of the Cathedral Close; (2) that there ought to be no competition whatever; that the primary consideration was not the plan, but the man, for the personality of the architect, his religious enthusiasm, his creative ability, his experience, management, etc., were of the utmost importance. In addition to this, Mr. Charles McKim and Mr. Burnham, in a strong letter [preserved in the Cathedral archives], expressed with great emphasis their judgment that to accord with the Government buildings of Washington, the Cathedral ought to be built in the style of the classic Renaissance.[41]

Consecration of the Close

Ascension Day, 1906. This day began as usual the open-air services on the Cathedral Close. As the whole debt on the land is now paid, there was a service of consecration of the Cathedral Close, commemorated by the Land Mark being set up this day, given by Mrs. Julian James, with the sundial upon it, which marks the seasons of the Christian Year. This Land Mark and Sundial were carefully set by Rev. Dr. Bigelow, of the Weather Bureau of the United States, on a meridian measured and marked on the Cathedral grounds by the instruments from the Naval Observatory. The Cathedral Foundation owes a great debt of gratitude to Professor Bigelow for all the pains and trouble he has taken to make the calculations and see that they are absolutely accurate.

The Cathedral Constitution

May, 1906. In this month, at a regular meeting of the Board, and after eighteen months of labor on the part of the Bishop, the committee of Trustees, Rev. W. L. DeVries and Rev. G.C.F. Bratenahl assisting, and also Mr. Arthur S. Browne, the constitution was thoroughly revised. To give an idea of the labor, all the statutes of the English Cathedrals were procured by me, on the advice of the

---

[41] As noted below, the decision for the Renaissance style was later reversed.

present ArchBishop of Canterbury, and carefully examined and collated. Over 2,000 typewritten pages were written by my secretary, Mr. Warner. All the statutes of American Cathedrals were studied, and finally this constitution was unanimously adopted by the Board of Trustees, who henceforth became the Cathedral Chapter. The trustees who gave me the most assistance in this difficult work were Rev. Dr. Harding, General Wilson and Mr. John A. Kasson. The constitution is elastic and very much is left to be added pro re nata.[42]

The Role of the Cathedral in the American Church

Perhaps I had better give some of the reasons for this prolonged consideration. The Cathedral (except as a building) is new in the American Church, and if properly organized it will supply a great want, that is, a sphere for Episcopal work. Hitherto the American Church, while technically Episcopal, is in effect parochial, for the Bishop is little more than (1) a parish visitor; (2) an ordinary; (3) a President of the Diocesan Convention. Missionary Bishops fill a larger sphere than Diocesan Bishops and have consequently more freedom as chief pastors of the flock. The consequence is that the pastoral office of the Diocesan Bishop is shorn of great possibilities in Diocesan work.

On the other hand, there are these considerations: (1) the present supra-parochial activities of the Church are sporadic and in some cases individualistic. They suffer because they are isolated from one another; (2) the supra-parochial potentialities of the Church are a great unutilized opportunity. No one can forecast the extended sphere of usefulness that would be created if this mine of wealth in Church effort were explored. New York parishes are now trying to do a Cathedral work at the expense of their pastoral work. A prominent Southern Bishop said to me: "New York parishes are no longer spiritual homes for the people; they are great eleemosynary institutions."

Now, the Cathedral, as the Bishop's Church, gives him a sphere for the exercise of his pastoral office with spiritual opportunities that he cannot have in any parish, where he would either be interfering with some rector, or else be awakening the jealousy of other parishes; and it is, at the same time, the Mother Church of the diocese, where all parishes are welcomed on equal terms, and where diocesan efforts both converge and radiate, and where missionary and educational efforts originate.

This is an ideal which belongs to the Primitive, not to the Mediaeval Church. The statutes of all the English Cathedrals, excepting perhaps Truro, fall

---

[42]Latin, for "to meet a particular emergency."

far below this ideal. European Cathedrals are all fettered by Mediaeval traditions and customs, which really paralyze the real work of a Cathedral. In America we are free, and it has been an immensely difficult task for us to separate (what we believe to be) the wheat from the chaff in those statutes. We finally concluded to make our constitution as short as possible, leaving it for those who come after to develop it pro re nata along the lines we have laid down. This will account for the lacunae that many parliamentarians and canonists will criticize. In so important a work, we thought it best not to legislate beforehand for contingencies which no one can foresee. All experience shows that the only safe rule in such legislation is the practical one of solviter ambulando.[43]

The question of the relation of the Cathedral to the Diocesan Convention has been a most perplexing one. The Diocesan Convention I have always felt to be "the Church in the Diocese," but the more we tried to act upon this principle, the more we found that there are certain aspects in which the Diocesan Convention does not fully represent the Church in the Diocese, just as in the American Constitution the Executive is different from the Legislative branch of the Government, while the President is amenable to Congress, so the Bishop, as diocesan executive, is different from the Diocesan Convention even while he is responsible to it.

In the American Church, the Bishop has heretofore been deprived too much of the power of initiative and the sphere for the exercise of the pastoral office, simply because he has never felt free to act apart from the Diocesan Convention. Now it was my first idea to bring the Cathedral in closest relations with the Convention, to give it the election—or at least the nomination—of the officers and trustees of the Cathedral, in a word, to put the Cathedral under the Convention, and thus defeat the very object that I had most at heart. But the Trustees almost to a man opposed this. They pointed to the Charter. They said that they could not discharge their duty under the charter if they were to commit the responsibility of filling vacancies or of enacting laws and statutes for the Cathedral to any other body, even the Convention of the Diocese. They consented to give the power of nomination to the Bishop, because he is, ex officio, president of the Board; but beyond this they refused to go.

Then my eyes were opened to see what I had not seen before. To do this with the Cathedral, the Bishop's Church, would be to give the Convention a power over the Cathedral that it did not have over any parish in the Diocese. It would make the Bishop less free than any rector. Instead of enlarging the Bishop's sphere of usefulness as chief pastor, it would curtail it. All this has been brought

---

[43] Probably *solvitur ambulando,* for "leaving room for future options."

about providentially. God has been leading us all by a path that we knew not.

Again, I see another result. The Washington Cathedral is not only the Cathedral of the Diocese. While diocesan, it is also the representative Cathedral of the whole American Church, and in that sense supra-diocesan. Some day this may become something more than a mere sentiment. I think this thought was always in Senator Edmunds' mind. It will be observed that we have touched upon this aspect of the Cathedral in the 150th paragraph of the Preamble.

I have always felt that the Cathedral should stand for the Anglican basis of Church unity, and the four offices of precenter, missioner, chancellor and almoner stand in connection with the four articles of the Lambeth Quadrilateral. At first I thought we might even go so far as to have one or two chancellors [as] representatives of Protestant evangelical bodies in the Chapter, even as we have had two Presbyterians on the Cathedral Board; but after two years of thought and consultations with Bishops, prominent rectors and church lawyers, I came with them to the absolute conclusion that this would be a mistake. We have, however, left places for clergy of other dioceses on the Council as "honorary canons," and also places for ministers of evangelical Protestant bodies in the Council as "Cathedral lecturers," and I hope the day is not far distant when we shall have representatives of both on the Cathedral Council. But that is a question to be left to the future, pro re nata.

Another great crux was how to provide for the appointment of dean and canons, when by our charter we were obliged to have fifteen trustees. The only way to do this was to elect the members of the Chapter for two years only. Then if one of these officers is wanted, he can be elected to fill a vacancy. Of course this means that a dean, etc., is only appointed for two years and undoubtedly this article of the constitution will have to be modified when the time comes. All this will take care of itself. At present we see no other way of meeting all the conditions of the situation. (The same difficulty occurs with regard to the Bishop Coadjutor.)

Selection of the Architect

June, 1906. At this time a meeting was held to formulate some plan for choosing the architects of the Cathedral, and on motion a committee was appointed, consisting of the Bishop, Dr. Harding, Dr. D. C. Gilman and Dr. Rives, to report in the autumn in writing. This committee had several meetings. As I was going to Europe, it was finally resolved that Dr. Rives and the rest should correspond with architects in America, while I was to see architects in Europe. We adopted the following plan: (1) As Gothic architecture requires special study, we were to limit ourselves only to Gothic architects. (2) We were to confine ourselves to those who could send in plans of work actually completed by them. This cut off all who could draw beautiful plans but had had no actual experience in Gothic construction. (3) We were to correspond both with English and American architects.

June 27 to July 10. In England the Bishop of Liverpool took me to see his Cathedral at St. James' Park, the foundation of which had just been laid, and he gave me a letter to the secretary of the board, who gave me other information and showed me the plans in detail. Afterwards I went to visit the Cathedrals of Litchfield, St. Alban's, Westminster Abbey, and Westminster Cathedral (Romanist). I failed to reach Lincoln, to my great disappointment, but went to Gloucester to see the things which had caused the downfall of Gothic architecture in England.

Then I had short conferences with the Bishops, namely, the ArchBishop of Canterbury, the Bishops of Southwark, Salisbury, Litchfield, etc., who all gave me many valuable points. I then saw a few architects, namely, Mr. Bodley, Mr. Reeves and Mr. Caroe. I tried to see Norman Shaw and another architect, but my time was too limited, and the two or three conversations I had with Mr. Bodley were so satisfactory and the reports I had of him were so unanimous as to his being the first Gothic architect of England today, that I really cared to go no further, especially as Mr. Bodley said that he would be willing to design our Cathedral in partnership with an American architect, and if the plan was approved by the Chapter, to build it.

On my way to Nauheim I stopped to see the Cathedrals of Antwerp, Cologne and Aix la Chapelle. At Cologne I noticed many points. At Nauheim and in crossing the ocean I read and re-read with great care the valuable volume on Gothic architecture in England by Francis Bond,[44] and made notes not only on this but regarding the points in the Cathedrals I have seen and tried to study. These are:

England: Westminster Abbey, St. Paul's, Southwark, Roman Catholic Westminster, St. Alban's, Rochester, Canterbury, Winchester, Salisbury, Wells, Exeter, Gloucester, Worcester, Litchfield, Chester, Liverpool, Carlisle, Manchester, Newcastle, Durham, Yorkminster, Lincoln, Peterborough, Ely, Norwich - 25.

Abbeys: Tewkesbury, Glastonbury, Furniss - 3.

France: Rouen, St. Duens, Amiens, Rheims, Laon, Notre Dame, St. Denis - 7.

Italy: Milan, Padua, St. Mark's, Venice, Duomo, Florence, Siena, St. Peter's, Rome,

---

[44]Francis Bond, *The Cathedrals of England and Wales* (London: B.T. Batsford, 1899)

5. The Private Record

St. Apollanaris, Nuovo, Ravenna, Torcello
Germany: Cologne, Aix la Chapelle, Basilici (Munich), Antwerp, Hof, Kirch, Innsbruck.

America: Albany, New York, and St. Patrick's (Roman Catholic) New York.

I once lectured for four years in my parish, once a week in winter, on the subject of architecture in general, and I never forgot the lessons and the information I thus gained. It has been invaluable to me now.

Spain: Cathedral of Seville.

Russia: St. Isaac's, St. Peter and St. Paul.

August, 1906. I returned from Europe, and on my way to Northeast Harbor I called at Boston on Mr. Cram of Cram, Goodhue & Ferguson, and on Mr. Henry Vaughan. At Northeast Harbor were Dr. Rives and Dr. Gilman, the latter ex-President of Johns Hopkins; also Bishops Doane and Mackay-Smith. Dr. Gilman, Dr. Rives and I had several meetings of a committee on the Cathedral. Dr. Rives had written to several American architects for designs of work completed by them, and several sent in specimens of their work, also Mr. Bodley of England. The undertaking seemed so vast that we resolved to invite all the trustees for a conference on August 29th or 30th, and those who came were Bishop Mackay-Smith, Dr. Gilman, Dr. Rives, Col. Truesdell and myself. Then we wrote to Mr. Bodley for more definite information. After this we sent out a very full letter describing all we had done, to all the members of the Chapter, suggesting Mr. Bodley and Mr. Vaughan as the Architects who were to prepare the design for Washington Cathedral.

October 10, 1906. On this date, at a meeting of the Chapter, after one hour's discussion, Messrs. Henry Vaughan and George F. Bodley were unanimously chosen as the architects, and a committee prepared at once a telegram to Mr. Bodley and a letter to Mr. Vaughan, announcing the fact. Both accepted at once. Mr. Vaughan came to Washington. I had a long conference with him, and finally Mr. Warner, my secretary, came in and took a stenographic report of our conversation.[45] After this I added several other points to the letter, forwarding two copies to Mr. Vaughan, who mailed one to London for Mr. Bodley. Mr. Bodley sailed from England November 21st, arriving in Washington about November 30th.

---

[45]The report of this conversation has not been found.

As I was away that day and he was to sail back on the same ship, the Oceanic, on December 4th, this only allowed us practically three days. He came with his first assistant architect, Mr. Hare. I dined with Messrs. Vaughan, Bodley and Hare at Dr. and Mrs. Rives' on November 30th. They had all spent the day on the Cathedral Close, studying its features.

December 1, 1906. On Saturday both architects and Mr. Hare met the Chapter at the Bishop's House, with the Cathedral Relief Model in the center of the room. Then Mr. Vaughan read the letter I had written to the architects (the typewritten report of my conversation with Mr. Vaughan) together with such suggestions and criticisms as Mr. Bodley desired to make. Mr. Bodley then made a long verbal explanation and criticism, saying that with these modifications he accepted the whole letter as a working basis, if the Cathedral Chapter agreed. They thereupon agreed unanimously, after making a few inquiries. This was most remarkable. To me it was nothing less than a proof of Divine guidance. I could scarcely have believed, six months ago, not only that the architects should have been the unanimous choice of the Board, but that the architects, Chapter and Bishop should have been of one mind regarding the whole general character of a Gothic Cathedral.

December 3, 1906. On Sunday I drove with the architects to the Cathedral Close. On Monday the members of the Chapter, with their wives, dined with the architects at the Bishop's House. I had one more conference with the architects on Tuesday morning, after which they all left for New York.

Completion of the Boys' Choir School

December, 1906. In this month the Choir School for Boys was finished, and also the enlargement of the Little Sanctuary for the Canterbury Ambon.

A Cathedral Publication

1907. There is such a demand for Cathedral news that we have decided to print an "occasional paper" to be called the "Cathedral Chimes." The first article in this is the revised constitution, to be followed by the supra-parochial work of the Diocese that is soon, it is hoped, to be organized under the auspices of the Cathedral.

New Gifts

In May [1907] the girls of the Cathedral School gave a "Calvary" or three steps to the Peace Cross, with a pulpit from which in future the sermons in the open air will be mostly delivered, as from the very first. This is to be called "The Salem." (See the wonderful comprehensive meaning of the word in Hebrew, to make peace, security, etc. etc.)

In the same month the chime of tubular bells given by Mr. and Mrs. G. S. Bowdoin, in memory of their daughter Fanny, were placed in the belfry of the Little Sanctuary, designed by Lansing Satterlee, the architect of the Little Sanctuary. They were rung for the first time on Whitsunday, 1907.

The Cathedral School

The commencement of the Cathedral School, under the new principal, Mrs. Barbour-Walker, marks a new era in the history of the school.

Progress on Architectural Plans

As the members of the Chapter were about separating for the summer, the second week in June [1907], Mr. Bodley hastened the plans and sent them by the Steamer Majestic. Mr. Floyd Jones was ready to receive them on their arrival. Secretary Cortelyou kindly notified the Custom House authorities not to detain them, as the law had been faithfully complied with. The express company forwarded them the same day by rail to Washington. Mr. Vaughan arrived in the morning. My carriage, with my secretary, was at the Georgetown Custom House when it was opened. In fifteen minutes the plans were on the wagon, and an hour after, when the Cathedral Chapter met at my house, the plans were displayed for consideration and Mr. Vaughan spent two hours in explaining them. I was prepared somewhat for the interior, because of the resemblance to the rejected plan of Mr. Bodley for Liverpool Cathedral, which I first saw in Mr. Bodley's London office and which first attracted me to him. But the exterior was a delightful surprise. It far exceeded all my expectations, for I knew that Mr. Bodley was severe and almost a purist in taste; but this exterior satisfied me in every respect. It more than fulfilled my expectations, and the view of the high windows of the apse on the outside was like a spring song; and although six weeks have now passed, the whole Cathedral, inside and outside, is as great a delight to me as ever. The only criticism as yet which I or any one has to find with the plans is that the West Towers seem not equal to the rest; but we have not yet seen the perspective drawings of the West Front.

We had expected to consider the plans all summer, but after considering them carefully, the Chapter adopted them three days after they had first seen them.

Then we thought it best to organize the Cathedral Council at once, that they, too, might feel that they had been consulted about the design. Accordingly the Council was organized the same week and adopted the plans. Afterwards all the clergy of the Diocese and the Churchmen's League were invited to see them. This sequence of events is remarkable, so much so that it must have been Providential, and I can only marvel at God's leading. In answer to prayer He has uplifted the Cathedral far above our most sanguine expectations and accomplished results that I never expected to see or dreamed of seeing in my own lifetime: (1) The Cathedral land was bought and paid for in seven years, 1898 to 1907; (2) the Cathedral Schools for Boys and Girls were both erected in that time; (3) in that time the sacred historical objects gathered out in the Cathedral Close interested the whole Church; (4) one month after the debt was paid we were able to secure the most prominent architects of America as an advisory commission; (5) that advisory commission reported against a "competition" unanimously; (6) the Cathedral Committee appointed by the Chapter were of one mind and the American architect, Mr. Vaughan; (7) I was unexpectedly enabled to go to Europe to see English architects and Mr. Bodley unexpectedly told me Mr. Vaughan had been his pupil; (8) the Cathedral committee, at Northeast Harbor, determined to recommend to the Chapter Messrs. Bodley and Vaughan unanimously, and I wrote long letters to each member of the Chapter, giving detailed reasons; (9) the Chapter, after careful consideration, appointed Messrs. Vaughan and Bodley unanimously; (10) Mr. Vaughan and I agreed on the plan of the Cathedral, and sent copy of our conversation to Mr. Bodley; (11) when Messrs. Vaughan and Bodley came to Washington and agreed to take this letter as a basis for plans, the Chapter agreed unanimously; (12) when the plans were completed they were unanimously accepted both by the Cathedral Chapter and the Cathedral Council. The Lord hath done marvelous things. I am bewildered when I think how He has brought so many strong men of many minds to agree so perfectly in the building of His House. Surely this is the work of the Holy Spirit, Who maketh men to be of one mind in an house.

Cazenovia, N. Y., July, 1907. The west front has arrived; like the rest of the Cathedral it has great inspiration; first, in the massive simplicity of the two towers. I have always longed to see a Gothic "campanile"; here it is most unexpectedly; second, in the grandeur of the central arch and two side arches. This makes the western facade of Washington more majestic than that of an English Cathedral—yes—Continental Cathedral, also. The great doorways have more than the cavernous depth of Rheims and the Amiens, without the portal, which always seems to me construction for effect—a trick of the trade. The size and proportions and measurement of parts is all right, but spiritually there is disproportion. The facade is too austere and too prison-like. It does not invite an entrance to God's House. Again, the towers have buttresses climbing to the top, an English fault, which makes the west towers of York, Canterbury and Westminster look clumsy. I have written

Mr. Bodley saying (1) that we do not want buttresses higher than the eaves of roof; we want the soaring Campanile line of Durham and Lincoln, not the uncertain, wavy outline of York; (2) we want a flight of steps before the west front, to take away the semblance of the west front standing on legs; (3) we want a different treatment of the gable. This is the Cathedral itself, not the protection (like the towers) or sheltering entrance, like the arches. The gable ought to be decorated like the tops of the towers. It ought to blend the note of welcome with that of awe. I have suggested a Bas Relief of the Cleansing of the Temple above the central arch and have written Mr. Bodley a letter about it.

July 12, 1907 (At Cazenovia). Events have followed each other with strange rapidity. Mr. Vaughan has returned from England, saying that the Cathedral plans were well advanced. Mr. Bodley and I have had frequent correspondence, in which I personally emphasized that the Cathedral should be joyous and triumphant, breathing the triumph of the Christian Faith.

The Foundation Stone

Twilight Park, August, 1907. Last June, the moment it was decided that the laying of the cornerstone was to be on September 29th, the Feast of St. Michael and All Angels, I wrote to Herbert Clark, who sent word to Antoin Thomas Gelat, drayoman, to procure a stone from the field behind the Church of the Nativity, Bethlehem. This he did in July. At the same time he had the scene photographed, and the endorsement of the United States Consul, Mr. Wallace, that the stone or stones (for being unable to send a single large stone to America before September 1st, he was obliged to send seven smaller ones in seven different boxes). These came so speedily that they have reached Washington in time. These were set in a large granite block to enclose them and prevent them from being crushed by the immense weight of the Altar and Reredos above them. They are on the under side of the granite, with the sentence "The Word was made flesh and dwelt among us" engraved upon them.

We have made many changes this summer on the Cathedral Close:

1. The Braddock Monument.
2. The Choir School.
3. The Girls' School.
4. The St. Hilda's Lodge.
5. The grading about the Choir School.
6. Open Air Service.
7. The Salem Place.
8. The Bronze Pulpit.

The Foundation Stone

Foundation Stone procession

6. THE FOUNDATION STONE

A few days after making the last entry in his *Private Record*, Bishop Satterlee returned to Washington from his summer home in the Catskills to oversee preparations for the foundation stone ceremony, which he and the cathedral trustees had set for September 29. Selecting the Feast of St. Michael and All Angels could be seen as no less than an appeal for heavenly support in this momentous first, if symbolic, step in construction of the Cathedral. There were, however, equally important earthly reasons for selecting that date. The International Convention of the Brotherhood of St. Andrew would bring hundreds of clergy and laity from all over the world to Washington on that day, as would the General Convention of the Episcopal Church that would meet in Richmond, Virginia, the following week. Months earlier Satterlee had invited Arthur Winnington-Ingram, the Bishop of London, and President Theodore Roosevelt to speak at the ceremony, and thirty-two bishops of the Episcopal Church were expected to attend on their way to Richmond. The president would speak for the nation. The bishops would represent the Episcopal Church at large. The presence of the Bishop of London, whose predecessors had exercised episcopal authority in the American colonies, would symbolize the Cathedral's ties to the worldwide Anglican Communion.

The Cathedral Council had designated prominent clergy and laymen to design the service; oversee the sale of platform tickets; direct the music; issue invitations; serve as chief ushers for both the foundation stone and brotherhood services; make luncheon arrangements; provide for hospitality and housing, medical services, and security; and distribute literature. During the summer all the buildings on the Close had been spruced up, walkways upgraded, and roadways improved. On August 24 the first sod was turned for an excavation eleven feet deep to contain the substructure for the foundation stone. A temporary wooden apse containing a platform and seats for three thousand people was built over the excavation, and the outer walls of the Cathedral itself were outlined with festoons of ropes and descriptive cards. By Friday, September 27, all the preparations on the Close were complete. Satterlee, the archBishop of the West Indies, and a representative of the Brotherhood of St. Andrew met the Bishop of London when he arrived at Pennsylvania Station in Washington that evening and escorted him to the White House, where he spent the night.[1]

On Saturday morning, as members of the Brotherhood assembled at the Church of the Epiphany for their corporate communion, the rain began to fall. The Weather Bureau prediction for rain on Saturday and Sunday proved true as cold showers turned to torrents during the night. Alone in his room, the bishop prayed for the rain to end, confident that the great day would bring fair weather.[2]

Sunday the 29th dawned wet and dismal as clergy and laity all over the diocese gathered at parish churches to celebrate Holy Communion at nine-thirty. At Satterlee's request, all later services in the parishes that day had been canceled. At the Jerusalem Altar in the Little Sanctuary Bishop Tuttle, the presiding bishop, was the celebrant. At Bishop Satterlee's chapel in his residence on Massachusetts Avenue, the celebrant was Bishop H. H. Montgomery, the secretary of the Society for the Propagation of the Gospel, with the bishops of London, Washington, the West Indies, and St. Albans in attendance. The Bishop of Los Angeles celebrated at St. Alban's Church on the Close for worshipers from the girls' school and the neighborhood, and for other visiting bishops and guests.[3]

By the time the services ended, the clouds had broken and thousands of people were making their way to Mount St. Alban. Hundreds arrived in automobiles, merchandise wagons, and carriages that stretched a half mile down Wisconsin Avenue. Others entered the Close from Massachusetts Avenue on the south or from Woodley Lane on the north. Drivers of bishops' carriages tied purple ribbons on their whips so that the police would wave them on to the Close. Hundreds of people had to walk up the long hill from Georgetown when every available streetcar could not accommodate the crowd. Coming through the oak grove near Wisconsin Avenue the throng moved east into the area that would become the nave of the Cathedral. As the noon hour approached, members of the Cathedral chapter, an associate justice of the Supreme Court, cabinet members, the commissioners of the District of Columbia, and representatives of the Senate, House, Judiciary, and the military services began to gather on the platform. Just before the procession started, President Roosevelt arrived with his wife and two of his children. At the last moment an ominous storm cloud gathered and a few drops of rain fell, but the sky brightened again as the service began.

Exactly at noon a trumpet fanfare based on a motif from Mendelssohn's "Hymn of Praise" started the procession from the west side of the Close down what would eventually be the center aisle of the Cathedral, marked off with posts and purple cords. A vested choir of 150 men and boys from four of the largest parishes in the city led the way with a section of the Marine Band, also in cassocks and cottas. Canon DeVries described the procession:

> The band and choirs passed around the altar site, where the foundation stone was to be laid, and ascended to their tiers at the rear of the center of the platform. But the clergy parted and allowed the Bishops, in the

160

order of their rank (the Presiding Bishop and the ArchBishop of the West
Indies walking together and leading, and the Bishops of Washington and
London immediately following, then the visiting Bishops, and after them
the American Bishops in the order of their consecration), and the Cathedral
Chapter and Council, to pass first to their places in the forefront of the center
of the platform. After them followed upwards of 75 or 80 of the diocesan
clergy, and sat between the Council and the choir. The visiting clergy, some
two hundred in number, including many of the best known presbyters of the
American Church, and a few from Canada and over sea, sat just west of the
altar site, in what will be the east end of the choir.

President Roosevelt speaking at the ceremony.

It was a magnificent site in that quadrangle, the platform enclosing three
sides of the Cathedral choir, along the lines of the north, east and south walls
of the Cathedral and open only on the west, and there indeed enclosed by

great throngs of people in the nave below, as it were, and the branching oaks filling in the places of the columns, pillars, arches and vaults in a rich, lustrous, leafy green.[4]

Following the lessons, Nicene Creed, and the supplications, the choirs and people sang "O Little Town of Bethlehem" while the architect and workmen began lowering the stone into the pit. At the same time Bishop Satterlee, with Henry Vaughan, the architect, and several others left the platform.

> Reaching the level and proceeding to the site of the altar the Bishop and his companions passed down into the great pit into which the foundation stone was descending. Before the stone reached the bottom its descent was arrested, the Bishop laid the mortar, and made in it at the center and four corners the sign of the cross, with the point of the trowel. Then the stone was set in place, the Bishop struck, and so proved it, three times with the Washington mallet and in the name of the ever blessed Trinity.[5]

After the Gloria in Excelsis Bishop Satterlee introduced President Roosevelt, who spoke briefly on the value of Christian fellowship in combating evil in the world. The Bishop of London added his greeting from the Church of England. Following the offertory hymns, Bishop Paret read the final collects and the presiding bishop gave the benediction. After the band played the Dresden Amen, the choirs and people sang "O Sion haste" and other recessional hymns as the procession slowly moved to the oak grove on the western side of the Close.

There was scarcely time for lunch before the procession of choirs, clergy, lay leaders, and now the full complement of the Marine Band, assembled to move to the amphitheater for the Brotherhood of St. Andrew service and the presentation and dedication of the Canterbury Pulpit.

The afternoon was well spent before the service ended and the great mass of people, estimated at more than 35,000, made their way home. For Henry Satterlee, this must have been the greatest day in his life, the successful culmination of eleven years of hard, sometimes frustrating, but in the end rewarding work.

After sending off the Bishop of London and his other guests, Satterlee took the train to Richmond for the opening session of the General Convention on October 2. On the fifth he was in Williamsburg to fulfill an obligation he had made earlier in the year to present a lectern given by President Roosevelt to Bruton Parish Church to hold a Bible given by King Edward VII. Satterlee had arranged an interview with the president to suggest the gift, which

Roosevelt agreed to make if the bishop would present it.[6]

Back in Washington Satterlee was swamped with diocesan and Cathedral business. Early in November he spent five days in his annual visitation to the parishes in Southern Maryland and returned once again to plans for the Cathedral. The Chapter had accepted the general plans drafted by Bodley and Vaughan, but there were many details still to be completed. When Bodley died suddenly on October 21, Satterlee moved quickly to have Vaughan appointed as cathedral architect. By December 5 the chapter had ratified Vaughan's appointment, and Satterlee was already in almost daily correspondence with him on details of design. The question of greatest concern to Satterlee was the seating capacity, which according to existing plans would be less than two thousand. He noted that there were many churches in America that held that number. The more he thought about it, the bishop concluded that seating for three thousand would be the minimum needed. To accomplish this number, he suggested extending the length of the transepts and placing galleries in the transepts. Vaughan found this idea completely unacceptable, but Satterlee would not relent. Eventually, by the end of January 1908, the bishop and the architect agreed on widening the nave to forty feet and placing a stone gallery in the transepts and West Gallery.[7] On major occasions, when the Cathedral is filled to capacity, the three balconies stand as a reminder of Satterlee's foresight.

The Cost of Commitment

On February 2, Satterlee attended a big missionary rally for the Washington Sunday Schools. On Monday, the tenth, he took the train to New York, as he did almost every month, to attend the meeting of the national Board of Missions. Already suffering with a heavy cold, he was determined to keep a speaking engagement with the cathedral committee in Providence, Rhode Island, on Wednesday, the twelfth. On Thursday, against the advice of his friends, he boarded the train for Washington, only to be delayed seven hours by heavy fog that prevented the transfer boat from crossing the Hudson River. Exhausted and ill, he insisted, over the protests of his family and physicians, on fulfilling his commitment to conduct confirmation services that weekend at two missions he had established for blacks in southeast Washington, at St. Monica's on Friday evening and at St. Philip the Evangelist on Sunday morning. His determination reflected the priority he gave to reaching out to the black population in the city, albeit in racially segregated missions.[8]

Physicians concluded on Monday that the bishop had a severe case of influenza, but as his condition grew worse during the week, it became evident that he was suffering from pneumonia. Soon after midnight on Friday the doctors informed him that the end was near. With his immediate family and the Rives, his closest friends from Calvary days,

The Church of the Ascension, where
Satterlee's funeral was held.

Satterlee expressed his reconciliation with death and bid farewell with a personal blessing for each individual present. Early on Saturday morning, February 22, he asked to receive Holy Communion and died with the words of the Sanctus, "Holy, Holy, Holy," on his lips.[9]

The daily papers on Monday reported in depth on the bishop's death and plans for the funeral to be held the next day at the Church of the Ascension at Twelfth Street and Massachusetts Avenue, NW. The church, which he had designated as his pro-cathedral until the new structure on Mount St. Alban could be built, was just two blocks from the bishop's residence on Thomas Circle. All day Monday scores of people of all denominations called at the residence to pay their respects. That evening a group of Washington clergy escorted the casket to the church. Clergy of the diocese maintained a vigil during the night around the casket in the chancel of the church, and beginning at seven on Tuesday morning, the Holy Communion was celebrated every hour until noon. By that time so many people had assembled in front of the church that they all but blocked Massachusetts Avenue. To accommodate the hundreds of mourners who could not be seated in the church, diocesan officials arranged for an overflow service at the nearby Church of the Incarnation at the same hour.[10]

Present when the service began were President and Mrs. Theodore Roosevelt, cabinet members, the Chief Justice, and members of Congress and the diplomatic corps. At two o'clock the combined choirs of two of the largest parishes in the city proceeded up Twelfth Street and entered the church to the strains of Chopin's funeral march. Then the choir moved forward without singing while Bishop Henry Potter of New York intoned the opening words of the burial service from the *Book of Common Prayer.* Following in the procession were the cathedral canons, members of the board of trustees and cathedral council, more than ninety of the diocesan clergy, and nine bishops. After Alexander Mackay-Smith, now bishop coadjutor of Pennsylvania, read the lesson, the choir sang the Te Deum, not usually used at Episcopal funerals but specifically requested by Bishop Satterlee. At his request there were no eulogies. After the Bishop of Tennessee read the appointed prayers, the service concluded with a hymn.

Joined by the hundreds of people who stood outside the church, the procession moved slowly west on Massachusetts Avenue to the Cathedral Close in what *The Washington Post* described as "one of the longest and most impressive ever seen in Washington." A large group of people had already gathered outside the Little Sanctuary. Bishop William Lawrence of Massachusetts read the committal service in the Little Sanctuary, where the body remained until Bethlehem Chapel was completed in 1912. There the tomb, in the chapel apse behind the reredos, was appropriately placed under the Jerusalem Altar and above the foundation stone.[11] On that stone succeeding generations built the great Cathedral that Satterlee's vision and leadership made possible.

THE SATTERLEE LEGACY

Few visitors coming to the Cathedral for the first time today have ever heard of Henry Satterlee or know anything about his place in the Cathedral's history. Unless they join a tour with one of the docents or listen to the audio cassettes, they will never hear Satterlee's name or see it on stone inscriptions. Without knowing it, however, visitors will encounter the tangible evidence of his presence from the moment they enter the Close. The very site on Mount St. Alban, high above the city of Washington, would not have been secured without him. Hearst Hall, the great west front of the Cathedral itself, the Herb Cottage, the Little Sanctuary, and the Lane-Johnston Building at St. Albans School bear the influence of his planning and architectural taste.

Stepping into the Cathedral itself visitors may note the wide, five-aisle nave and in the transepts and west end the balconies that Satterlee insisted upon. In the crossing visitors encounter multiple examples of Satterlee's influence: the steps leading up to the Great Choir, the crucifix on the rood beam, the open design of the rood screen, the Canterbury Pulpit, and the absence of a lantern in the central tower, to which Satterlee gave the name "Gloria in Excelsis." Satterlee's influence was decisive in the design and placement of the two chapels on either side of the Great Choir, the Glastonbury cathedra, and the Jerusalem Altar with its triumphant cross without a corpus.

Underlying Satterlee's influence in creating all of these material objects was his elite sense of high style and quality. Standing as a prayer to God in stone, wood, glass, and iron, the Cathedral could only exhibit the very best examples of design, materials, artistry, and craftsmanship. This tradition of excellence that Satterlee established was honored by George

Bodley, Henry Vaughan, Philip Hubert Frohman, and Richard T. Feller during the decades of design and construction, and that tradition is still maintained in the Cathedral today. Every stone, every carving, every stained-glass window, every piece of embroidery, and every hinge and door handle reflects Satterlee's insistence on the very best.

Satterlee's impact on the Cathedral extends far beyond these material objects incorporated in the structure. During his Washington years, Satterlee reminded his colleagues that his intention was not just to erect a magnificent building but to make it a vital center for carrying the Christian Gospel to the nation and the world. The Cathedral, he declared, was to have three defining purposes. It was to be "A House of Prayer for all People," "The Chief Mission Church of the Diocese," and "A Great Church for National Purposes."

These three definitions were not the product of Satterlee's experience in Washington but came out of his earlier ministry in Wappingers Falls and New York City. He applied them in slightly different contexts in Washington, and they took on new meaning in the life of the Cathedral after his death. Since 1908, successive bishops, deans, canons, architects, and precentors have applied Satterlee's propositions in different ways, but they remain central in the Cathedral's mission.

A HOUSE OF PRAYER FOR ALL PEOPLE

Creating "A House of Prayer for All People" was a cardinal aim of Satterlee's ministry from the beginning. He was not the originator of this definition, crafted from verses in the Old and New Testaments, but he never tired of evoking it. At Wappingers Falls it defined his efforts to bring into the reach of the Church a broad spectrum of people from aristocrats on their Hudson River estates to local farmers, immigrant families, and the scores of young women working in the town's mills. Not content simply to provide services in the local church, Satterlee set out to attack, as he put it, "the real problem of a working man's life."[12] The young rector with his lay helpers improved sanitary conditions in workers' dwellings, opened a village library, set up a home for working girls, organized clubs and debating societies for working men, and, most of all, tried to make the parish church "a warm spiritual home."

Satterlee's success in bringing people from all social classes into one Christian community made him a logical choice to be rector of Calvary Church, a "society" parish that also included Calvary Chapel, whose congregation was mostly blue-collar workers. To these established institutions Satterlee added Galilee Mission, which provided food, lodging, and educational resources to people in the slums on the lower East Side. In his efforts to build "a house of prayer for all people," Satterlee was frustrated by the pew rent system. In 1895 he admonished the parish that "private ownership even of a pew in the house of which Christ Himself says, 'My house shall be called a house of prayer for all people,' is felt to be contrary to the Gospel by outsiders, who have come to regard pewed churches in the light of private religious club houses. . . ."[13]

There was no doubt in Satterlee's mind that the Cathedral was to be "A House of Prayer for All People." That declaration meant that all people, whatever their religious background, would be welcome to worship there. He was not suggesting, however, that the Cathedral be non-denominational. It would be Episcopal in its liturgy and doctrine, but Satterlee held out the hope that the Cathedral would become a magnet attracting other Christian denominations to the Episcopal Church. The basis for union was the Chicago-Lambeth Quadrilateral. In a sermon at Trinity Church, New York, in January 1900, Satterlee asserted that the Cathedral was not to be "a mere monument to sectarianism, but it may be a witness to Christian unity, unity based upon Holy Scriptures and the Apostolic Creed, the holy sacraments and the apostolic order." He declared "the Episcopal Church was peculiarly fitted to build a National cathedral, because it combines in itself the Protestant and Catholic tendencies, and is the lineal descendant and successor of the primitive Church, as it was in the first four centuries before Church and State were ever heard of, and before the medieval novelties of Roman Catholicism had appeared."[14] The Cathedral in the nation's capital, in Satterlee's words, was to be "a witness before the whole country of Christian unity with an Anglican basis."[15]

Satterlee's bold assertion seems naive today, but it was credible for Episcopalians at the turn of the century. As Professor Frank Sugeno has pointed out, during the nineteenth century most Episcopalians "generally agreed that the church order of the Episcopal Church was a better vehicle for the propagation of the Christian faith than that of other churches. . . . Episcopalians were becoming convinced that their church had a special vocation of carrying their church order throughout the land. To some the vocation was to become the Church of America."[16]

Although Satterlee's dream was not realized as he conceived it, the Cathedral has become "A House of Prayer for All People" in ways he never imagined. Other Christian denominations are invited to conduct services in the Cathedral. It has provided a worship home for Jewish and Polish Catholic congregations. Since the terrorist attack on the World Trade Center and Pentagon in 2001, the Cathedral has strengthened ties with other faiths by inviting Muslims, Buddhists, and other non-Christian religious leaders to preach and take part in Cathedral services. While maintaining the Anglican tradition of the Quadrilateral, the Cathedral is now more fully "A House of Prayer for All People" than ever before in its history.

THE CHIEF MISSION CHURCH OF THE DIOCESE

Satterlee's deep commitment to missions, both foreign and domestic, remained at the center of his ministry to the day of his death. Thus, it is not surprising that mission would be one of his three directives for the Cathedral. Of the three, the mission directive has been most difficult to apply. At the time he prescribed it, he was thinking primarily in terms of establishing missions for new parishes west of Rock Creek Park, an area then served only by St. Alban's Church as far north as the District line. To direct this work, Satterlee named his protégé Philip Rhinelander canon missioner of the Cathedral. As diocesan bishop, Satterlee also took steps to bring the dozen rural missions in the diocese under his direct control in an effort to revive and strengthen them. His death in 1908 largely aborted this effort.[17]

During the decades when construction was the primary focus, mission was not one of the standing functions of the Cathedral, although the chapter did appoint canon missioners, like Rhinelander, who ministered to the needs of individuals and congregations in the diocese. Since the 1990s, as the bishop, dean, and chapter turned their attention from construction to a redefinition of program, more attention has been given to mission. This is a work still in progress, but Satterlee's directive has not been forgotten.

A GREAT CHURCH FOR NATIONAL PURPOSES

As Washington emerged as the capital of a new world power in the last decade of the nineteenth century, it seemed inevitable to many Episcopalians that the city would be the site of a new diocese with its own cathedral, and farsighted, ambitious churchmen like Douglas and McKim saw that cathedral as serving a national purpose. For Satterlee, this expectation was not only obvious but unavoidable. On the most practical level, he early realized that the Cathedral could not be built without financial support on the national level. In his "parlor meetings" in the large cities of the Northeast, he pitched his appeal as a competition to match the attempts of the Roman Catholic and Protestant Churches to establish a foothold in the nation's capital. In his correspondence and publications he relied on the words "National Cathedral."[18]

For Satterlee, however, the term was much more than a fund-raising slogan. If the Cathedral was to be "A House of Prayer for All People," it would have to be a national institution, potentially the seat of the presiding bishop and the administrative center of the Episcopal Church nationally. He knew full well that creating a national church would require overcoming the stubborn parochialism that he railed against in the *Private Record*, but it seemed that the Cathedral itself could help turn the Church in a national direction.

Satterlee's idea of a national church was neither new nor original. In the 1830s Anglican leaders in the Oxford Movement saw the Church of England as potentially a great national institution that could provide a moral guide for society at large and thus provide a rallying point for uniting the denominations. At the end of the century, Anglican clergy such as W. H. Freemantle and Bishop Brooke Fox Westcott (whom Satterlee cited in *A Creedless Gospel*) proposed a national church, committed to social action, that would be a national agency for the improvement of the English people. Freemantle's book, *The World as a Subject of Redemption,* was popular in America, especially after he published a revised edition in 1898, just at the time Satterlee was beginning his fund-raising campaign. But Satterlee, like other Americans, was cool to the idea of the Church functioning as a national welfare agency as well as to Freemantle's suggestion of an established church. What did appeal to Satterlee was Freemantle's prediction that the national church would help to unify all the Protestant denominations in America, perhaps around the Episcopal Church.[19]

Probably of even greater influence on Satterlee than Westcott and Freemantle was his long-time mentor and advisor, William Reed Huntington. Satterlee's long-standing commitment since 1888 to the Chicago-Lambeth Quadrilateral as a standard for unification of the Protestant denominations around the Episcopal Church clearly reflected Huntington's views. A decade later, in 1898, Huntington published a new book, *A National Church,* that suggested a framework for such an institution. Huntington saw the national church as a federal structure that would organize churches at the county, state, and national level, an organization that would accommodate Episcopal parishes and dioceses. He admitted that questions of worship and polity would be more difficult to resolve, but he held out the hope that in time, perhaps in a century, the United States would have a national church based on Episcopal forms of organization, worship, and polity.[20]

We can only guess that Satterlee found Huntington's last book interesting but too theoretical and speculative. For Satterlee the Cathedral was to be a tangible and compelling centerpiece of a national Episcopal Church uniting the Protestant denominations. Satterlee's vision of the national church was never realized, certainly not as a unified body of the Protestant churches or even as a national Episcopal Church. The many attempts during the following four decades to build a national structure for the Episcopal Church around the Washington Cathedral all failed except for the General Convention's designation of the Cathedral as the seat of the presiding bishop in 1940.

If Satterlee's pamphlets and sermons did not light the way to a national church, they did help to define the Cathedral as "A Great Church for National Purposes." The word "national" appeared in the name of the National Cathedral School for Girls in Satterlee's own lifetime and in the National Cathedral Association, created in 1910 as an evolution of his city and state committees. While honoring the separation of church and state, Satterlee's successors continued to recruit the Marine Band for services, not only on state occasions but also for dedications of Cathedral fabric. During the 1920s and early 1930s Bishop James E. Freeman launched a national publicity campaign to promote the Cathedral as "America's Westminster Abbey." In the years after World War II, Bishop Angus Dun and Dean Francis B. Sayre took public stands on national political issues. Beginning with President Wilson's funeral in 1924, Washington Cathedral became the accepted venue for state funerals and national services in times of tragedy or celebration. In 1989, as construction of the building was nearing completion, Bishop and Dean John T. Walker began using the term "Washington National Cathedral" on Cathedral letterhead and all publications. This change was perhaps intended as the first signal that the Cathedral was moving from eighty-three years of construction into a new era focused on mission, outreach, and ecumenism.

If Satterlee is unknown to the public at large, his influence continues to permeate the life of the Cathedral to the present day. Every bishop who succeeded him has invoked Satterlee's words on great occasions, and worshipers in every Cathedral service are surrounded by artifacts in stone, wood, and iron that reflect his presence. But his primary legacy may well be the Foundation Stone itself. As Christopher Row has pointed out, the stone is "both the literal foundation of the building and the institutional foundation of the Cathedral as a wider organization. . . . The foundation stone is the symbolic underpinning for the entire Cathedral, yet here it is the literal foundation for the twelve stones—hewn from Solomon's Temple quarries—which constitute the High Altar of Washington Cathedral."[21] The Cathedral rests on the Foundation Stone Satterlee laid, and it will stand, God willing, as he put it, "for generations to come."

NOTES ON SOURCES

PRIMARY SOURCES

The largest collection of manuscript sources relating to Bishop Satterlee is in the archives of Washington National Cathedral and the Episcopal Diocese of Washington. Record Group 2 in the Diocesan Archives (DWA) contains four cubic feet of records relating to Satterlee's official acts and correspondence as Bishop of Washington and five cubic feet of personal correspondence with family, friends, and fellow clergy. Included in the collection are essays and theses that Satterlee wrote during his school days. The correspondence files appear to contain virtually every letter Satterlee received after coming to Washington. There are also copies in Satterlee's handwriting of scores of letters he sent to others. The files also contain a few diaries covering short periods of time, a scrapbook of newspaper clippings, and genealogical data on the Satterlee family going back to Norman times but not including his own generation. In boxes 18-20 are the full texts of more than two hundred sermons that Satterlee preached at Zion and Calvary. As bishop he no longer had time to write out full texts but preached from notes, some of which are in the collection.

The Cathedral Archives (WNC) contains scores of documents written by or related to Satterlee's work in creating the Cathedral. The most pertinent records are in Record Group 117, historical records, and Record Group 162, relating to art, architecture, and construction.

Copies of the typescript of the *Private Record* are filed in both the diocesan and the Cathedral archives.

St. Mark's Library at General Theological Seminary in New York City contains a dozen documents related to Satterlee. The records of Calvary Church, now housed in the parish hall of St. George's Church in New York City, include a complete set of the Calvary *Year Books* published during the years of Satterlee's rectorship and a scrapbook related to Satterlee's work at Calvary. The *Year Books*, some running to almost three hundred pages, are a rich source on the Satterlee years at Calvary.

The parish archives of Zion Church in Wappingers Falls, New York, contains a complete set of vestry minutes during Satterlee's years there and perhaps a score of manuscripts relating to the history of the parish. The collection also includes several *Year Books* that Satterlee published during his rectorship. The Grinnell Library, across Main Street from the church, contains a few records related to Irving Grinnell.

SECONDARY SOURCES

The only published biography of Satterlee is Charles Henry Brent's *A Master Builder: Being The Life and Letters of Henry Yates Satterlee, First Bishop of Washington* (New York: Longmans, Green, 1916). Brent is particularly good on Satterlee's background, student days, and ministry at Zion Church and Calvary. Brent probably wrote this portion of the book in 1911 or soon thereafter, when he had access to Mrs. Satterlee's recollections and some documents that do not appear in the Satterlee papers in the Archives of Washington National Cathedral. The second half of the book was probably written in 1915 and early 1916, when Brent was pressing to complete it before Mrs. Satterlee's death. The latter chapters consist mostly of long quotations from documents at hand with little attempt to put events in context. Like most biographies of nineteenth-century clerics, Brent's book is sharply focused on church affairs with virtually no reference to the larger scope of history, but it remains an indispensable record of Satterlee's life.

Copies of all the books written by Satterlee are in the library of the Cathedral Archives: *A Creedless Gospel and the Gospel Creed* (New York: Charles Scribner's Sons, 1895); *New Testament Churchmanship and the Principles Upon Which It Was Founded* (New York: Longmans, Green, 1899); *The Building of a Cathedral* (New York: Edwin S. Gorham, 1901); and *The Calling of the Christian and Christ's Sacrament* (Washington: Church Militant Publishing Co., 1902). In addition to these books, Satterlee wrote a stream of promotional pamphlets preserved in the Cathedral Archives. He also commissioned the writing and publication of two books related to major events in the early history of the Cathedral: *The Peace Cross Book* (New York: R. H. Russell, 1899); and William L. DeVries, *The Foundation Stone Book: Washington Cathedral, A. D. 1907* (Washington: Privately published, 1908).

Many books and articles describing the Cathedral were published as construction progressed during the twentieth century. Of these, two are essential for understanding the evolution of architectural design.

Richard T. Feller's, *Completing Washington Cathedral For Thy Great Glory* (Washington, D.C., 1989) is a rich treasure house of information and data on the architecture, design, construction, and iconography of the Cathedral. Christopher D. H. Row's "A World Without End: Philip Hubert Frohman and the Washington National Cathedral" (Ph.D. diss, Harvard University, 1999), focuses on Frohman but in the first two chapters contains a brilliant analysis of the theological basis for the design of the Cathedral and Satterlee's role in the original work by Bodly and Vaughan. Row's book also includes descriptions of and comments on architectural design not available elsewhere.

Other secondary sources containing information on Satterlee are:

> The Journals of the Episcopal Diocese of New York, 1874-1896
> The Journals of the Episcopal Diocese of Washington, 1895-1910
> The Journals of the General Convention of the Episcopal Church
> The Churchman, a weekly on Episcopal Church news published in New York City, 1880-1908
> The Living Church
> New York Times
> New York Herald
> The Washington Post
> Washington Evening Star

END NOTES

CHAPTER 1

1. As quoted in Edwin C. Burrows and Mike Wallace, *Gotham: A History of New York to1898* (New York: Oxford University Press, 1999), 452.

2. E. Digby Baltzell, *Judgment and Sensibility: Religion and Stratification* (New Brunswick, NJ: Transaction Publishers, 1994), 56.

3. Edward Satterlee to Henry Yates Satterlee (HYS), Oct. 26 [1873], Dec. 26, 1873; to Jane Lawrence Satterlee (JLS), Mar. 6, 1874, all in Diocese of Washington Archives, Record Group 2, Box 14, Folder 3 (DWA, 2-14-3).

4. Bishop Satterlee described his mother in a note he dictated many years later, DWA, 2-12-17.

5. Charles H. Brent, *A Master Builder: Being the Life and Letters of Henry Yates Satterlee, First Bishop of Washington* (New York: Longmans, Green, 1916), 1-8.

6. Ibid., Albany city directories, microfiche, 1833-34, 1845-46, Library of Congress.

7. Burrows and Wallace, *Gotham,* 712-17; Brent, *A Master Builder*, 9-10; New York City directories, microfilm reels 1 (1861-62) and 2 (1868), Library of Congress.

8. HYS to his aunts from Vienna, Nov. 28, 1858, quoted in Brent, *A Master Builder*, 11-12.

9. The lack of punctuation and the crossed-out words and phrases suggest that this and other documents in the file are drafts that were later copied in clear form for submission in class. All the essays noted here are in DWA, 2-14-5.

10. HYS, notes on first day at Columbia, DWA, 2-14-5. This file also contains copies of his essays and other

works as well as letters from college friends.

11. Brent, *A Master Builder,* 14-15. Three letters from members of Congress in the summer of 1862 are in DWA, 2-14-6. All state that no appointments to the Academy were available.

12. Jane Satterlee to HYS and Jane Churchill Satterlee, Feb. 29, 1872, DWA, 2-14-3.

13. The Power of the Will, DWA, 2-14-5.

14. Brent, *A Master Builder,* 16-17.

15. Robert W. Prichard, *A History of the Episcopal Church* (Harrisburg, PA: Morehouse Publishing, 1991), 84-90, 118-23.

16. Ibid., 161-63; *Journal of the General Convention* (JGC), 1865, 320-22.

17. JGC, 1862, 344.

18. "The Report of the Board of Trustees of the General Theological Seminary," JGC, 1865, 278-302.

19. R. William Franklin, "Puseyism in the Parishes of Leeds and Wantage Contrasted," *Anglican and Episcopal History* 62 (Sept. 1993): 377-82; John R. Griffin, "Dr. Pusey and the Oxford Movement," *Historical Magazine of the Episcopal Church* 42 (June 1973): 139-53.

20. Judith Proctor, "'. . . an honest table is one that has four legs': The Liturgical Skirmishes in the Diocese of Maryland in 1843," *Anglican and Episcopal History* 68 (Dec. 1999): 443-45; Prichard, *A History of the Episcopal Church,* 148-50.

21. E. Clowes Chorley, *Men and Movements in the American Episcopal Church* (New York: Charles Scribner's Sons, 1946), 194-227.

22. Powel Mills Dawley, *The Story of General Theological Seminary: A Sesquicentennial History,* 1817-1967 (New York: Oxford University Press), 212-18.

23. Frederick D. Huntington to HYS, Dec. 7, 1895, DWA, 2-12-13.

24. Brent, *A Master Builder,* 16-17.

25. Zion Church, Vestry Minutes, Aug. 4, 1865; Brent, *A Master Builder,* 19-21.

26. Burrows and Wallace, *Gotham,* 866-67, 904. The best source on the Grinnell family is Carol M. Bell, "The Grinnell Library Association of Wappingers Falls, New York, 1867-1940," (M.A. thesis, Long Island University, 1975), 9-13. On Satterlee's early association with Grinnell, see Prescott Evarts, Address at Dedication Services of the Grinnell Memorial Window, Dec. 15, 1923, Zion Church Archives; Grinnell's obituary, *New York Times,* May 12, 1930.

27. HYS to his mother, Sept. 14, 1862, DWA, 2-14-5.

28. Martin Bruegal, *Farm, Shop, Landing: The Rise of a Market Society in the Hudson Valley,* 1780-1860 (Durham: Duke University Press, 2002).

29. Frank Hasbrouck, *A History of Dutchess County New York* (Poughkeepsie, NY: S. A. Matthieu, 1909), 465-69.

30. James Riker, Jr, *The Annals of Newtown, in Queens County,* New York (Lamberville, NJ: Hunterdon House, 1982), 285-88; New York (City), Borough of Queens, *Description of Private and Family Cemeteries in the Borough of Queens* (New York: Topographic Bureau, 1932), 18-22; U.S. Federal Census, 1850, New York City, 18th Ward, 245; *New York Times,* Oct. 1, 1862, 8; Burrows and Wallace, *Gotham,* 87, 178, 372, 545, 574.

31. Brent, *A Master Builder,* 19. There are voluminous family letters in DWA, 2-11-17.

32. Brent, *A Master Builder,* 23.

33. Suzanne Keller, *Beyond the Ruling Class: The Strategic Elites in Modern Society* (New Brunswick, NJ: Transaction Publications, 1991), 4.

34. HYS, draft autobiography, undated, DWA, 2-14-9.

35. Minutes, General Parish Meeting, Zion Church, Aug. 6, 1867; Barbara Griffin, Draft History of Zion Parish, both in Zion Church Archives.

36. Many of Satterlee's sermons at Zion are in DWA, 2-18-16 to 2-19-3. As an example of his pastoral work, see Abby D. Cobb to HYS, Jan. 13, 1874, DWA, 2-6-15. On his Sunday School book, see HYS, *Christ and His Church: Questions and Answers on the Life of Christ and His Teachings, St. Paul's Missionary Journals, the Early Church, the Ancient British Church, the History of the Bible and Prayer Book and the Christian Year* (New York: E. P. Dutton, 1882). A copy is in St. Mark's Library, General Theological Seminary, New York.

37. Brent, *A Master Builder,* 38-43; Irving Grinnell to HYS, Aug. 14, 1873, DWA, 2-14-15.

38. Zion Church Archives has copies of several of the *Year Books* published between 1875 and 1880.

39. Zion Parish, Year Book, 1879-1880, Zion Church Archives; Brent, *A Master Builder,* 50-51; Griffin, Draft History, 5.

40. Vestry Minutes, Zion Church, Feb. 6, 1880.

41. HYS to Mary Catlin, Mar. 6, 1880, in Brent, *A Master Builder,* 57-62.

42. Brent, *A Master Builder,* 65. On payment of the parish debt, see James Marlor to HYS, Feb. 2, 1884, DWA, 2-15-7.

CHAPTER 2

1. Charles H. Brent, *A Master Builder: Being the Life and Letters of Henry Yates Satterlee, First Bishop of Washington* (New York: Longmans, Green, 1916), 69, 79; Horatio Potter to Henry Yates Satterlee (HYS), Feb. 24, 1870, Diocese of Washington Archives, Record Group 2, Box 14, Folder 10 (DWA, 2-14-10); Henry C. Potter to HYS, Mar. 31, 1873, DWA, 2-15-8; HYS Diary, Feb. 18, 1896, DWA, 2-21-1.

2. Brent, *A Master Builder,* 33, 42; HYS to Henry C. Potter, Feb. 17, 1898, Bishops' Correspondence, Item 335, St. Mark's Library, General Theological Seminary, New York.

3. HYS to Bishop Tuttle, Feb. 13, 1882; HYS to James Emott, Feb. 16, 1881; HYS to Rector, Trinity Church, New Haven, undated draft; HYS to Bishop Stevens Perry, Jan. 30, 1882; C. C. Tiffany to HYS, Feb. 14, 1882; all in DWA, 2-14-14.

4. Robert Prichard, *A History of the Episcopal Church*

(Harrisburg, PA: Morehouse Publishing, 1991), 184-88; E. Clowes Chorley, *Men and Movements in the American Episcopal Church* (New York: Charles Scribner's Sons, 1946), 284-314; New York Times, Sept. 6, 1881, Oct. 30, 1982, 8-4.

5. HYS to Wardens and Vestrymen of Zion Church, Apr. 29, 1882, Zion Church Archives.

6. HYS statement quoted in Brent, *A Master Builder*, 79-80.

7. HYS, handwritten note, undated, DWA, 2-14-9.

8. Brent, *A Master Builder*, 81.

9. James Sheerin, *Henry Codman Potter: An American Metropolitan* (New York: Fleming H. Revell Co., 1933), 19-40.

10. W. S. Rainsford, *The Story of a Varied Life: An Autobiography* (New York: Doubleday, Page, 1922), 203-18; Elizabeth Moulton, *St. George's Church, New York* (Privately printed, 1964), 62-68.

11. Brent, *A Master Builder*, 129-30.

12. Brent, *A Master Builder*, 96-102; HYS, "The Advent Mission of the Episcopal Church," Harper's Weekly 29 (Nov. 25, 1885): 778-79; Tuttle to HYS, Apr. 7, 1887, DWA, 2-6-24; *New York Times*, Mar. 31, 1885, 8-3.

13. *New York Times,* Jan. 4, 1886, 8-3.

14. Rainsford, Story of a Varied Life, 232-55; Edwin C. Burrows and Mike Wallace, *Gotham: A History of New York to 1898* (New York: Oxford University Press, 1999), 1053-55.

15. Brent, *A Master Builder*, 90.

16. HYS to My Dear Lord Bishop, Aug. 14, 1884, and HYS to D. L. Moody, Aug. 14, 1884, both in DWA, 2-14-9.

17. Brent, *A Master Builder*, 90, 104.

18. Year Book of Calvary Parish, 1888, 98-150; Journal of the Diocese of New York, 1886 (New York: Diocese of New York, 1887), 136-37.

19. Brent, *A Master Builder*, 82-85.

20. Quoted in Brent, *A Master Builder*, 84-85.

21. Hamilton Schuyler, *A Fisher of Men, the Life of Churchill Satterlee, Priest and Missionary: An Interpretation of His Life* (New York: Edwin S. Gorham, 1905), 1-32.

22. Philip H. Burch, Jr., *Elites in American History: the Federalist Years to the Civil War* (New York: Holmes & Meier, 1981), 145, 196; Burrows and Wallace, *Gotham*, 123, 576, 657, 720.

23. Arthur Mann, "British Social Thought and American Reformers of the Progressive Era," *Mississippi Valley Historical Review* 42 (Mar. 1956): 672-87; Burrows and Wallace, *Gotham*, 1170-80.

24. Brent, *A Master Builder*, 121; Schuyler, A Fisher of Men, 18; Gertrude Himmelfarb, *Poverty and Compassion: The Moral Imagination of the Late Victorians* (New York: Alfred Knopf, 1991), 235-43; Paul T. Phillips, *A Kingdom on Earth: Anglo-American Social Christianity, 1880-1940* (University Park: Pennsylvania State University Press, 1996), 60, 89-90.

25. Brent, *A Master Builder*, 121, 134-37; HYS to Mr. Ingram, July 1, 1892, DWA, 2-14-12.

26. For a description of the Bethel Green project, see *New York Times*, Jan. 22, 1893, 17-7.

27. HYS to J. Lewis Parks, Feb. 4, 1897, DWA, 2-12-8.

28. *New York Times,* Nov. 11, 1892, 10-1; Mar. 24, 1893, 1-5.

29. *New York Times,* Mar. 19, 1893, 9-5; Mar. 25, 1893, 8-5.

30. Calvary Year Book, 1890-1891, 74; Calvary Year Book, 1891-92, 183; The Churchman 71 (Feb. 2, 1895): 156; Stephen S. Garmy, Calvary Church, New York City: A Guide to the Church [parish pamphlet], 7.

31. Burrows and Wallace, *Gotham*, 1186-87.

32. Burrows and Wallace, *Gotham*, 1185-88; Cavalry Year Book, 1895, 113; Brent, *A Master Builder*, 116-17.

33. Calvary Year Book, 1892-1893, 143; Calvary Year Book, 1895, 23-28. To make his point, Satterlee conflates the wording of Isaiah 57:6 and Matthew 21:13.

34. Rainsford, *Story of a Varied Life,* 233-309; Moulton, *St. George's Church,* 67-82.

35. HYS, *A Creedless Gospel and the Gospel Creed* (New York: Scribner's, 1895), 26.

36. George E. Hodges and John Reichert, *The Administration of An Institutional Church: A Detailed Account of the Operation of St. George's Parish in the City of New York* (New York: Harper Brothers, 1906), 1; Phillips, *A Kingdom on Earth*, 70-72.

37. Journals of the Diocese of New York, 1883, 119-20; 1885, 48-54, 121-28; 1886, 4.

38. Calvary Year Book, 1889, 178.

39. Brent, *A Master Builder*, 139-42; "Report of the Provisional Committee on Church Work in Mexico," DWA, 2-5-35; HYS to Jane Satterlee, Oct. 1892, DWA, 2-15-8.

40. Evidently, Brown chose to overlook the Episcopal Church's continuing dependence on the Church of England; Prichard, *A History of the Episcopal Church,* 188-89. This section draws heavily on Prichard, 173-76, 184-93. See also John Frederick Woolverton, "William Reed Huntington and Church Unity: The Historical and Theological Background of the Chicago-Lambeth Quadrilateral" (Ph.D. diss., Ann Arbor: University Microfilms, 1964), 40-44; John W. Suter, *Life and Letters of William Reed Huntington* (New York: Century Co., 1925).

41. The Chicago and Lambeth statements of the Quadrilateral appear in the 1979 *Book of Common Prayer,* 876-77.

42. Brent, *A Master Builder*, 162-63, 263; James L. McElrath, "The Theme of Church Unity in the American Church Congresses, 1874-1933," *Historical Magazine of the Episcopal Church* 42 (Sept. 1973): 218-19.

43. *New York Times*, Sept. 22, 1895, 20-4; Oct. 1, 1895, 13-6; Oct. 2, 1895, 8-5.

44. *New York Times,* Oct. 11, 1895, 16-3; Oct. 14, 1895, 5-1.

45. Brent, 190-206; DWA 2-12-14 contains an extensive file of documents Satterlee collected. On press coverage, see the *New York Sun*, Nov. 18, 1896, 1-1; *New York Times,* Nov. 18, 1896, 6-1; London *Daily Chronicle,* Nov. 21, 1896; London *Daily News,* Nov. 21, 1896; Washington *Evening Star*, Jan. 5, 1896, copies of all are in DWA, 2-12-14.

46. Diocese of Washington, *Journal of the Primary Convention,* 1895, 56-57, 63-64, 67-69; *New York Times,* Dec. 6, 1895, 8-4.

47. *New York Times*, Dec. 7, 1895, 2-3; *New York Herald,* Dec. 7, 1895, copies in DWA, 2-6-21. Three examples of many letters received: Arthur Chilton Powell to HYS, Dec. 9, 1895; J. A. Buck to HYS, Dec. 12, 1895; Clarence Buel to HYS, Dec. 9, 1895, all in DWA, 2-15-2.

48. HYS, "Pro and Contra Washington" and "Pro and Contra Calvary," undated, both in DWA, 2-6-18.

49. Brent, 14-80: *The Living Church,* Apr. 4, 1896. A copy of the service leaflet for the consecration is in DWA 2-5-29.

50. Brent, 180.

CHAPTER 3

1. *Who's Who in America* 11 (1920-21): 800; Douglas to the Vestry Committee, St. John's, June 13, 1889, Douglas Papers, St. John's Church, Washington, D.C. (STJ).

2. Stetson Conn, *Washington's Epiphany: Church and Parish,*1842-1972 (Washington: Church of the Epiphany, 1976), 77.

3. Douglas and McKim to William Paret, Bishop of Maryland, Oct. 27, 1890, Washington National Cathedral Archives, Record Group 117, Box 1, Folder 2 (WNC, 117-1-2). Charles C. Glover, a prominent banker and member of St. Alban's Church, claimed in 1927 that he was the originator of the idea and discussed it with laymen and Bishop Paret (E. N. Lewis, "Important Historical Facts of Washington Cathedral, Based on Personal Reminiscences of Charles C. Glover," May 11, 1927, WNC, 112-1-2 (Glover Account)).

4. David A. Kavelage, *Cathedrals in the Episcopal Church in the U.S.A.* (Cincinnati: Forward Movement, 1993), 20, 23; William R. Whittingham, Plan for Northminster Cathedral, 1839 (?); Whittingham to his parents, Apr. 3, 1843; S. J. Donaldson to Whittingham, May 14, 1869, all in Diocese of Maryland Archives; Richard G. Hewlett, "The Creation of the Diocese of Washington and Washington National Cathedral," *Anglican and Episcopal History* 71 (September 2002): 358.

5. *Baltimore Sun*, June 2, 1871, 4; Maryland Journal, 1871, 13-14.

6. Paret to Douglas and McKim, Oct. 28, 1890, WNC, 117-1-4.

7. Douglas to Paret, May 16 and 21, 1891, with copy of indenture attached, WNC, 117-1-4; Maryland Journal, 1891, 29.

8. Douglas to Paret, Sept. 21, 1891, WNC, 117-1-4.

9. Douglas to Paret, July 2, Nov. 18, Dec. 10, 1891; Glover to Paret, Dec. 15, 1891. In his letter to Paret, Glover listed the names of the twenty-two laymen who attended the meeting; three were absent. McKim to Paret, Dec. 6, 1891; Herman V. Viele, secretary of the site committee, and Douglas, chairman, to Paret, Dec. 18, 1891; Douglas to Paret, Nov. 24, Dec. 19, Dec. 21, 1891, all in WNC, 117-1-4.

10. M. E. Mann to Paret, June 23, 1892, WNC, 117-1-6.

11. Douglas, Glover, Henry E. Davis, McKim, John H. Eliott, and John W. Kasson to Paret, Oct. 13, 1892; Douglas to Paret, Oct. 14, 1892; McKim to Paret, Oct. 31, 1892, all in WNC, 117-1-6. The charter bills were introduced as S. 3391 and H.R. 9471, 52nd Cong., 1st sess.

12. Douglas to Paret, June 1, 1892, WNC, 117-1-15.

13. Douglas to Paret, Feb. 1895, WNC, 117-1-18.

14. McKim to Paret, Jan. 12 and 18, 1893; Douglas to Paret, Mar. 30, 1893; John A. Kasson to Paret, Nov. 21, 1893, all in WNC, 117-1-8; Paret to Douglas, Feb. 6, 1893, WNC, 117-1-16; Douglas to Paret, Apr. 15, 1894, WNC, 117-1-10; W. R. Huntington to Paret, May 4, 1893; Henry C. Potter, Bishop of New York, to Paret, May 5, 1893, WNC, 117-1-16.

15. Douglas to Paret, Dec. 7, 1893, and reply, Dec. 28, 1893, both in WNC, 117-1-8.

16. T. A. Hand to Paret, May 2, 1892, WNC, 117-1-6; McKim to Paret, May 26, 1894; Douglas to Paret, May 31 and June 7, 1894, all in WNC, 117-1-10; George Truesdell to Paret, May 20, Sept. 6, and Sept. 14, 1893, all in WNC, 117-1-8; Paret to Douglas, July 12, 1893, WNC, 117-1-16.

17. Paret to Douglas, Apr. 1, 1893, WNC, 117-1-16; Douglas to Paret, Apr. 13, 1893, Oct. 22, 1893, both in WNC 117-1-8.

18. George F. Edmunds to Paret, Apr. 3, 1893, WNC, 117-1-4.

19. Maryland Journal, 1893, 49-50.

20. The Washington Post, May 27, 1895, 8.

21. Ibid.

22. Baltimore Sun, May 30, 1895, 2; The Washington Post, May 30, 1895, 2; Maryland Journal, 1895, 16-17.

23. Journal of the General Convention, 1895, 15, 33, 192, 205, 225.

24. Constance M. Green, Washington, Capital City, 1879-1950 (Princeton: Princeton University Press, 1963), 3-17.

25. Chapter Minute Book, Dec. 10, 1894, vol. 1, 55; Hearst to Douglas, Dec. 10, 1894, WNC, 134-7-5.

26. Chapter Minute Book, Apr. 25, 1895, vol. 1, 60. A copy of the contract appears on p. 61. Flagg, memorandum submitted with the Cathedral Plan, n.d., WNC, 117-3-12.

27. Britton to Douglas, Apr. 30, 1895, WNC, 117-3-4.

28. Chapter Minute Book, May 3, 1895, vol. 1, 65-68.

29. Paret to Britton, May 21, 1895, and Britton's reply, May 24, 1895, WNC, 177-2-7.

30. McKim to Hearst, May 14, 1895, WNC, 134-7-5, and reply, June 3, 1895, WNC, 134-7-1.

31. Britton and Wilson to Douglas, June 3, 15, 26, and July 2, 1895, and to Paret, June 9, 1895, all in WNC, 117-3-4; W. C. Noyes and Glover to Paret, June 8, 1895, WNC, 117-2-7; Douglas to Paret, June 16, 1895, and Paret to Britton, July 5 and 20, 1895, all in WNC, 117-2-6.

CHAPTER 4

1. Henry Yates Satterlee (HYS) to Rev. A. B. Hunter, St. Augustine's School, Raleigh, NC, Jan. 19, 1901, Roberts Collection, Calendar 180, St. Mark's Library, General Theological Seminary. There is a rich collection of correspondence on the conference of Southern bishops in 1907 in the Diocese of Washington Archives, Record Group 2, Box 3, Folders 20 to 22 (DWA 2-3-20 to DWA 2-3-22). For Satterlee's definitive statement on race relations in the Church, see his address to the Convention of the Diocese of Washington, May 15, 1907, 33-42.

2. Satterlee to Britton, Mar. 4, 1896, Washington

National Cathedral Archives, Record Group 117, Box 2, Folder 7 (WNC, 117-2-7).

3. On Barber, see I. B. Holley, Jr., "How Asphalt Paving Came to the Urban United States," *Technology and Culture* 44 (Oct. 2003): 709-13. On Satterlee's earlier financial commitments, see Chap. 1, p. 19, and Chap. 2, pp. 25, 34.

4. Journal of the General Convention, 1898, 174.

5. William C. Woodward to HYS, Mar. 20, 1900, DWA, 2-8-14; *The Church Militant*, Nov. 1898, 184.

6. *The Peace Cross Book* (New York: R. H. Russell,1899). Copy in the Cathedral Archives.

7. *Washington Post* article on the incident, May 13, 1903.

8. HYS, The National Episcopal Cathedral at the Capital of the United States, printed pamphlet, 1898, WNC, 129-4-3.

9. HYS to Jane Satterlee, Jan. 12, 1900, DWA, 2-15-6.

10. Satterlee's correspondence with William Douglas Caroe, the designer, is in WNC, 162-15-1.

11. Chapter 5, p. 92.

12. Lawrence and Doane to HYS, both dated Dec. 11, 1905, WNC, 162-18-12.

13. HYS to Board of Trustees of the Cathedral of St. John the Divine, n.d., DWA, 2-12-7; *New York Times*, Feb. 22, 1891, 3.

14. HYS to the Trustees, Dec. 28, 1905, WNC, 162-18-6.

15. Ibid.

16. Henry Yates Satterlee, *The Building of a Cathedral* (New York: Edwin S. Gorham, 1901), 23-24.

17. List of Advantages and Disadvantages of the Proposed Site, n.d., WNC, 117-3-12.

18. HYS to the Trustees, Dec. 28, 1905, WNC, 162-18-6.

19. Chapter Minutes, Dec. 29, 1905, vol. 2, 23-25; Lawrence to HYS, Jan. 1, 1906, WNC, 162-18-12.

20. HYS to Dr. Fiske, Feb. 2, 1906, WNC, 162-18-12;

Constance McLaughlin Green, *Washington, Capital City, 1879-1950* (Princeton University Press, 1963), 133-40.

21. HYS to Burnham, Apr. 4, 1906, WNC, 162-18-12.

22. HYS, Report to the Board, marked "Strictly Confidential," n.d., but clearly after May 5 and before May 21, 1906, WNC, 162-18-12; Chapter Minutes, May 21, 1906, vol. 2, 38. The complete text of the report appears in Christopher D. H. Row, "World Without End: Philip Hubert Frohman and the Washington National Cathedral" (Ph.D. diss., Harvard University, 1999), UMI Dissertation Abstracts, 245-49.

23. Burnham to HYS, June 25, 1906, WNC, 162-18-12.

24. HYS to Burnham, Aug. 21, 1906, WNC, 162-18-12.

25. HYS to Burnham, Aug. 27, 1906, WNC, 162-18-12.

26. HYS to William Lowndes and other members of the Board of Trustees, Aug. 22, 1906, WNC, 162-18-6.

27. Walpole to HYS, Sept. 21, 1906, WNC, 162-18-12.

28. HYS to Bodley and HYS to Vaughan, both Oct. 8, 1906, WNC, 162-18-7.

29. HYS to Bodley, Jan. 11, 1907, WNC, 162-18-7.

30. Bodley to HYS, Mar. 27, Apr. 4, 1907, both in WNC, 162-18-7. The emphasis on the word "transmitted" is Bodley's.

31. HYS to Bodley, Apr. 8, 1907, WNC, 162-18-7.

32. HYS to Bodley, Apr. 23, 1907, WNC, 162-18-7. Row discusses in detail the exchange of correspondence on the eleven points (Row, "World Without End," 92-94).

33. HYS to Vaughan, Dec. 12, 1906; Vaughan to HYS, Dec. 14, 1906, Mar. 5, 1907; HYS to Vaughan, May 17, 1907, all in WNC, 162-18-7; Row, "World Without End," 121-25, 255-56.

34. Vaughan to HYS, May 23, 31, 1907, WNC, 162-18-7.

35. Chapter Minutes, June 7, 1907, Vol. 2, 61. Row, 10-19; HYS, *A Creedless Gospel and the Gospel*

Creed, New York: Charles Scribner's Sons, (1895), 195-260.

36. HYS to Bodley, June 8, 1907, WNC, 162-18-7; Chapter Minutes, June 5, 7, 1907, Vol. 2, 58-67.

37. Row, 97.

CHAPTER 5

No endnotes

CHAPTER 6

1. William L. DeVries, *The Foundation Stone Book: Washington Cathedral, A. D. 1907* (Washington: Privately published, 1908), 15-28.

2. Charles H. Brent, *A Master Builder: Being the Life and Letters of Henry Yates Satterlee, First Bishop of Washington* (New York: Longmans, Green, 1916), 394.

3. DeVries, *The Foundation Stone Book*, 39-40.

4. Ibid., 42-43.

5. Ibid., 46.

6. Henry Yates Satterlee (HYS) to William A. R. Goodwin, Mar. 6, 1906; William Loeb, Jr., Secretary to the President, to HYS, Aug. 29, 1907, both in Diocese of Washington Archives, Record Group 2, Box 8, Folder 3 (DWA 2-8-3).

7. HYS to Jane Satterlee, Nov. 8, 1907, DWA, 2-5-35; HYS to Vaughan, Oct. 21, Dec. 26, 1907; and Jan. 3, 21, 27, 30, 31, 1908; Vaughan to HYS, Dec. 30, 1907; and Jan. 6, 28, 30, 1908, all in Washington National Cathedral Archives, Record Group 162, Box 18, Folder 10; excerpts are included in Brent, *A Master Builder,* 448-55.

8. *New York Times,* Feb. 23, 1908.

9. *The Washington Post,* Feb. 23, 1908.

10. Ibid., Feb. 24, 25, 26, 1908; *Washington Times,* Feb. 23, 25, 1908; *Washington Evening Star*, Feb. 24, 1908; *Washington Herald*, Feb. 26, 1908.

11. Brent, *A Master Builder,* 405.

12. HYS, manuscript biographical statement, written sometime after 1896, DWA, 2-11-10.

13. Calvary Year Book, 1895, 23-28.

14. *New York Sun*, January 29, 1900.

15. *New York Times,* January 29, 1900.

16. Frank E. Sugeno, "The Establishmentarian Ideal and the Mission of the Episcopal Church," *Historical Magazine of the Protestant Episcopal Church* 53 (Dec. 1984): 288.

17. Rhinelander was appointed in 1901. See Chapter 5, 122.

18. HYS, The National Episcopal Cathedral at the Capital of the United States, pamphlet, probably winter, 1898, WNC, 129-4-3.

19. This paragraph is based largely on Paul T. Phillips, *A Kingdom on Earth: Anglo-American Social Christianity, 1880-1940* (University Park PA: Pennsylvania State University Press, 1996), 163-58.

20. Ibid., 169-74; John Frederick Woolverton, "William Reed Huntington and Church Unity: The Historical and Theological Background of the Chicago-Lambeth Quadrilateral," (Ann Arbor: University Microfilms, 164), 301-12, 346; William Reed Huntington, *A National Church* (New York: Charles Scribner's Sons, 1898), 55-73.

21. Christopher D.H. Row, "World Without End: Philip Hubert Frohman and the Washington Cathedral," Ph.D. Dissertation, Harvard University, 1999, UMI Dissertation Abstracts, 17.

Biographical Notes

Anderson, Bishop
Charles Palmerston Anderson, 1863-1930; rector, Grace Church, Oak Park, Illinois, 1891-1900; Bishop of Chicago, 1900-1930.

Andrews, Bishop
Launcelot Andrewes, Bishop of Winchester, England; most prominent of the translators of the King James or "Authorized Version" of the Bible, in 1611.

Babcock, S. D.
Samuel D. Babcock, 1822-1902; New York banker, on vestry at Calvary Church.

Baldwin, Bishop
M.S. Baldwin, Bishop of Huron, Ontario.

Bangs, Miss
Lois A. Bangs, principal of Academic Classes for Girls, New York City; co-principal, National Cathedral School, 1900-1906.

Barber, Mr. A. L.
Amzi Lorenzo Barber, 1843-1909; educator and industrialist; professor of natural philosophy, Columbian University (George Washington University), 1868-1872; owner of Barber Asphalt Paving Co., Washington; introduced asphalt pavement in many cities in the United States and Europe.

Barbour-Walker, Mrs.
1867-1950; principal, National Cathedral School, 1906-1913; established schools in the Philippines; with the American Red Cross and YMCA in France during World War I; dean, William Smith College, 1919-1929.

Barringer, Victor C., Mrs.
Nee Maria Massey, a major early donor to the Cathedral.

Battershall, Dr.
Probably Walton Wesley Battershall, 1840-1920; rector of various parishes in upstate New York, including St. Peter's, Albany, 1874-1920; Doctor of Divinity, 1866.

Bell, Mr.
Charles James Bell, 1858-1929; cousin of Alexander Graham Bell; senior member, Bell & Co., bankers; founder and president, American Security & Trust Co.; chairman, McKinley inaugural committee; trustee, Washington Public Library; president, board of education, District of Columbia; original Cathedral trustee, 1899-1929.

Bigelow, Rev.
Frank Hagar Bigelow, 1851-1924; astronomer and meteorologist; professor of meteorology, U.S. Weather Bureau; ordained priest, 1880; assistant minister, St. John's Church, Washington, from 1891; held chair of solar physics at George Washington University; designed the sundial on the Cathedral grounds; wife was Mary Ellen Bigelow (Spalding), a major early donor to the Cathedral.

Boardman, Miss
Mabel Thorp Boardman, 1860-1946; second woman to receive a master's degree at Yale University; socially prominent activist and civic leader; reorganized and revitalized the American Red Cross; member, board of incorporators, American Red Cross, 1900; national secretary, 1919-1944; started the nursing system of the Red Cross; first woman commissioner of the District of Columbia, 1920-1921; remains interred in the Cathedral.

Boardman, Mr.
William Jarvis Boardman, 1832-1915; father of Mabel Thorp Boardman.

Bodley, George Frederick
Sir George Frederick Bodley, 1827-1907; prominent English Gothic architect; designed parts of King's College, Cambridge, and Liverpool Cathedral; first architect of Washington Cathedral.

Bond, Francis
Died 1918; author of *Cathedrals of England and Wales* and other books on English Gothic architecture.

Bowdoin, George, Mrs.
Née Julia Grinnell.

Bowdoin, George S.
George Sullivan Bowdoin, 1842-1913; New York banker and railroad executive; married Julia Irving Grinnell, sister of Irving Grinnell (q.v.); personal friend of Satterlee; member, J.P. Morgan & Co.; major contributor to Cathedral of St. John the Divine, New York City, and Washington Cathedral; member, New York committee of Washington Cathedral.

Bratenahl, Rev. George
George Carl Fitch Bratenahl, 1862-1939; businessman in New York City, 1883-1893; studied for ministry under Satterlee; ordained priest, 1898; rector of St. Alban's Church, Washington, 1898-1912; canon, Washington Cathedral, 1903-1916; dean, 1916-l936; Cathedral trustee, 1907-1939.

Brent, Bishop
Charles Henry Brent, 1862-1929; curate, St. Paul's Cathedral, Buffalo, 1887; St. John the Evangelist, Boston, 1888-1891; assistant minister, St. Stephen's, Boston, 1891-1901; close friend of Satterlee; Bishop of the Philippine Islands, 190l-1918; declined election as Satterlee's successor as Bishop of Washington, 1908; author of *A Master Builder*, a biography of Bishop Satterlee (Longmans Green, 1916).

Brewster, Bishop
Chauncey Bunce Brewster, 1848-1941; rector, Christ Church, Rye, New York, 1873-1881; Christ Church, Detroit, 1881-1885; Grace Church, Baltimore, 1885-1888; Grace Church, Brooklyn, 1888-1897; Bishop of Connecticut, 1897-1928.

Britton, Alexander T., Col.
Alexander Thompson Britton, 1835-1899; Civil War veteran; lawyer in Washington from 1865; member of a presidential commission to codify public land laws; director of several banks and railroads; incorporator of the Cathedral Foundation, 1893; original Cathedral trustee, 1894-1899; chairman of the Cathedral's first building committee.

Bruce, Matilda V., Miss
A major early donor to the Cathedral and National Cathedral School.

Buckingham, Mrs.
Née Margaret C. Freeman, d. 1946; married Benjamin H. Buckingham, lived at 1525 H Street, NW, Washington; sister of Isabel Freeman (q.v.).

Burnham, Daniel Hudson
1846-1912; noted Chicago architect; designer of the World's Columbian Exposition, 1892; member, District of Columbia Park Commission, 1902

Butler, Nicholas Murray
1862-1947; scholar and educator of international renown; president of Columbia University, 1901-1945, and five other colleges; member, New Jersey state board of education, 1887-1895; organized the College Entrance Examination Board; commissioner of Paris Exposition, 1889; chairman, Lake Mohonk Conference on International Arbitration, 1907-1912; awarded half of Nobel Peace prize in 1931; awarded thirty-nine honorary degrees from American and foreign universities; decorated by fifteen foreign governments; member of numerous scholarly societies; author of twenty books and many published essays and addresses.

Butler, William Allen
1863-1923; lawyer; member of firm of Butler, Wychoff & Reid, New York City; director of Hanover Fire Insurance and other companies; trustee, American Fine Arts Society.

Caroe, Mr.
William D. Caroe, resident architect of Canterbury Cathedral; directed the sculpting of the Canterbury Pulpit at Washington Cathedral.

Chew, "Brother"
John H. Chew, rector of St. Alban's Church, Washington, 1865-1881; grandson of Bishop Claggett.

Chew, Dr.
Samuel Claggett Chew, 1837-1915; physician; professor of medicine, University of Maryland; great grandson of Bishop Claggett.

Claggett, Bishop
Thomas John Claggett, 1743-1816; first Bishop of Maryland, 1792-1816; first Episcopal bishop consecrated in the United States.

Clark, Bishop
Thomas March Clark, 1812-1903; rector, Grace Church, Boston, 1836-1843; St. Andrew's, Philadelphia, 1844-

1847; Trinity Church, Boston, 1847-1851; Christ Church, Hartford, 1851-1854; Bishop of Rhode Island, 1854-1903; presiding Bishop of the Episcopal Church, 1899-1903.

Clark, Senator
William Andrews Clark, 1839-1925; western mine owner, merchant banker, and railroad executive; president, Montana state constitutional convention, 1884 and 1889; United States senator from Montana, 1899-1907.

Clarke, Casper P.
Sir Caspar Purdon Clarke, 1846-1911; director, South Kensington Art Museum, London; director, Metropolitan Museum of Art, New York, 1905-1910; friend of Satterlee's father.

Colt, Mrs. Samuel
Elizabeth H. Colt, daughter of the Rev. William Jarvis of Middletown, Connecticut; wife of Samuel Colt, 1814-1862, inventor of the Colt revolver, 1856.

Cortelyou, Secretary
George Bruce Cortelyou, 1862-1940; law reporter in New York City, 1883-1885; assistant secretary to President Theodore Roosevelt, 1901; Secretary of the Treasury, 1907-1909.

Coxe, Bishop
Arthur Cleveland Coxe, 1818-1896; rector of Calvary Church, New York City, 1862-1865; Bishop of Western New York, 1865-1896; close friend of Satterlee and responsible for bringing him into the Episcopal Church.

Cram, Mr.
Ralph Adams Cram, 1863-1942; prominent Boston architect; designed St. Thomas Church, New York City, and Calvary Church, Pittsburgh; supervising architect, Princeton University; consulting architect, Cathedral of St. John the Divine in New York City; author of books on English and Gothic architecture; partner in Cram, Goodhue & Ferguson.

Croswell, Dr.
James Greenleaf Croswell, 1852-1915; professor of classical languages at Harvard, 1883-1887; headmaster, Brearley School.

Crozier, Gen.
William Crozier, 1855-1942; career soldier and inventor; chief ordnance officer of Peking relief expedition; president, U.S. Army War College, 1912-1913; general and chief of ordnance, U.S. Army, 1901-1919; inventor of military ordnance; delegate to the International Peace Conference at The Hague, 1899.

DeVries, Dr.
William Levering DeVries, 1865-1937; missionary, Howard County, Maryland, 1894-1896; private chaplain to Bishop Satterlee, 1896-1908; rector, St. Mark's Church, Washington, 1896-1911; canon and chancellor, Washington Cathedral, 1911-1929; canon and precentor, 1929-1937; trustee of Washington Cathedral; author of *The Foundation Stone Book*, 1908.

Dewey, Admiral
George Dewey, 1837-1917; lieutenant, U.S. Navy, during the Civil War; promoted to commodore, 1896; commander of U.S. Asiatic Fleet, Manila Bay, 1898; promoted to admiral, U.S. Navy, 1899; Cathedral trustee, 1899-1917.

Dix, Dr.
Morgan Dix, 1827-1908; son of John A. Dix, U.S. senator from New York, Secretary of the Treasury, and governor of New York; rector, Trinity Church, New York, 1862-1908; clerical delegate to eight General Conventions.

Doane, Bishop
William Croswell Doane, 1832-1913; rector, St. Mary's Church, Burlington, New Jersey, 1853-1860; St. John's, Hartford, 1860-1864; St. Peter's, Albany, 1867-1869; Bishop of Albany, 1869-1913; founded St. Agnes School, Albany, 1870; lecturer, English literature, Trinity College, Hartford, 1864-1867; long-time friend of Satterlee.

Dodge, W. E.
William Earl Dodge, 1832-1903; merchant, industrialist, and philanthropist; chairman of the National Commission of Arbitration; president of the YMCA; active in religious and benevolent societies.

Donald, Dr.
E. Winchester Donald, 1848-1904; rector, Church of the Intercession, New York City, 1875-1882; rector, Church of the Ascension, New York City, 1882-1892; university preacher, Harvard University, 1892-1896; rector, Trinity Church, Boston, 1892-1904.

Douglas, Dr. George W.
George William Douglas, 1850-1926; assistant, Calvary Church, New York City, 1877; vicar, Trinity Church, New York City, 1879-1886; rector of St. John's Church, Washington, 1889-1892; drafted the constitution of Washington Cathedral, 1892-1893; incorporator of the Cathedral Foundation, 1893; original Cathedral

trustee, 1894-1896; rector, Trinity Church, New Haven, Connecticut, 1895-1898; senior canon, Cathedral of St. John the Divine, New York City, 1904-.

Dudley, Bishop
Thomas Underwood Dudley, 1837-1904; assistant minister, Christ Church, Baltimore, 1869-1875; chancellor, University of the South, 1893; Bishop of Kentucky, 1875-1904.

Dyer, Herman
Heman Dyer, 1833-1900; priest and professor; president, Western University of Pennsylvania, 1843-1844; general manager, Evangelical Knowledge Society; editor of Episcopal *Quarterly Review,* 1854-; declined bishopric of Kansas, 1862; retired, 1880; member, influential Clerical Club of New York City.

Edmunds, Senator
George Franklin Edmunds, 1828-1919; lawyer; member, House of Representatives from Vermont, 1854-1859; U.S. senator from Vermont, 1866-1891; incorporator of the Cathedral Foundation, 1893; original Cathedral trustee, 1894-1896.

Elliott, Dr.
John H. Elliott, rector, Church of the Ascension, Washington, 1884-1904; Cathedral trustee, 1896-1903.

Farrand, Beatrix
1872-1959; daughter of Frederick Rhinelander and Mary Cadwalader (Rawle) Jones; married Max Farrand, 1913; landscape designer and founding member of the American Society of Landscape Architects; designed gardens for Yale, Princeton, and Dumbarton Oaks.

Flagg, Mr.
Ernest Flagg, 1857-1947; prominent New York architect; designed St. Luke's Hospital in New York, the Corcoran Gallery of Art in Washington, D.C., and many other buildings.

Flannery, Mr.
Lott Flannery, Washington carver who carved the Peace Cross and the Glastonbury Cathedra.

Freeman, Miss Isabel C.
Died 1929; sister of Margaret C. (Mrs. Bruce) Buckingham (q.v.); major early donor to the Cathedral.

Frisby, Rev. Dr.
William Barroll Frisby, 1854-1902; rector of Church of the Advent, Boston.

Garrett, Robert, Mrs.
Née Mary Frick; prominent Baltimore socialite and wife of the president of the Baltimore & Ohio Railroad; chair, Baltimore committee on the Cathedral; lived at 11 W. Mt. Vernon Place, Baltimore.

Gibson, Mr.
Robert W. Gibson, 1854-1927; British architect, naturalized U.S. citizen; architect, Albany Cathedral, National Cathedral School; contributed drawings of the Glastonbury Cathedra.

Gillespie, Gen.
George Lewis Gillespie, 1841-1913; Union officer in the Civil War; awarded the Congressional Medal of Honor; engineering officer on general staff, Army of the Potomac, 1862-1864; command of Atlantic Coast defenses during the War with Spain, 1898; chief of engineers, U.S. Army, 1901; major general, 1904; member, Lighthouse Board of the District of Columbia.

Gilman, Dr. D. C.
Daniel Coit Gilman, 1831-1908; educator; professor of physics and political geography, Yale University, 1856-1872; president, University of California, 1872-1875; first president, Johns Hopkins University, 1875-1901; first president, Carnegie Institution of Washington, 1901-1904; Cathedral trustee, 1904-1908.

Glover, Mr.
Charles Carroll Glover, 1846-1936; prominent Washington businessman and philanthropist; president, Riggs National Bank; treasurer, Corcoran Gallery of Art, Washington, D.C.; led movement to establish Rock Creek Park, Potomac Park, and Zoological Park; vestryman, St. Alban's Church, Washington; incorporator of the Cathedral Foundation, 1893; original Cathedral trustee, 1894-1934; major Cathedral donor.

Goldsborough, Mr.
Richard A. Goldsborough, prominent Washington attorney and vestryman at St. Alban's Church, Washington, D.C.

Green, Mr.
Bernard Richardson Green, 1843-1914; civil engineer, supervised construction of the Washington Monument, the Library of Congress, the Natural History Museum, the War and Navy Building, and other government buildings in Washington.

Grinnell, Irving
1838-1921; grandnephew of Washington Irving and son of Moses Hicks Grinnell, a wealthy New York shipping magnate, who was a member of Congress and collector of the Port of New York; educated at Columbia University; prominent landowner in Dutchess County, New York; member and senior warden for thirty years

of Zion Church, Wappingers Falls; long-time friend of Satterlee.

Grosvenor, Dr.
William Mercer Grosvenor, 1863-1916; rector, Trinity Church, Lenox, Massachusetts, 1890-1895; rector of Church of the Incarnation, New York City, 1895-1911; dean, Cathedral of St. John the Divine, New York City, 1911-1916.

Hadden, Alexander
One of Satterlee's bright young men at Calvary Church; personal secretary to Satterlee in New York and Washington; probably the son of Dr. Alexander M. Hadden, d. 1912; prominent New York physician and member of the Cathedral committee in New York.

Hall, Dr. Charles H.
Charles Henry Hall, 1820-1895; rector of churches on Long Island and West Point, New York, 1844-1847; rector, St. John's Church, Johns Island, South Carolina, 1847-1856; rector, Church of the Epiphany, Washington, 1856-1869; rector, Holy Trinity Church, Brooklyn, New York, 1869-1895.

Hamlyn, Mrs. Charles
Née Huybertie Lansing Pruyn; married Charles Sumner Hamlyn, a Boston lawyer and civic leader, 1898; a member of the Boston committee on the Cathedral.

Harding, Rev. Dr.
Alfred Harding, 1852-1923; born in Ireland, came to United States in 1863; assistant, Trinity Church, Geneva, New York, 1882-1883; assistant, St. Paul's Church, Baltimore, 1883-1887; rector, St. Paul's Church, Washington, 1887-1909; Cathedral trustee, 1903-1909; Bishop of Washington, 1909-1923.

Hare, Bishop
William Hobart Hare, 1838-1909; rector, St. Paul's Church, Chestnut Hill and other Philadelphia parishes, 1862-1870; secretary and general agent, Foreign and Domestic Missionary Society of the Episcopal Church, 1870-1872; Bishop of South Dakota, l873-1909.

Hayes, Charles H.
Assistant minister, Pro-Cathedral Church of St. Mark, Washington, D.C., 1896-1900.

Hearst, Senator
George Hearst, 1820-1891; successful prospector in California gold rush of 1850; engaged in mining, stock raising, and farming; member, California state assembly, 1865-1866; owner, *San Francisco Chronicle*; U.S. senator from California; father of William Randolph Hearst.

Hearst, Phoebe A.
Phoebe Appelman Hearst, 1842-1919; wife of Senator George Hearst, mother of William Randoph Hearst; teacher and philanthropist; set up kindergarten classes and working girls' clubs in San Francisco, Washington, D.C., and Lead, Colorado; regent of the University of California; provided initial funding for the National Cathedral School.

Hodges, Dr.
John Sebastian Bach Hodges, 1830-1915; rector, Church of the Holy Communion, Chicago, 1859-1860; rector, Grace Church, Newark, New Jersey, 1860-1870; rector, St. Paul's Parish, Baltimore, 1870-1906; incorporator of the Cathedral Foundation, 1893; original Cathedral trustee, 1894-1896; composer of services, chants, anthems, and hymn tunes.

Howell, Mr.
Richard L. Howell, born 1882; rector of St. Margaret's Church, Washington, 1897-1898.

Hunniwell, Mr.
Possibly James Frothingham Hunnewell, 1832-1910, a Boston merchant and author; or Walter Hunnewell, 1844-1921, Boston banker and trustee.

Huntington, Dr.
William Reed Huntington, 1838-1909; rector, All Saints' Church, Worcester, Massachusetts, 1862-1882; rector, Grace Church, New York City, 1883-1909; one of the most distinguished clergymen in the Episcopal Church at the turn of the century; ecclesiastical reformer and principal author of the Chicago Quadrilateral.

Hyde, Thomas
1839-1919; member, St. John's Church, Georgetown; vice president, Riggs National Bank; Cathedral treasurer, 1894-1900; Cathedral trustee, 1900-1919.

Irwin, Miss Agnes
1841-1914; dean of Radcliffe College, 1894-1909.

Julian-James, Mrs.
Née Cassie Mason Myers; major early donor to the Cathedral; memorialized by the Cathedral sundial.

Johnson, Reverend
Edward D. Johnson, deacon, 1898; rector, Grace Church, Georgetown, 1899-1900.

Johnson, Bishop
Joseph Horsfall Johnson, 1847-1928; rector, Holy Trinity Church, Bristol, Rhode Island, 1879-1881; St. Peter's, Westchester, New York, 1881-1886; Christ

Church, Detroit, 1886-1896; Bishop of Los Angeles, 1896-1928.

Johnston, Harriet Lane, Mrs.
1826-1906; niece and official hostess for President James Buchanan; widow of Henry Elliott Johnston, a Baltimore banker and railroad builder; provided funds for the establishment of the boys' school that became St. Alban's.

Jones, Beatrix. See Farrand.

Kaiser, William
Probably William Keyser; in Baltimore Social Register, 1899; married Mary Brent; lived at 1009 Calvert Street, Baltimore; incorporator of the Cathedral Foundation, 1893.

Kasson, Gen.
John Adam Kasson, 1822-1910; lawyer and diplomat, first assistant postmaster-general of the United States, 1861-1862; U.S. commissioner to the International Postal Congress, 1863, 1867; U.S. congressman from Iowa, 1863-1867, 1873-1877; minister to Austria, 1887-1881, to Germany, 1883-1885; special envoy to international conferences, 1885-1889; incorporator of the Cathedral Foundation, 1893; original Cathedral trustee, 1894-1920; major Cathedral donor.

Kibbey, Miss Bessie J.
1857-1949; lifelong D.C. resident and philanthropist; chair, for fifty years, of admissions committee, Washington Home for Incurables; donated money for the city's first playground; gave the Cathedral's Carillon; lived at 2025 Massachusetts Avenue.

Knower, Mr.
Probably Benjamin Knower, a member of the Cathedral's New York City committee; lived at 4 E. 77th Street, New York.

L'Enfant, Major
Pierre Charles L'Enfant; 1754-1925; George Washington's architect for the City of Washington.

Lawrence, Bishop
William Lawrence, 1850-1941; rector, Grace Church, Lawrence, Massachusetts, 1876-1884; professor, Episcopal Theological School, 1884-1893; dean, 1888-1893; Bishop of Massachusetts, l893-1927.

Loeb, Secretary
William Loeb, Jr., 1866- 1937; secretary to President

Theodore Roosevelt, 1903-1909; later collector of customs in New York City.

Mackay-Smith, Bishop
Alexander Mackay-Smith, 1850-1911; assistant, St. Thomas Church, New York, 1880-1887; Archdeacon, Diocese of New York, 1887-1893; rector, St. John's Church, Washington, l893-1902; Bishop of Pennsylvania, 1902-1911; Cathedral trustee, 1894-1907.

McKim, Charles
Charles F. McKim, 1847-1909; architect and partner in firm of Mead McKim and White, New York City.

McKim, Dr.
Randolph Harrison McKim, 1842-1921; served in the Confederate army during the Civil War; chaplain, Virginia cavalry, 1864-1865; rector, Christ Church, Alexandria, 1867-1875; rector, Holy Trinity Church, New York City, 1875-1886; rector, Trinity Church, New Orleans, 1886-1888; rector, Church of the Epiphany, 1888-1920; leader of the Washington delegation in the Diocese of Maryland, 1890-1895; incorporator of the Cathedral Foundation, 1893; original Cathedral trustee, 1894-1920; leading candidate in the election of the first Bishop of Washington.

McLaren, Bishop
William Edward McLaren, 1831-1905; Presbyterian minister, 1860-1870; ordained an Episcopal priest, 1872; rector in Cleveland, Ohio, 1872-1875; Bishop of Illinois, 1875-1877; Bishop of Chicago, 1877-1895; founded Western Theological Seminary, Chicago, 1883.

McMillan, Senator
James McMillan, 1838-1902; railroad and shipbuilding executive; president of Detroit board of park commissioners and board of estimates; U.S. senator from Michigan, 1889-1902.

McVickar, Bishop
William Nielson McVicar, 1843-1910; rector, Holy Trinity Church, Harlem, New York, 1868-1875; Holy Trinity, Philadelphia, 1875-1897; Bishop of Rhode Island, 1898-1910.

Merrill, Dr. Selah
1837-1909; Congregational minister, 1864; chaplain, 48th U.S. colored infantry, 1864-1865; studied in Germany, 1868-1870; archaeologist, American Palestine Exploration Society, 1874-1877; discovered and excavated the second wall of Jerusalem; curator,

Biblical Museum, Andover Theological Seminary; U.S. Consul, Jerusalem, 1882-1885, 1891-1893, 1898-1907.

Morgan, Mr.
John Pierpont Morgan, 1837-1913; banker, financier, and philanthropist; vestryman and senior warden, St. George's Church, New York, 1868-1913; major donor to schools, museums, and the Cathedral of St. John the Divine, New York City.

Morton, Governor and Mrs. Levi
Levi P. Morton; member, House of Representatives from New York, 1879-1881; vice president of the United States, l889-1893; incorporator of the Cathedral Foundation, 1893; governor of New York, l895-1896.

Newlands, Mr. Francis J.
Probably Francis Griffith Newlands, 1848-1917; lawyer, member, House of Representatives from Nevada, 1893-1903; U.S. senator, 1903-1917; chairman, Senate Committee on Corporations organized in the District of Columbia, 1893-1894.

Nourse, Mr. James
James Burns Nourse, 1828-1917.

Nourse, Mr.
Probably Charles Joseph Nourse, 1825-1905; secretary of the Cathedral's New York City committee; lived at 245 Lexington Avenue, New York City; incorporator of the Cathedral Foundation, 1893; original Cathedral trustee, 1894-1910.

Nuttall, Bishop
Enos Nuttall, 1842-1916; ArchBishop of the West Indies; consecrated, 1880.

Packard, Rev.
Probably Thomas Jones Packard, 1854-1912; on faculty of Virginia Theological Seminary, 1904-1905.

Page, Mr. Thomas Nelson
1853-1922; lawyer, Richmond, Virginia, 1875-1893; U.S. ambassador to Italy, 1913-1919; author of numerous books on the Civil War period, including novels and stories from Southern point of view.

Paret, Bishop
William Paret, 1826-1911; rector, Trinity Church, Elmira, New York, 1866-1868; Christ Church, Williamsport, Pennsylvania, 1868-1876; Church of the Epiphany, Washington, D.C., 1876-1885; Bishop of Maryland, 1885-1911; incorporator of the Cathedral Foundation,

1893; original Cathedral trustee, 1894-1896.

Park, General
John Grubb Parke, 1827-1900; Civil War veteran; Army engineer; Washington businessman, 1889-1900; director, Washington & Georgetown Street Railway Co. and National Safe Deposit Co.; manager, Columbia Hospital; president, Society of the Army of the Potomac; first secretary of the Cathedral Foundation; original Cathedral trustee, 1894-1900.

Parke, Mrs.
Ellen Parke, née Ellen Bright; wife of General Parke.

Partridge, W. Ordway
William Ordway Partridge, 1861-1930; sculptor and author; lecturer on fine arts, George Washington University, 1897-1903; works include memorial statues in Chicago and New York and the baptismal font for the Cathedral.

Pellew, Mr.
Henry Edward Pellew; 1828-1923; born in England, emigrated to United States in 1873; social reformer; organized bureau of charities, New York City, with Theodore Roosevelt, Abram S. Hewitt, and others; organized night refuges, circulating library coffee houses, and tenement house reform in New York; member, St. John's Church, Lafayette Square; founder of Keble College, Oxford; incorporator of the Cathedral Foundation; original Cathedral trustee, 1894-1905.

Penick, Bishop
Charles Clifton Penick, 1843-1914; Bishop of Cape Palmas, 1877-1883; rector, St. Andrew's Church, Louisville, Kentucky; St. Mark's Church, Richmond, Virginia.

Pepper, George Wharton
1867-1961; Philadelphia lawyer; professor of law, University of Pennsylvania, 1894-1910; trustee of the university, 1911-1961; chairman, Pennsylvania Council on National Defense during World War I; member, Pennsylvania Commission on Constitutional Revision, 1920-1921; U.S. senator from Pennsylvania, 1922-1927; member, Cathedral chapter, 1923-1958.

Pinkham, Bishop
W. C. Pinkham, 1844-1928; consecrated Bishop of Saskatchewan, 1887.

Potter, Bishop
Henry Codman Potter, 1835-1908; rector, Grace

Church, New York City; secretary, House of Bishops, 1865-1883; Bishop of New York, 1883-1908.

Powell, Dr.
Arthur Chilton Powell, rector, Church of the Atonement, Cincinnati, 1879-1882; St. John's Church, York, Pennsylvania, 1882-1888; Grace Church, Baltimore, 1888-.

Pruyn, Miss
See entry for Mrs. Charles Hamlyn.

Pyne, Percy R., Mrs.
Née Albertina Taylor, d. 1900; wife of Percy Rivington Pyne, financier and philanthropist; close confidant of Satterlee and key member, Calvary Church, New York; early Cathedral donor.

Rhinelander, Philip M.
Philip Mercer Rhinelander, 1869-1939; grew up in Calvary Church, New York; priest-in-charge, Chapel of the Good Shepherd and St. Alban's Church, Washington, 1896-1903; professor, Berkeley Divinity School, Middletown, Connecticut, 1903-1907; professor, Episcopal Theological School, Cambridge, Massachusetts, 1907-1911; Bishop of Pennsylvania, 1911-1923; Cathedral trustee, and warden, College of Preachers, 1921-1937; brother-in-law of Constance Satterlee, daughter of Bishop Satterlee.

Rives, Dr. and Mrs.
William Cabell Rives, 3rd, 1850-1938; born in Paris, the son of the U.S. Minister to France; educated at Harvard and Oxford; supported Satterlee missions in New York City, 1885-1895; came to Washington with Bishop Satterlee, 1896; anonymous donor of the Peace Cross, 1898; supported hospital missions of the Diocese of Washington; member of the Cathedral chapter, 1905-1938; wife was Mary Frederica Rhinelander, sister of Philip M. Rhinelander, q.v.

Russell, Archibald D., Mrs.
Née Albertina Pyne, d. 1918; daughter of Mrs. Percy Rivington Pyne; chair, Cathedral committee in New York City; early Cathedral donor; husband, Archibald Russell, was a Cathedral trustee, 1918-1919.

Russell, Henry, Mrs.
Née Hope B. Ives, a member of the Cathedral committee in Providence, Rhode Island.

Ryerson, Arthur, Mrs.
Née Emily Borie, a leader on the Cathedral committee in Chicago.

Satterlee, Constance
1874-1948; daughter of Bishop Satterlee; married Frederick H. Rhinelander, brother of Philip Rhinelander (q.v.), 1910; member and chair, Cathedral committee in New York City, 1914-1943, 1943-1945.

Satterlee, Churchill
1857-1904; son of Bishop Satterlee; graduate, Columbia University, 1890; General Theological Seminary, 1893; rector, Grace Church, Morganton, North Carolina, 1895-1901; rector, Trinity Church, Columbia, South Carolina, 1901-1904.

Satterlee, Lansing
Edward Lansing Satterlee, d. 1918; nephew of Bishop Satterlee; graduate, Columbia School of Architecture; studied at Paris Ecole National et Speciale des Beaux Arts; designed chapel for Zion Church, New York City, the McKinley Memorial, New Hamburg, New York, and the Little Sanctuary and All Hallows Gate at Washington Cathedral.

Shaw, Norman
Richard Norman Shaw, 1831-1912; English architect and author.

Shields, Professor
Charles Woodruff Shields, 1825-1904; theologian, author; ordained Presbyterian minister, 1849; pastor, Presbyterian churches in Hemstead, Long Island, and Philadelphia, 1850-1865; ordained priest, Episcopal Church, 1898; professor of science and religion, Princeton University, 1865-1900.

Smith, Rev. George Williamson
1836-1925; ordained priest, 1864; chaplain, U.S. Naval Academy, 1865-1868; rector of Church of the Redeemer, Brooklyn, 1881-1883; president, Trinity College, Hartford, 1883-1904; assistant minister, St. John's Church, Lafayette Square, Washington, 1905-1925.

Stetson, Francis L.
Francis Lynde Stetson, 1846-1920; lawyer in New York City; member, Stetson, Jennings & Russell, 1894; general counsel and director, numerous railroads, industrial corporations, and banks.

Street, Mrs.
Mrs. William A. Street, 43 Park Avenue, New York City; née Lucy Morgan.

Tompkins, Rev. Floyd W.
Floyd Williams Tomkins, 1850-1932; missionary in the

West, 1875-1883; rector, St. James' Church, Keene, New Hampshire, 1883-1884; minister-in-charge, Calvary Chapel, New York, with Satterlee, 1884-1888; rector, Christ Church, Hartford, 1888-1891; St. James' Church, Chicago, 1891-1894; Grace Church, Providence, Rhode Island, 1894-1899; Church of the Holy Trinity, Philadelphia, 1899-1932.

Trask, Mr. Spencer
1844-1909; New York banker; corporate director of railroads and other companies; trustee, General Theological Seminary, New York City.

Truesdell, Col.
George Truesdell, 1842-1921; civil engineer; Civil War veteran who enlisted as a private, promoted through the ranks to lieutenant colonel when he resigned in 1869; organizer and president of the Eckington and Soldiers' Home Railways Company, Washington; commissioner of D.C., 1894-1897; prominent businessman on the boards of many banks and other enterprises; incorporator of the Cathedral Foundation, 1893; an original Cathedral trustee, 1894-1921.

Tucker, Bishop
Beverley Dandridge Tucker, 1846-1930; rector, Richmond County, Virginia, 1873-1882; St. Paul's, Norfolk, Virginia, 1882-1906; Bishop of Southern Virginia, 1906-1930.

Tyndal
William Tyndale, 1492(?)-l536, English reformer and martyr.

Vanderbilt, Cornelius
1843-1899; grandson of Cornelius ("Commodore") Vanderbilt; banker and railroad magnate.

Vanderbilt, W. K.
William Kissam Vanderbilt, 1849-1920; capitalist and railroad official; director, Metropolitan Opera; founder, Vanderbilt Clinic.

Walpole, Rev. Dr. G. H. Somerset
George Henry Somerset Walpole; tutor, Scolae Cancellarii, Truro, England, 1877-1882; St. Mary's Pro-Cathedral, Auckland, New Zealand, and warden, St. John's College, New Zealand, 1882-1889; professor of theology, General Theological Seminary, New York, 1889-1896; principal, Bede College, Durham, England, 1896-1903.

Westcott, Bishop
Brooke Foss Westcott, Bishop of Durham, 1825-1901;

biblical scholar and a leader in the movement to create the "Revised Version" of the Bible, 1861-1885; memorialized on the Canterbury Pulpit.

Westinghouse, Mrs.
Née Marguerite Erskine Walker; wife of George Westinghouse, the inventor, 1846-1914.

Wetmore, Miss
Could be either Edith or Maud Wetmore, daughters of George Peabody Wetmore, who married Edith M. Keteltas; winter address, 1609 K Street, Washington, D.C.

Wetmore, Mrs. George P.
Wife of George Peabody Wetmore, 1846-1921, governor of Rhode Island, 1885-1886, and U.S. senator, 1894-1913.

Whipple, Bishop
Henry Benjamin Whipple, 1823-1901; rector, Zion Church, Rome, New York; Church of the Communion, Chicago; Bishop of Minnesota, 1859-1901; member, Indian treaty commissions; founder, St. Mary's Hall, Shattuck Military School, and Seabury Divinity School, Minnesota; trustee, Peabody Fund.

White, Mrs. Joseph
Née Matilda Bishop; lived at 15 E. 24th Street, New York; probably a member of Calvary Church.

Whittaker, Bishop
Ozi William Whitaker, 1830-1911; rector, St. John's, Gold Hill, Nevada, 1863-1865; St. Paul's, Englewood, New Jersey, 1865-1867; St. Paul's, Virginia City, Nevada, 1867-1869; missionary Bishop of Nevada, 1869; Bishop of Pennsylvania, 1886-1911.

Williams, Bishop
John Williams, 1817-1899; Bishop of Connecticut, 1851-1899; presiding Bishop of the Episcopal Church, 1887-1899.

Wilmer, Skipworth
Skipwith Wilmer, prominent Baltimore churchman, convention delegate, Church of the Holy Innocents, Baltimore; residence, 913 N. Charles Street, Baltimore.

Wilson, General
John Moulder Wilson, 1837-1919; brigadier general; winner of the Congressional Medal of Honor; superintendent of West Point, 1889-1893; chief of engineers, 1897-1907; in charge of building important engineering works after Civil War, including Washington

Monument; incorporator of the Cathedral Foundation, 1893; an original Cathedral trustee, 1894-1916.

Wycliffe
John Wycliffe, l320(?)-l384; English religious reformer and Bible translator.

ACKNOWLEDGMENTS

This book is the product of a team effort by volunteers in the Cathedral Archives. Assisting me in early research relating to Satterlee's *Private Record* were Veronica Daugherty and the late Lawrence Olson, who searched out personal data on the hundreds of individuals listed in the Biographical Notes. Later on, Margaret D. Lewis brought her vast knowledge of the history of the Diocese of Washington and the National Episcopal Church to bear on our research. Marianne Ruch applied her extraordinary knowledge of cathedral records to unearth elusive data. Jesse Wilson, curator of photographs, provided scores of images for possible use in this book.

I am especially indebted to Diane Ney, a skilled writer, author, and editor, who helped not only to polish the text but also to resolve questions of organization and style.

Elody Crimi, a talented artist and photographer, designed and produced the book. Patient and enthusiastic, Elody made the creation of the book a fascinating and creative adventure.

In addition to the volunteers, friends in the Washington area made important contributions. Donna Wilkes, with great accuracy, keyed Mrs. Satterlee's typescript into a digital format. Margaret Shannon saved me dozens of trips to the Library of Congress and other collections for facts needed to round out parts of the story, including how the *Private Record* came to be produced. Gail Mathews' sharp eyes and pencil captured dozens of small errors in final proofreading.

Marilyn N. Hewlett, my helpmate and best critic, patiently read and marked up innumerable drafts of sections of the manuscript over the last decade. I will dearly miss her on future projects.

As a novice in writing church history, I turned to experts in the academia for help. Robert W. Prichard at Virginia Theological Seminary; Robert Bruce Mullin at General Theological Seminary in New York, Peter W. Williams at Miami University in Ohio, and two anonymous readers for a university press, critiqued an early version of the manuscript and guided me through the complexities of the Oxford Movement, the raging debates over churchmanship, and the arcane structure of the Episcopal Church in the nineteenth century. In the process they saved me from numerous embarrassing errors.

Archivists and record custodians helped me find key documents and manuscripts in their collections. I am especially indebted to the late F. Garner Ranney, archivist of the Episcopal Diocese of Maryland; Barbara Griffin, archivist of St. James' Church, and the staff of the Grinnell Library in Wappingers Falls, New York; Isaac Gewirtz, director of special collections at St. Mark's Library, General Theological Seminary; Julia Randle, archivist, Bishop Payne Library, Virginia Theological Seminary; Linda Sheehan at St. George's Church, New York; and Stephen S. Garmy, vicar of Calvary Church, New York.

As the Cathedral's historiographer and archivist for more than twenty years, I have enjoyed an extraordinary privilege in having unrestricted access to the rich collection of records that support this history. As archivist, however, I have never been a member of the staff but rather a volunteer who took on this project on his own initiative. Thus the book is the product of my own personal endeavor and bears no imprimatur by the Cathedral. Without the advice and help of all those noted above and many others, it would not have been possible to write this book. For all the remaining errors and omissions, I am solely responsible.

INDEX

PICTURE CREDITS

All photographs and pictures to be credited to the Washington National Cathedral Archives except as listed below.

Cover photo by Elody R. Crimi, © 2007

Chapter 1 divider page, painting, p. xii, "Becalmed off Halfway Rock," by Fitz Hugh Lane, 1860. Impage © Board of Trustees, National Gallery of Art, Washington.

Photo, p. 13, Wappingers Falls, Library of Congress

Photo, p. 18, Street Scene, Wappingers Falls, Library of Congress

Chapter 2 divider page, photo, page 20, Lower East Side, NY, 1920s, Do You Graphics

Illustration, p. 26, Henry Codman Potter, *Centennial History of the Protestant Episcopal Church in the Diocese of New York, 1785 - 1885*, New York, D. Appleton, 1886

Illustration, p. 31, Galille East side buildings of Calvary Church, *New York Times*, April 15, 1886

Chapter 4 divider page, photo, p. 60, Tenleytown Road Trolley, 1890s, Historical Society of Washington, D.C.

Photo, page 91, Connecticut Avenue Bridge over Klingle Run, Historical Society of Washington, D.C.

The following photographs are to be credited to Charles H. Brent, *A Master Builder*, Longmans, Green, 1916:

p. 3 Yates mansion
p. 15, Irving Grinnell
p. 15, Saterlee as assistant Minister
p. 16, Zion Church
p. 22, Calvary Church, New York
p. 24, Satterlee as rector, Calvary Church
p. 25, Interior, Calvary Church